MONETARY THEORY AND MONETARY POLICY IN THE 1970s

Monetary Theory and Monetary Policy in the 1970s

HG225
S425
1970

PROCEEDINGS OF THE 1970
SHEFFIELD MONEY SEMINAR

EDITED BY

G. CLAYTON

J. C. GILBERT

R. SEDGWICK

OXFORD UNIVERSITY PRESS

1971

*Oxford University Press, Ely House, London W.*1

GLASGOW NEW YORK TORONTO MELBOURNE WELLINGTON
CAPE TOWN SALISBURY IBADAN NAIROBI DAR ES SALAAM LUSAKA ADDIS ABABA
BOMBAY CALCUTTA MADRAS KARACHI LAHORE DACCA
KUALA LUMPUR SINGAPORE HONG KONG TOKYO

PRINTED IN GREAT BRITAIN BY
WILLIAM CLOWES AND SONS LIMITED
LONDON, COLCHESTER AND BECCLES

PREFACE

This book contains the papers and proceedings of the Sheffield Seminar on Monetary Theory and Monetary Policy in the 1970s, held in September 1970. The idea of the Seminar was to provide a forum for contributions to monetary theory and its policy implications, including lines for future development. We have included an introduction, giving a bird's-eye view, and brief summaries of the informal discussions of the papers with the intention of recording the more important points made, but without usually attributing views to particular participants. As will be seen from the list of participants, academic economists and members of the staffs of the Treasury, the Bank of England and the banks attended. This book may be regarded in some ways as a companion volume to *Money in Britain, 1959–1969*, edited by David R. Croome and Harry G. Johnson (Oxford University Press, 1970), which contains the papers and proceedings of the Radcliffe Report—Ten Years After Conference held in October 1969 at Hove.

We wish to thank Shell International Petroleum Company Limited for their generous financial support of the Seminar and Mr. Alan F. Peters of that Company for his initiative and kindly help in many ways. The University of Sheffield also gave financial support which is much appreciated. We also wish to thank all the participants who by their presence contributed to the success of the Seminar, Professor Harry G. Johnson for his personal help, and Mr. Peter K. Else and other colleagues in the Division of Economic Studies. Lastly we are grateful for Mrs. C. Joan Cawdron's efficient secretarial help.

University of Sheffield　　　　　　　　　GEORGE CLAYTON
January, 1971　　　　　　　　　　　　　JOHN C. GILBERT
　　　　　　　　　　　　　　　　　　ROBERT SEDGWICK

CONTENTS

I

INTRODUCTION

THIS is an exciting time for monetary economics. The contributions to the Money Seminar are very helpful for an understanding of the present position of monetary economics. It will be seen that some progress is made, and lines for the future development of monetary theory and its implications for monetary policy are indicated. The centre-piece of current controversy remains the relative advantages of the income–expenditure and the quantity theory of money approaches. A wide range of opinion was represented at the Seminar. Although such supporters of Radcliffian Keynesianism as Professor N. Kaldor and Dr. A. B. Cramp[1] were unable to be present, we were fortunate to have the leading new monetarist, Professor Milton Friedman, with us. It can be argued that these two approaches are complementary, not competitive, in the general body of monetary theory. At any rate, since Wicksell divided aggregate demand into the two categories of expenditure on consumption goods and on capital goods, an analysis of aggregate demand in terms of some basic constituents has been seen to be important and helpful to an understanding of an economy. On the other hand, the quantity theory of money as developed in terms of the concepts of the velocity of circulation and demand for money to hold has been important in monetary theory, and its resuscitation and development by Friedman and the other new monetarists have been fully justified. In terms of their predictive value the two approaches appear to be more competitive. The multiplier which relates autonomous expenditure, assuming the problem of its definition has been overcome, to consumption or income appears to be unstable in the short-run and not easily predicted. The velocity of circulation, while by no means stable, does appear to be more predictable in view of the econometric studies showing a

[1] N. Kaldor, 'The New Monetarism', *Lloyds Bank Review*, July 1970; A. B. Cramp, 'Does Money Matter?', M. Friedman, 'The New Monetarism: Comment', N. Kaldor, 'Reply', *Lloyds Bank Review*, Oct. 1970.

stable demand for money function. Professor David E. W. Laidler in his paper discusses the famous study by M. Friedman and D. Meiselman, 'The Relative Stability of Monetary Velocity and the Investment Multiplier in the United States, 1897–1958',[2] and the controversies to which it gave rise. Further work is required on the definition of the control variable, autonomous expenditure or the supply of money, and the related study of the functional relationships.

Professor Robert W. Clower in his paper, 'Theoretical Foundations of Monetary Policy', argues strongly for much more analysis of a monetary economy in micro-economic rather than in macro-economic terms. He does not regard monetary policy as a sensitive or reliable instrument of control at present and urges that research should be undertaken into the dynamics of observable processes of monetary adjustment and the related possibilities of economic control. Professor Frank P. R. Brechling in his discussion of Professor D. E. W. Laidler's paper supports this approach saying that he would welcome analyses of the micro-dynamics of monetary behaviour which would give us a deeper understanding of the role of money in modern economies. Professor Harry G. Johnson in his discussion paper opposed this line, arguing that the strength of monetary theory depended upon the general analysis and not on concern with the institutional details of a monetary economy. Professor Milton Friedman in the general discussion showed no more interest in the technology of monetary exchanges than in the technology of a pin-making factory, while Clower reiterated the importance of detailed analysis of monetary trading processes.

Clower explains how the Walrasian conception of exchange precludes the use of a single commodity as a means of payment and substitutes a conception of the economic system which involves a means of payment. Undoubtedly, static and dynamic equilibrium systems can be developed to include a means of payment. It is this function of money which is emphasized by Clower, although a means of payment must also be a store of value, a temporary abode of purchasing power. He defines money not empirically but theoretically 'in terms of explicitly postulated restrictions on trading alternatives that assign a special role to certain commodities as payment media in organized markets' (p. 17 below). For the United States and the United Kingdom he defines money as

---

[2] M. Friedman and D. Mieselman, in Commission on Money and Credit, *Stabilization Policies* (Englewood Cliffs, N.J.: Prentice Hall, 1963).

currency, demand deposits (current accounts), and trade credit. In trade credit Clower includes credit card and overdraft facilities, departmental store credit and travellers' cheques, as well as commercial paper and book credits. Professor W. Brian Reddaway in his discussion of Professor Andrew D. Bain's paper points to the difficulty of monetary control because of the absence of convenient discontinuities between money and near-monies. Thus it is not surprising to find Johnson preferring an alternative definition, and Professor George L. S. Shackle in his discussion paper arguing that time deposits (deposit accounts) and unused overdraft permission should be included, while trade credits should be excluded, if we accept the definition that money is a means of payment. Shackle points out that the process of increasing trade credit is the putting off of the making of payments and that it is in influencing the velocity of circulation that trade credit plays its part. Surely theoretical and empirical definition of money are a matter of convenience, and 'assets' which could possibly be included on the supply side and are not must be taken into account on the demand side.

Professor Milton Friedman in his paper, 'A Monetary Theory of Nominal Income', develops the quantity theory of money to derive a theory of nominal income rather than a theory of prices or real income for the purpose of analysing short-period changes. He combines Keynes's idea that the current market interest rate is largely determined by the rate that is expected to prevail over a longer period with Irving Fisher's idea [3] that the nominal or money rate of interest (the current market interest rate) depends on the real rate of interest and the expected change in the price level. In this model Friedman assumes that the difference between the anticipated real interest rate and the anticipated rate of real growth is determined outside the system, an alternative to the full employment and rigid price assumptions of the quantity and Keynesian income–expenditure theories. He has a model of nominal income into which prices and quantity do not enter separately. An advantage of this model is that it allows for 'equilibrium' situations in which prices may be rising or falling and real and nominal interest rates diverge. The simple monetary theory of nominal income puts in the centre of the stage 'the relation between the flow of income at each point in time and the past history of the quantity of money'

[3] Fisher's real rate of interest doctrine goes back to Marshall, Ricardo and Thornton. See F. A. Hayek, *Prices and Production* (London: George Routledge and Sons, Ltd., 2nd ed., 1935), p. 23, n. 2.

(p. 52 below). The time path of nominal income is determined, but the division of changes in nominal income between prices and quantity is not.

Sir Roy Harrod in his discussion paper pointed out that Keynes held that, although there were special occasions when the rate of interest was determined by the views of asset holders about the future, it was in general determined by the money supply and demand for liquidity. One of his main criticisms of Friedman's system for the determination of nominal income was that it made no reference to the degree of wages-push which some economists think a primary determinant. Harrod supported Keynes in denying Irving Fisher's view that prospective inflation is added to what would otherwise be the money rate of interest. He argued that a certain prospect of inflation could have no effect on the rate of interest while uncertainty about it would raise the rate of interest. (The latter point is in line with Keynes's theory of liquidity preference, although not specifically mentioned by him.) The former point was combatted in the general discussion, it being argued that the equilibrium between bonds and equities would involve a higher money rate of interest on bonds. The opportunity cost of holding common money and current accounts is higher, owing to the negative rate of interest because of rising prices. The equilibrium, therefore, also involves less money in real terms being held, giving a higher marginal utility of 'convenience'.

Professor Thomas Wilson in his discussion paper regards the explanation of the determinants of money income without specifying the respective contribution of changing output and changing prices as the central difficulty of Friedman's approach. The analysis of economic change will be much affected by the relative importance of changes in real income. Changes in income distribution may have an important effect on the propensity to save. Wilson, like Harrod, regards the omission of cost inflation as a serious defect and writes, 'It surely will not do to leave out of account pressures on the side of supply in attempting to provide an explanation of changes in the flow of money income' (p. 68 below). Cost inflation and the possibility of an incomes policy were stressed in the general discussion, but Friedman stressed the importance of the quantity of money.

Professor David E. W. Laidler's paper, 'The Influence of Money on Economic Activity—a Survey of some Current Problems', is a wide-ranging study of recent econometric work in monetary economics, in which particular attention is paid to the currently unsettled questions and the lines of research which could be adopted for their solution. Taking a simple Hicks–Hansen macro-economic model, he argues that reduced form studies do not tell us much about the relative advantages of the income–expenditure and quantity theory approaches. He writes, 'reduced form studies can only complement an examination of structural relationships and are in no way a substitute for it' (pp. 89–90 below). Professor Frank P. R. Brechling in his discussion paper argues that reduced form comparisons can only shed limited light and stresses the danger of assuming that the money supply is purely exogenous. Dr. Douglas Fisher in his discussion paper makes use of what he describes as *ad hoc* adjustment mechanisms and considers that his findings 'suggest that the burden of proof is on anyone who wishes to treat the money stock as exogenous' (pp. 143–44). Fisher also discusses the evidence of the stability of the demand for money and submits that it is under a cloud.

There was much debate in the general discussion on reduced form versus structural (behavioural) equations, Friedman stressing the advantages of the former. Against the well-known criticisms of reduced form equations, the supporters argue that although it would be nice to have a complete theory in the form of a set of structural equations, there are great difficulties, time is short, and the short-cut is safe. Repetition of reduced form studies taking different episodes in time and place gives strong support to the method. This question is by no means settled.

Laidler concludes his detailed discussion by stating that the importance of the quantity of money as a determinant of the level of economic activity is firmly established. He states as the justification of his position that we have convincing evidence for the United States, if not yet for Britain, that variations in the quantity of money took place independently of the variation in the level of income to which they are related, and evidence that a transmission mechanism working through a stable demand for money function and a relationship between interest rates and expenditure can be shown to exist (pp. 122–23 below). Attention is drawn to his discussion of recent work on the widely diffused influences of interest rates on expenditure and the importance of time lags (adjustment and/or expectation lags) in the demand for money and expenditure functions. An explicit theoretical basis for further work on lags must be developed so that we can have 'an explicit theory of income determination that has time lags between changes in policy variables and changes in the level of income as an integral part of its structure' (p. 109). Laidler also refers to our lack of knowledge relating to the time paths of output and prices as 'perhaps *the* crucial gap in short-run macroeconomic theory' (p. 119).

Associated with Laidler's emphasis on the transmission mechanism and his reference to the lag effects of monetary and fiscal policies is the general problem of the degree of importance to be attached to the methods by which the supply of money may be increased. It is interesting to note that in 1752 David Hume envisaged that 'by miracle, every man in Great Britain should have five pounds slipped into his pocket in one night,'[4] while in 1969 Milton Friedman supposes a helicopter miracle, the helicopter flying over a community and dropping dollars from the sky.[5] Such is the continuity of economic thought. Keynes had a more complicated vision of the Treasury filling old bottles with bank notes, burying them in disused coal-mines, and determining the conditions under which they could be dug up again.[6]

In the main, attention must of course be directed to the injection of new supplies of money into an economy by open-market operations and by fiscal policy. In the discussion papers we find Shackle asking, 'if we do succeed in altering the flow, what difference to the effects of this will be made according as we alter the flow by *stock* or by *velocity*?' (p. 34 below), and Brechling stating, 'Not much is known about the differences in the short-run and long-run effects of these methods [budget deficits and open-market operations] of introducing money into the economy' (p. 140). Wilson refers to Friedman's omission of the government, having in mind the link between public finance and changes in the money supply. He writes, 'It is not at all clear how the changes in M assumed by Professor Friedman are brought about in his stateless economy.... But the manner of distribution is surely bound to have some effect on the response unless, indeed, we are considering a very long period...' (p. 168). In general discussion Clower considered the method of injection important, while Friedman thought it did not matter,

[4] David Hume, *Essays Moral, Political and Literary* (London: The World's Classics, Grant Richards, 1903), p. 307.

[5] M. Friedman, *The Optimum Quantity of Money and Other Essays* (Chicago: Aldine Publishing Company, 1969), pp. 4–5.

[6] J. M. Keynes, *The General Theory of Employment Interest and Money* (London: Macmillan and Co. Ltd., 1936), p. 129.

although it might be important for the first round. This debate which has a long history will continue well into the 1970s.

With Professor Andrew D. Bain's paper on 'Monetary Control Methods in the United Kingdom' the Seminar directed its attention from mainly theoretical considerations towards the practical problems faced by the monetary authorities in operating monetary policy in the existing financial environment, and in the process opened up a veritable Pandora's Box of controversial and unsolved issues. At least there was a substantial measure of agreement on one point, namely, that, irrespective of the appropriate targets chosen by the monetary authorities, the existing battery of controls, with its concentration on the activities of the commercial banks, has seriously impaired the efficiency of financial intermediation. It was widely felt that any reform of the methods of monetary control should give a high priority to the need to improve the efficiency of the financial mechanism.

It is difficult to quarrel with Bain's warning at the outset that proposed changes in the methods of control must take account of the present institutional framework if they are to be taken seriously. Similarly, the majority of the discussants were prepared to accept Bain's policy objectives, although some demurred at his suggestion that the *prime* objective should be to 'create conditions which are conducive to a high rate of economic growth' (p. 156 below) and felt that this was better left to market forces. Mr. A. R. Nobay, one of the primary discussants, was particularly sceptical of the desirability of an objective function, including a growth rate.

In accepting the need for reform of the existing system of reliance on an amalgam of general and specific controls Bain squarely faces the issue that it is inequitable to the commercial banks and has inevitably led, as the Radcliffe Committee predicted,[7] to the rapid growth of forms of financial intermediation which have the chief merit that they by-pass the existing controls. In such circumstances reformers have the choice between recommending the abandonment of specific controls in favour of general ones and extending the net of specific controls to cover as many financial institutions as possible.

Before outlining his own proposals Bain reveals his bias against sole reliance on general controls on the grounds that 'it would need open market operations on a massive scale and involve very large changes in interest rates to obtain the desired response' (p. 161

[7] *Radcliffe Report*, Comnd. 827, para. 504.

below). His fears echo the objection which the Radcliffe Committee made to the use of widely fluctuating rates of interest, namely that it would gravely weaken the stability of the intricate and highly developed network of financial institutions.[8] Mr. Brian Griffiths, an exponent of control solely through open market operations, is naturally sensitive to this objection, and counter-attacks, not entirely convincingly, with the argument that 'existing holders of gilts will tolerate wider short-run variations in their prices, provided they are compensated with a higher average return' (p. 188). On this issue it is as well to recognize our ignorance about the short-run demand and supply inelasticities in financial markets and the degree to which any potential interest rate instability would be reduced by the activities of speculators.

Bain finds himself in agreement with Griffiths' objectives of ensuring greater equity in the impact of control on different financial institutions and of increasing the competitiveness of the British banking system, but argues that a cash ratio system would face formidable obstacles in practice, not least of which is the Bank of England's responsibility for debt management. He therefore concludes that Griffiths' scheme is not the best way of achieving his objective.

Bain then examines the alternative approach, as exemplified by Professor J. S. G. Wilson's proposal for blocking leakages in the present system of monetary control mainly by granting the monetary authorities power to specify the maximum rates of interest payable on the liabilities of certain financial institutions.[9] The basic difficulty with such an approach is that an extension of the mechanism of control to remove unfair competition with the banks by existing non-bank financial intermediaries is likely in time to stimulate the growth of new non-bank intermediaries outside a wider network of control, thus creating a new source of unfairness to the detriment of the efficiency of the financial system as a whole. Moreover, it is likely to obstruct the entry of existing financial institutions, like building societies, into retail banking which is desirable for the furtherance of the objective of a more competitive banking system. One has the suspicion, as Bain suggests, that Wilson's scheme suffers from the major disadvantage that it would

[8] *Radcliffe Report*, Cmnd. 827, para. 491.
[9] J. S. G. Wilson, 'Regulation and Control of the United Kingdom Banking and Financial Structure', Banca Nazionale Del Lavoro, *Quarterly Review*, June 1969, pp. 128–45.

tend to ossify the existing structure and inhibit financial innovation.

Bain's own solution for reforming the system of monetary control in the United Kingdom relies on reinforcing open-market operations in gilt-edged securities and the control of key interest rates with the application of a set of asset ratios to a wide range of financial institutions. His basic proposal is that financial institutions would be required to hold in their portfolios public sector debt equal to some specified minimum proportion of their liabilities. The philosophy underlying this proposal is that it is more logical for control to be directed at certain deposit-creating activities than at the banks or particular institutions. Professor W. Brian Reddaway, one of the primary discussants, while sympathizing with this approach, raises some formidable objections to Bain's scheme. The major one concerns the threat to the effectiveness of such a mechanism of monetary control arising from the existence of large holdings of public debt outside the financial institutions in the hands of 'people who are quite prepared to sell some of it to the financial institutions' (p. 180 below). Professor Friedman in the subsequent discussion suggested that the credibility of the scheme could be restored if Bain were to include cash explicitly in the public sector asset ratio, thus maintaining control via high-powered money. Reddaway also argues that Bain's scheme requires a good deal more amplification if certain administrative difficulties are to be resolved. At the end of this session there was widespread agreement that Bain had squarely recognized the dilemma facing the monetary authorities but had not as yet succeeded in devising a practicable solution.

The next session witnessed a not unsuccessful attempt by a practising banker, Mr. John E. Wadsworth, to bring the academic participants down to earth with the presentation of his paper on 'The Nature and Uses of Bank Liquidity'. In this paper he discusses the evolution of the concept of liquidity as applied to the banking system. As was revealed by the controversy aroused by the emphasis of the Radcliffe Committee on the significance of the general liquidity effect, it presents difficulties, although it must obviously be a concern of the authorities. Analytically it is troublesome not only because it is not measurable—nor even easy to define—but because it is neither an objective nor a tool of policy but something in between. Wadsworth and the two primary discussants, Mr. Roger F. G. Alford and Professor J. Michael Parkin, go to considerable pains to unravel some of the complexities of this awkward concept. Both Wadsworth and Alford emphasize that it is misleading to concentrate on the liquidity of individual assets, while Parkin makes the useful point that the term liquidity may be attached to either the level of the liquidation cost of an asset or its variability. This distinction serves to emphasize the fact that the liquidity of assets varies over time (p. 222 below).

Having disposed of definitional problems, Wadsworth moves on to an interesting examination of the enormous swings which have taken place in the components of liquid assets in recent years, owing to increased lending by way of commercial bills despite the extension of ceilings to this form of lending also and a sharp diminution in the volume of Treasury bills. He further points out that the development of parallel markets has added to liquidity requirements, because of the tremendous growth of the intermediaries operating in these markets, and predicts that bankers will have to adopt flexible policies to maintain the liquidity of their balance sheets in a swiftly changing financial environment.

The other main topic of Wadsworth's paper is the function of both cash and liquidity ratios in regulating deposits, which he prefers to direct controls on the grounds that they allow more competition. He avers that, despite the Governor of the Bank of England's evidence to the Select Committee on the Nationalised Industries, the ratios have not been an effective curb on deposit creation but have served the purpose of easing the problems of debt management and of providing a base upon which the requirements of Special Deposits can be imposed. However, he concedes that the pressure on bank liquidity during the past eighteen months has created a new situation in which the liquidity ratio could conceivably operate as an effective regulator of deposits. Looking to the future Wadsworth expresses a preference for a mechanism of control based on liquidity ratios which could be varied in both directions and extended to cover other financial institutions.

The paper proved to be an effective catalyst, for it provided the stimulus for a provoking discussion of the theory and practice of monetary control, much of it due to Parkin's contribution. Parkin argues that in the present state of knowledge the most precise control of deposits can be obtained by controlling the stock of cash and that there is no purpose in having a multiplicity of ratios for the purpose of improving monetary control. The validity of this argument hinges on his implicit assumption that the volume of high-powered money is given by the authorities, but this is disputed by those members of the Seminar in closest touch with policy decisions. In particular it is stressed that arguments on the role and function of cash or liquidity ratios are only about subsidiary technical matters, whereas the major problem is the volume of high-powered money which the authorities feel obliged to create in view of their debt management problems. Rightly or wrongly, the authorities in existing circumstances believe that the demand for public sector debt is unstable and that an active open market operations policy is only too likely to lead to instability in interest rates. Thus the Seminar was once again brought face to face with the problem of instability of financial markets. This problem was not resolved, although one discussant introduced a new element by arguing that international competition and capital flows could be relied upon to prevent interest rate instability.

The final paper, given by Professor John H. Williamson, which was entitled 'On the Normative Theory of Balance-of-Payments Adjustment', was intended to be a recognition by the organizers of the Seminar that discussions of monetary theory and policy in the U.K. environment cannot be profitably pursued on the assumption that we are dealing with a closed economy. Williamson presents a paper which is novel in the sense that it is a pioneering attempt to apply the Ramsey[10] model to balance of payments problems. An essential element in his paper is that previous treatments of the balance of payments adjustment problem have placed excessive emphasis on the total balance of payments position including the capital account and that, consequently, policymakers can be led into the error of ignoring changes in the foreign net worth of the economy. This has led to a predilection for short-term adjustment policies which are undesirable in terms of long-run goals and, in fact, render them less attainable. A difficulty raised by Williamson's model, which occupied part of the subsequent general discussion, is concerned with the indeterminancy of the time horizon during which the economy is directed along an adjustment path towards a steady-state optimal solution. However, Williamson argues that, given the assumption of high rates of interest, the time horizon is likely to be between 5 and 10 years.

Mr. Peter M. Oppenheimer, one of the primary discussants, while acknowledging the novelty of Williamson's approach, puts forward various criticisms including, *inter alia*, what are, in his view,

[10] F. P. Ramsey, 'A Mathematical Theory of Saving', *Economic Journal*, Dec. 1928.

excessively severe strictures on Professor Robert A. Mundell's ideas,[11] the treatment of the domestic capital stock as if it were being determined independently of the external capital stock, and the welfare aspects of inflation. Mr. Marcus H. Miller, the other primary discussant, emphasizes, firstly, that particular care needs to be exercised in measuring changes in a country's international net worth and, secondly, that the maximization of welfare requires the application of the theory of portfolio selection to the composition of international assets and debts. Other discussants took up these points but also called attention to the desirability of more rigorous analysis of the role of exchange rate flexibility in Williamson's model.

Thus the Seminar moved to its appointed end in a climate of opinion which combined satisfaction with the amount of light which had been thrown on some dark corners of the monetary environment with an uncomfortable awareness of how much we still have to learn about the impact of monetary variables on the economy.

[11] R. A. Mundell, 'The Appropriate Use of Monetary and Fiscal Policy for Internal and External Stability', *I.M.F. Staff Papers* 9, 1962.

II

THEORETICAL FOUNDATIONS OF MONETARY POLICY

ROBERT W. CLOWER

Discussion Papers
(*a*) HARRY G. JOHNSON
(*b*) G. L. S. SHACKLE

II

THEORETICAL FOUNDATIONS OF MONETARY POLICY

ROBERT W. CLOWER

(Professor of Economics, Northwestern University)

DISCUSSIONS of monetary policy traditionally have proceeded on the assumption that the distinctive feature of a money economy is the existence of institutional arrangements that assign an exclusive role to certain commodities as means of payment in organized markets. In sharp contrast with this procedure, formal treatments of monetary theory traditionally have started from premises that preclude explicit consideration of alternative technologies of exchange and related questions of market organization. Historically, therefore, specialists in monetary policy have had little intellectual guidance from specialists in monetary theory. In recent years, however, monetary theorists have become increasingly aware of the shortcomings of their conceptual tools and have taken important steps to overcome them.[1] The statement of a definitive monetary theory is still a long way off, but the main outlines of an intellectually satisfying theory seem now to be discernible in the literature. My purpose in this paper is to give a common sense account of this emerging theory and to indicate some of its implications for contemporary discussions of monetary policy.

I. THE DEFINITION OF MONEY

The most significant development in the recent literature is a growing consensus of opinion among monetary economists about

[1] Cf. Harry G. Johnson, 'Recent Developments in Monetary Theory—A Commentary', in *Money in Britain 1959-1969*, edited by D. R. Croome and H. G. Johnson (London: Oxford University Press, 1970), pp. 95-100.

the proper definition of money.[2] The main difficulty in the past has been for monetary theorists to emancipate themselves from pre-conceptions carried over from conventional value theory, the whole of which rests on an essentially Walrasian conception of exchange as a virtual process in which the trading plans of a set of individuals are costlessly coordinated by a central authority whose only explicit function is to determine a vector of exchange rates that will permit individuals to carry out, at least in principle, a series of mutually consistent and beneficial barter transactions.[3] This conception of market exchange precludes assignment of a specialized role to any single commodity as a means of payment, for its logic implies that any good may be traded directly for any other good, which is to say that all commodities are perfect substitutes as means of payment. The natural consequence is to divert attention away from the function of money as a medium of exchange and to focus attention instead on its function as a store of value. From here it is but a short step to the conclusion that all assets are 'more or less money'; hence, that the definition of money is an empirical rather than a theoretical problem and must be decided accordingly on the basis of evidence as to which of a set of alternative definitions performs best in applications.[4]

Most of these perplexities vanish if we substitute for the Walrasian paradigm a conception of the economic system that permits us to view monetary exchange as a phenomenon involving the existence of a set of independent markets in each of which units of one particular commodity can be traded directly only for units of one or more other commodities that custom or law has specifically designated as means of payment. On this view, 'money' consists of the class of all commodities that serve as means of payment in organized markets, and the definition of this class constitutes an

[2] See Johnson, loc. cit. My comment is based more on impressions derived from unpublished papers by Brunner and Meltzer, Niehans, Saving, Hahn, and others than on published work.

[3] Cf. Sir John Hicks, *Critical Essays in Monetary Theory* (Oxford: The Clarendon Press, 1967), p. 6; Axel Leijonhufvud, *On Keynesian Economics and the Economics of Keynes* (New York: Oxford University Press, 1968), Chapter 2; E. C. H. Veendorp, 'General Equilibrium Theory for a Barter Economy', *Western Economic Journal*, Mar. 1970, pp. 1–3, 21–2; and R. W. Clower, 'Is There an Optimal Money Supply?', *Journal of Finance*, May 1970, pp. 425–7.

[4] See Milton Friedman and Anna J. Schwartz, 'The Definition of Money', *Journal of Money, Credit, and Banking*, Feb. 1969, pp. 1–14; and David Laidler, *The Demand for Money* (London: International Textbook Company, 1969).

essential preliminary in the formulation of any theoretical model.[5] There is nothing novel in this procedure. In Walrasian equilibrium analysis, it is assumed implicitly if not explicitly that there exists just one organized market and that within this market all commodities are universally acceptable as means of payment.[6] Similarly, in traditional (and modern) discussions of barter trade, it is commonly argued that a distinct market corresponds to each possible pairwise combination of individuals and commodities. Only during the past few years, however, have monetary theorists come gradually to recognize that trading arrangements in a money economy correspond more closely to the completely decentralized process envisioned in traditional treatments of barter exchange than to the completely centralized process implicit in Walrasian models.[7] Unanimity of opinion on this issue has yet to be attained, but present indications are that, in future discussions of monetary theory, 'money' will be defined theoretically in terms of explicitly postulated restrictions on trading alternatives that assign a special role to certain commodities as payment media in organized markets.[8]

It is one thing, of course, to establish a theoretical definition of money and quite another to decide what collection of objects in the real world should be considered to correspond to the definition. Two main questions arise in this connection: first, what markets in the real world are to be regarded as organized; second, what

[5] This rather obvious point seems first to have been made in my 'Reconsideration of the Microfoundations of Monetary Theory', *Western Economic Journal*, Dec. 1967. Its full significance was not clear to me, however, until I read Joseph Ostroy's *Exchange as an Economic Activity* (Ph.D. dissertation, Northwestern University, 1970), *passim*.

[6] Standard accounts of macroeconomics obscure this fact by referring not only to excess demand functions for goods, labour, bonds and money but also to 'markets' for each of these 'goods' (see, for example, Don Patinkin, *Money, Interest, and Prices*, second edition (New York: Harper-Row, 1965)). Walras recognized this problem in early sections of his *Elements*, for he begins by postulating the existence of 'trading posts' for various possible pairwise combinations of exchangeable commodities; but in later lessons he anticipates modern confusion by speaking as if there were a one-to-one correspondence between 'markets' and 'commodities'.

[7] On this, see Veendorp, op. cit., and Ostroy, *passim*; Jurg Niehans, 'Money in a Static Theory of Optimal Payment Arrangements', *Journal of Money, Credit, and Banking*, Nov. 1969, pp. 706–25.

[8] This theme underlies virtually all work on monetary theory that I have seen in draft form over the past two years—a biased sample, no doubt, but one that includes contributions from some twenty graduate students and an even larger number of established theorists.

commodities routinely serve as means of payment in such markets?
I do not wish to minimize the difficulty of these questions, but in
my opinion both can be answered satisfactorily in relation to the
objectives of any given investigation by direct inspection of trading
patterns and payment procedures in various sectors of the economy.
For the United States and the United Kingdom, for example, it
seems clear that for most practical purposes, 'money' should be
considered to include trade credit as well as currency and demand
deposits.[9]

The fruitfulness of a particular definition of money will depend,
of course, not only on its definition and empirical interpretation but
also on the definition and empirical interpretation of other concepts
of monetary theory. This point merits emphasis, for it underlies
what is perhaps the central theme in recent contributions to
monetary theory, namely, that the main shortcomings of conventional theory derive from faults not in empirical interpretation but
in theoretical specification.[10]

II. THE DEMAND FOR MONEY

Widespread acceptance of a definition of money that emphasizes
its role as a means of payment would be of little consequence were
this changed perspective not associated with important advances
in the theoretical understanding of market exchange processes in
the real world. Perhaps the best way to approach this subject is to
observe that the existence of organized markets in which certain
commodities play an exclusive role as means of payment does not
permit us to assert that there will exist a positive demand for such
commodities for purposes of exchange. On the contrary, to establish
theoretically that there exists a positive demand for money, we
must introduce a number of additional assumptions. This may be

[9] The essential issue here is whether the tender of any given financial instrument
permits a buyer to take delivery of a commodity from a seller. On this criterion,
trade credit qualifies as money—trade credit being interpreted to include credit
card and overdraft facilities, department store credit and travellers' checks, as
well as commercial paper and book credits. On the same criterion, time deposits
and other financial claims that are perfect or near-perfect substitutes for money
only as stores of value unambiguously fail to qualify as money. Cf. Arthur B.
Laffer, 'Trade Credit and the Money Market', *Journal of Political Economy*,
Mar./Apr. 1970, pp. 239–67.

[10] Cf. R. W. Clower, *Readings in Monetary Theory* (London: Penguin Books,
Ltd., 1969), Parts III and IV.

seen most easily by supposing (contrary to common sense) that it costs individuals nothing to engage in the activity of exchange. Then an individual's choice among alternative trading arrangements will depend simply on his tastes and initial commodity endowment and on those of his potential trading partners. The properties of this kind of economy have been explored intensively by Joseph Ostroy,[11] whose findings confirm the intuitive notion that individual pursuit of gains from trade almost always will lead to some indirect trading and show that informational requirements associated with even the simplest chains of multilateral barter are quite horrendous. But this being so, it is virtually impossible to establish precise criteria to compare the potential efficiency of alternative sets of trading arrangements. As matters stand, therefore, we cannot hope to make out a general case for the superiority of monetary over other kinds of trading arrangements; that is, we cannot assert that money *will be* used even in an economy where it *might be* used.[12]

The most obvious way to get around this difficulty is to suppose that it costs each individual something in terms of time or effort to engage in the activity of exchange. In keeping with earlier discussions of this problem by Baumol, Tobin, Demsetz, and others, we may suppose that trading costs associated with the pairwise exchange of any two commodities generally comprise two components: a fixed charge to reflect costs of search and bargaining that are independent of quantities exchanged; a variable charge to reflect costs of storage and transport that depend directly on quantities traded. Other things being equal, individuals will have an incentive, on the one hand, to trade infrequently and in large lots in order to minimize fixed trading costs per unit of time and, on the other hand, to trade frequently in small lots in order to minimize variable trading costs. It follows that total trading costs per unit of time will be a U-shaped function of average holdings of inventories of any given commodity. The position and form of these functions will vary, depending on the mode of market organization and on the commodity pairs exchanged. In systems that admit only of direct barter, for example, search and bargaining costs are likely

---

[11] Op. cit.

[12] Milton Friedman's recent attempt at formal analysis of the problem of monetary optimality (*The Optimum Quantity of Money and Other Essays* (Chicago: Aldine Press, 1969)) is logically vitiated by his failure to recognize, much less deal with, this problem.

to be extremely high for all commodity pairs by comparison with systems that permit indirect barter; and systems that involve unorganized barter among individuals are likely to entail higher trading costs than systems that involve pairwise exchange of any two commodities at organized trading centres.[13]

It has never been demonstrated formally, but it is easy to convince oneself intuitively, that trading cost functions will be uniformly lower for all commodities if trades are carried out in markets where only a few specially designated commodities can be exchanged directly for all other commodities than if trades take place in less regimented circumstances. For only if trade is highly organized can individuals consistently avoid holding inventories of virtually all commodities and yet be sure that in any desired trade there will always be a double coincidence of wants. I shall not dwell further on this subject, for I have little to add to what has already been said in recent contributions to the transactions cost literature. Here it will suffice to suppose, albeit arbitrarily, that a 'quantum jump' in trading costs separates monetary from other systems of trade so that the mere existence of organized markets for monetary exchange effectively ensures that other possible modes are never utilized.[14]

Even on this assumption, we cannot show that there will exist a positive demand for money. As a technical matter, an individual can always reduce his average holdings of money to any desired level, however small, by so synchronizing his sales and purchases in organized markets that money receipts are almost instantly reflected in money expenditures. But if trading costs are U-shaped functions of average holdings of commodity inventories, it is easy to show that individuals normally will not aim at perfect synchronization of sales and purchases. For, in general, the minimum point of the trading cost function for one commodity will not occur at a value of average inventory holdings that coincides with the value of average inventory holdings at the minimum point of the trading cost function for any other commodity or collection of other commodities. In general, therefore, individuals will find it desirable to avoid perfect synchronization of purchases and sales. This implies the existence of a positive demand for money for purposes of exchange. In effect, money is just one among many trade inven-

---

[13] On this see Sir John Hicks, op. cit.; R. W. Clower, *Readings in Monetary Theory*, pp. 7–14.

[14] Cf. Kevin C. Sontheimer, 'A Technological Representation of Money', University of Buffalo Discussion Paper (mimeo), 1970.

tories, and average holdings of money for trading purposes are determined jointly with average holdings of all other commodities.[15]

The factors governing desired holdings of money and other inventories will include, among other things, current holdings of inventories, desired average rates of production and consumption of each commodity, actual and imputed rates of interest, and anticipated rates of change of prices. Current as distinct from desired inventory holdings will be governed by prevailing market conditions that affect realized purchases and sales and realized rates of production and consumption. To formulate an explicit formal model that accurately portrays the dynamics either of individual or market behaviour in a monetary economy is obviously an extremely difficult task—so difficult that it has yet to be carried out for any but special cases.[16] Nevertheless, it seems clear on the basis of existing work that formal analysis of these problems will yield little qualitative information that is not already obtainable from more informal analysis of the sort presented here. In particular, there is no reason to suppose that conclusions from dynamic models of individual inventory-holding behaviour will differ significantly from common sense inferences that can already be drawn from static models. All the same, if monetary theory is ever to provide a reliable guide to policy action, explicit formal models must be developed.

My discussion thus far—like most of the literature on monetary theory—rests on the tacit assumption that money consists of a single commodity like gold or fiat currency. To come to grips with any practical problem, we clearly must be willing to contemplate more realistic situations in which money consists of currency, demand

---

[15] Cf. R. W. Clower, op. cit. (1970).

[16] The essential problem is to devise models that permit us explicitly to analyse price–quantity behaviour in economic systems where trade takes place at other than equilibrium prices—what are commonly (but, in my opinion, inappropriately) called 'non-tatonnement models'. Thus far only limited progress has been made in this direction. Cf. Herschel Grossman, 'Theories of Markets Without Recontracting', *Journal of Economic Theory*, Dec. 1969, pp. 476–9; Herschel Grossman, 'A General Disequilibrium Model of Income and Employment', *American Economic Review*, Mar. 1971; and Peter Frevert, 'Disequilibrium in a Macroeconomic Model', in *Papers in Quantitative Economics*, Quirk and Zarley, ed., University of Kansas Press, 1968. Reference should also be made to recent (but as yet unpublished) work by Richard W. Ruppert and Robert Russell ('Intermarket Spillover of Excess Demand and the Stability of Non-tatonnement Adjustment Processes'), and by John Ledyard ('Growth, Stability, and a Disequilibrium Action Process').

deposits, and trade credit—the last item being especially important since it is used as means of payment in virtually all business transactions. In principle, there are few difficulties in this area. To account for positive holdings of different kinds of money, it is only necessary to recognize that trading costs will depend to some extent on modes of payment, and that trading cost functions associated with one mode of payment normally will not lie uniformly below trading cost functions for other modes. Thus different modes of payment may coexist in a money economy even under stationary conditions. This is a matter of some importance because the proliferation of payment modes in any actual economy typically entails the use of one kind of money as a reserve for others. The pyramiding of monetary instruments would be of little importance in a stationary world, but (as history shows) it can become crucially important in situations of monetary disequilibrium.

III. THE ROLE OF MONEY IN ECONOMIC ACTIVITY

The preceding discussion assigns money a passive rather than active role in the determination of real economic magnitudes, for the great bulk of outstanding stocks of means of payment will consist in any advanced economy of claims whose nominal quantity is endogenously determined by factors over which no individual or government authority can exercise effective short-run control. This is not to say that money is unimportant, either in terms of the long-run effects upon real economic welfare of monetary trading arrangements or in terms of the short-run effects upon real economic magnitudes of autonomous changes in various components of the money stock. However, it does suggest that the task of identifying causal interrelations among real and monetary magnitudes is considerably more complicated than some theories of monetary phenomena might lead us to suppose.

Let us approach this subject by distinguishing two classes of monetary economies: the first, economies in which there exist no non-monetary financial assets; the second, economies in which the bulk of all financial assets consist of claims that are not money. The simplest case of an economy without non-monetary financial assets is one in which money consists either of privately produced nuggets of gold (inside money) or fiat currency notes issued and declared to be legal tender by some central authority (outside money). On either assumption, holdings of money will be governed by conditions of taste and technology that determine individual holdings of commodity inventories. Of course, changes in nominal stocks of money associated with changes in mining technology or with new issues of fiat notes will induce transient adjustments in both real money balances and in commodity inventories. In this simple system, however, the demand for money clearly will be a stable function of a few key variables, so we should not expect money to play an independent role in determining real magnitudes even if the economy is subject to frequent random shocks. The single-asset monetary economy is the appropriate frame of reference for those who regard money as a 'temporary abode of general purchasing power', for in this kind of economy the function of money is purely that of a trade inventory.[17]

The role of money becomes more complex if we admit the existence of two kinds of money commodities, one consisting of, let us say, privately produced gold nuggets, the other of privately issued promises to pay a stated number of gold nuggets on demand. Under stationary conditions of taste and technology, the performance characteristics of this model should be essentially the same as those of a single money-asset model: for in normal circumstances individuals' would regard private notes as good substitutes for gold as means of payment. Except in a system where notes were backed 100 per cent by gold, however, random shocks might set off monetary expansions or contractions in which money played a temporarily independent role via changes in the ratio of notes to gold. One can even conceive of inventory cycles in connection with this model, for the existence of commodity inventories together with fractionally-backed issues of private notes opens the door to speculative investment in inventories in periods of monetary expansion and to panic attempts to exchange notes and inventories for gold in periods of monetary contraction.

If we consider a more general model in which privately granted but non-negotiable trade credit routinely serves as money in most exchange transactions, the potential speculative impact of autonomous or induced changes in negotiable components of the money supply becomes painfully obvious. In ordinary circumstances, there will be a fairly stable monetary pyramid with gold at the apex, gold-backed notes in the middle, and gold- and note-backed trade

---

[17] This view, popularized by Milton Friedman, is implied by but does not itself entail a means-of-payment conception of money: cf. Harry Johnson, op. cit., p. 100.

credit at the bottom. But suppose that an exogenous shock produces an unanticipated increase in stocks of some inventories which, in turn, leads some individuals to reduce new orders. The initial effect may well be to expand trade credit as sales fall and inventories continue to rise; but soon there must be a sharply increased demand for notes and gold to meet the demands of trade creditors, and after this point a monetary contraction of major proportions may well ensue.

Arguments conducted on the basis of plausible rather than demonstrative reasoning do not prove anything, of course, but proof is not my object. On the contrary, my purpose is to emphasize that in any but the simplest single money-asset world, the use of money as a temporary abode of purchasing power in normal circumstances entails its potential use as a semi-permanent form of investment in abnormal circumstances. The economic significance of this conclusion depends on the extent to which changes in the demand for money directly impinge upon current flows of income and expenditure. If holdings of money balances were not closely linked with and sensitively dependent upon holdings of commodity inventories, the direct influence of monetary changes upon production and consumption activity would surely be slight. If modern trends in monetary theory are on the right track, however, the links connecting money holdings with commodity inventories are so close as to guarantee that monetary changes will invariably exert a direct and important influence upon production and consumption flows.

So much for monetary systems without non-monetary financial assets. The more general case of systems in which a major portion of all financial assets consists of non-monetary claims does not admit of any but brief and superficial treatment here. It goes without saying that such systems will be more vulnerable to speculative influences than economies without developed capital markets. Exactly as in simpler systems, changes in the demand for money will influence production and consumption decisions directly via their impact upon holdings of commodity and money inventories. Such changes will also directly affect fixed investment decisions, via their effect upon security markets;[18] for there is no

[18] For a persuasive analysis of this sphere of monetary influence, see Patrick Hendershott and George Horwich, 'The Monetary-Interest Rate Mechanism and its Policy Implications: A Critique of Milton Friedman' (Purdue University mimeo, 1970).

difference in principle between inventories of fixed capital and inventories of working capital and finished goods,[19] and in a money economy all inventory decisions will be affected directly by changes in money flows that alter either the level or composition of the stock of money. The monetary influences will also affect real economic magnitudes via familiar channels—interest rates, wealth effects, and so forth—but not, I suspect, in ways that can be inferred from the existing literature. For the very essence of the role of money in economic activity lies in the fact that it *constrains* rather than *facilitates* market exchange of other commodities in situations of widespread disequilibrium—and contemporary economic theory provides no techniques to analyse such situations.

IV. MONETARY POLICY

The bearing of the preceding discussion on the issue to which this paper is addressed, namely, the present state of the theoretical foundations of monetary policy, may be summed up in a phrase: the foundations don't exist. This being the case, my paper cannot include comments about the constituents of a 'rational' scheme of monetary policy, for surely we cannot deal effectively with such delicate issues except on the basis of a reasonably precise, logically coherent, and empirically acceptable conception not merely of the role of money in economic activity but also of related dynamic interrelations among real and monetary magnitudes. The emergence of such a conception is, I think, clearly foreshadowed in the recent literature; but the promise has yet to be realized. As of the present time, therefore, I have no basis other than 'hunch' and 'feel' for affirmative pronouncements about contemporary policy issues. However, I think some fairly definite remarks of a negative kind are in order—and also some comments about desirable directions for future research.

First, the negative remarks. Contemporary discussion of monetary policy centres upon the work of Milton Friedman, the leading apostle of a school of thought that David Fand has aptly described as 'monetarist'.[20] The growing influence of this school is regarded by some as a triumph of scientific truth over Keynesian dogma, by others as a regrettable retreat into orthodoxy, by yet others as the

[19] Cf. Hicks, op. cit., Chapter 3.
[20] David I. Fand, 'A Monetarist Model of the Monetary Process', *Journal of Finance*, May 1970, pp. 275–89. Also see Johnson, op. cit., pp. 84 ff.

replacement of one fashion in half truths by another. My position—
as reflected in earlier comments—is best described as 'sympathetic'
to the last of these possibilities. But let me elaborate.

The basic assumption of the monetarist school—according to
both its leading exponent and its leading supporters—is that there
exists a stable demand function for money, money being interpreted for most purposes as currency and commercial bank demand
and time deposits.[21] No doubt this is an essential point of departure;
a school of thought that denies the assumption is obviously in
serious trouble before it begins. But this assumption taken by itself—
or even in conjunction with a set of other assumptions that guarantee
the existence of monetary equilibria corresponding to arbitrarily
given initial conditions—leads absolutely nowhere in the discussion of monetary policy unless it is combined with numerous
other assumptions about the structure and dynamic response of the
economic system to changes in the stock of money and other
controllable policy parameters.[22] If the assumption of a stable
demand function for money and related comparative statics
propositions constituted the only fixed stars in the monetarist
universe, therefore, we might conclude without further ado that
the monetarists were hopelessly lost in space.

In truth, monetarist doctrine involves numerous other components; specifically, a large collection of so-called 'empirical
hypotheses' about the relation between short-run changes in the
stock of money and short-run changes in overall economic activity.
Unfortunately, this category of hypotheses is not one that has been
catalogued and dealt with by specialists in logic. Presumably these
empirical hypotheses could be restated as logical propositions and
subjected to conventional tests of consistency to ascertain whether
they merit further testing in the light of empirical evidence—a
procedure that is surely standard in other areas of empirical science.
However that may be, no such procedure has been followed by
monetarist writers. Acting on the classic maxim that truth follows
more surely from error than from confusion, James Tobin has
attempted to put some of the monetarist 'empirical hypotheses' into
a form where they can be subjected to conventional tests of logical

[21] Harry G. Johnson, 'Monetary Theory and Policy', *American Economic Review*,
June 1962, p. 351.
[22] Cf. M. L. Burstein, *Economic Theory: Equilibrium and Change* (London and
New York: Wiley and Sons, 1968), Chapter 13, esp. pp. 289–90 and pp.
296 ff.

consistency and factual relevance;[23] but his attempt has been dismissed by Prof. Friedman as 'imprecise, inaccurate and misleading'.[24] I pass no judgement on this exchange, except to remark that the burden of effort in arriving at a precise, accurate and authoritative account of monetarist doctrine has yet to be accepted and borne by any monetarist writer.

I shall not dwell further on a line of argument the implications of which should already be evident. Since the monetarist school has not provided an explicit formal account of the dynamics of monetary adjustment, the uncommitted student of monetary economics can hardly help but regard the bulk of monetarist literature as so much sound and fury, signifying little more than the personal charm, dialectical skill and encyclopedic factual knowledge of its chief apostle, Milton Friedman. The monetarist literature is important— and highly so—for the questions it forces us to ask about observed patterns of behaviour; but it is worth almost nothing as far as answers to these questions, or guidance in seeking answers, is concerned.[25]

So much for negative comments. Since (as indicated earlier) my own grasp of short-run monetary dynamics is at best only slightly more firm than that of the monetarists, I shall not state my own prejudices about monetary policy and related matters. It seems to me that the first duty of academic economists is to confess ignorance about matters on which they are in fact ignorant. To be sure, I may be the only academic student of monetary economics who *is* so ignorant in this area as to feel that he must eschew any but the blandest public statements about policy issues; but I suspect that I have plenty of company. So let me go one step beyond my denial of allegiance to the monetarist camp of policy proposals and declare my lack of allegiance to any other camp, Keynesian or otherwise. I am committed in truth to just one proposition, which is that I know too little about monetary dynamics to commit myself to any

[23] James Tobin, 'Money and Income: Post Hoc Ergo Propter Hoc', *Quarterly Journal of Economics* 84, May 1970, pp. 301–17.

[24] Milton Friedman, 'Comment on Tobin', *Quarterly Journal of Economics* 84, May 1970, p. 327.

[25] This observation is not in any way intended to detract from the scientific importance of Prof. Friedman's work, but rather to put it into perspective and to question its immediate usefulness as a basis for theoretical and empirical research by less talented writers. For a more elaborate appraisal and appreciation of Prof. Friedman's contributions to monetary economics, see my 'Monetary History and Positive Economics', *Journal of Economic History* 24, Sept. 1964, pp. 364–80.

systematic scheme of monetary policy, passive or active, that has been or might be proposed at this time.

This is already an over-long and discursive paper, so I shall conclude with a brief comment about directions for future research. The conception of a money economy that I have outlined does not encourage me to regard monetary policy as a sensitive or reliable instrument of economic control at the present time. Nor do I believe that its potential merits, or lack thereof, can be properly assessed on the basis of time-series and cross-section evidence of the sort that is presently available. Accordingly, I see little point in ever more elaborate statistical analyses of alternative demand functions for money or in similar studies of full-scale econometric models. However, I think we might learn a good deal about the dynamics of observable processes of monetary adjustment, and about related possibilities for economic control, if we had access to information of the sort that would be provided by a continuous cross-section sample of a representative selection of transactors whose asset holdings, sales, purchases, and income and expenditures were recorded in detail on a monthly or quarterly basis. Much of the theoretical and empirical research required to ensure proper design of such a sample, and accurate definition and measurement of relevant sample data, has already been carried out, but with other objectives in mind and without explicit reference to a generally acceptable theory of monetary phenomena. It is in this direction— the elaboration of a scheme of data collection and processing that will permit reliable empirical testing of alternative formal models of monetary adjustment—that I see some hope of future progress in monetary theory and policy and a possible end to the inconclusive debates that have plagued monetary economics for nearly two centuries. In the absence of work along these lines, I see no hope at all.

Discussion Papers

(*a*) HARRY G. JOHNSON

(*Professor of Economics, London School of Economics/University of Chicago*)

CLOWER'S paper starts with the proposition that, until very recently, monetary theorists have started from 'premises that preclude explicit consideration of alternative technologies of exchange and related questions of market organisation', and hence have provided very little guidance for specialists on monetary policy, I believe on the contrary that this has been the strength of monetary theory—that it has concentrated on general principles of analysis of a monetary economy, on the assumption that such an economy exists in reality, and has not allowed itself to be captivated by the fascination with institutional detail that so frequently blinds policy practitioners to the real nature of what they are doing. Certainly the prevailing tradition of British monetary research, which has dined out far too long on the strength of lunches in the City and, if attainable, at the Bank of England, provides little support for the view that monetary theory is at its most useful when it is most intimate with the institutional detail of the monetary authority's policy environment. The function of theory is not to furnish superficial descriptive realism for the policy-makers—who will always know more about their own realities than the theorist can hope to achieve—but to show that beneath the superficial details are operating general principles of a logical and cognizable kind. I therefore do not necessarily accept Clower's assumption that the re-examination of the foundations of monetary theory that has been occurring recently is a forward step towards more policy-relevant theory.

Clower is, of course correct in criticizing the application of conventional general equilibrium value theory to monetary economics, an application which disregards the fundamental point that everything does not exchange for everything else, but instead money exchanges for goods and goods for money. The new work which has investigated the reasons for and advantages of this social arrangement is certainly both interesting and useful, and atones for over-facile initial assumptions made by past theoretical writers. But there is a danger of throwing the baby out with the bathwater. The work Clower describes is in one sense merely an extension of the Baumol-Tobin inventory-theoretic approach to the demand for money to the recognition that money-holding is an alternative not only to the holding of inventories of other financial assets, but to the holding of inventories of goods (and services?). As such it yields a determinate 'demand for money', even though that demand is not a utility-motivated demand for money *per se* but a by-product of an optimizing approach in which money-holding is the lesser of two evils, and a purely transitional phenomenon, for any individual economic unit. The former characteristic is of normative but not positive significance; the latter has always been recognized by monetary theorists, but disappears on aggregation and hence lends itself to formulation in terms of a desired normal or average stock of money. Moreover, these characteristics are easily absorbed into the 'utility' approach to the demand for money, which has the advantage over the inventory approach of being able also to absorb the 'store of value' as well as the 'transactions' demand for money.

It is true enough, as Clower argues, that in the course of processes of monetary disturbance the normal relations between stocks of money holdings and flows of transactions become disturbed. But this is a well-known fact, and the real question is the empirical one of whether one can use these normal relations for the prediction of the outcome of such disturbances.

The crucial point to which Clower's emphasis on the new approach to fundamental monetary theory leads him is the idea that trade credit ought to be included in the total of 'money'. This contention stems from his emphasis on the 'means of payment' function of money. If we are concerned with the very short-run question of how large a demand for current goods and services the public could exercise, then trade credit is a relevant consideration— though what matters here is *unused* trade credit, not total trade credit; and the argument has a close similarity to the contention often advanced in relation to the British banking system in the immediate post-war period, that unused overdrafts should be counted as part of the money supply in addition to deposits. And the key question, which Clower does not adequately discuss, is whether the volume of trade credit is related in a stable fashion to other indices of overall economic activity, and whether expansion or contraction of the use of trade credit is sufficiently closely related to general monetary expansion or contraction for the effects of its existence to be absorbed by the conception of a legged process of adjustment to monetary change or by the notion of an interest-elastic demand for money. Instead, by dwelling on the theoretical possibilities of use of trade credit creating problems for monetary management (over how long a run?) Clower panders to the propensity of the monetary authorities to believe that monetary management is incredibly difficult, and that whatever they have in fact done must have been more intelligent than anything else they might have done—or than either doing nothing, or following the advice of theorists to aim at long-range stable growth of the money supply.

The importance Clower attributes to the inclusion of trade credit in the money supply obviously follows from his emphasis on the transactions function of money, and the ability money furnishes to acquire goods without providing other goods in exchange. And it raises some fundamental issues, since Clower challenges the empirical approach to the determination of what is and what is not money on the grounds of the transactions function. But he does not argue the matter out. True enough, an unused overdraft facility or unused trade credit enables me to buy goods that I could not afford to buy from my normal flow of income, and so enables me to make purchase decisions destabilizing to the economy. But, in contrast to the use of my money balances, use of my overdraft facility or trade credit entails the accumulation of a debt that I must eventually repay, whereas I am under no obligation to rebuild my pocket cash or deposit balance. Money can alternatively be defined as assets I can exchange for goods without incurring a debt and a repayment obligation. This definition has empirical applic-ability. Clower's alternative approach to the definition of money in terms of the total of assets and borrowing rights that I can convert into goods and services without let or hindrance does not.

Discussion Papers

(*b*) G. L. S. SHACKLE

(*Emeritus Professor of Economics, University of Liverpool*)

IF the controlling of money is to provide a means of controlling the economy, *money* has to be something which passes two tests. It must itself have, or it must transmit, powerful effects on the economy; and it must itself be susceptible to control in appropriate respects. These two requirements give us, perhaps, a sort of map-maker's fix on the definition of money. Neither requirement alone is sufficient, and, of course, there is no presumption that such a 'money' can be identified or shown to exist. We might proceed by reviewing some suggestions as to what *money* can mean. Definitions in words are necessarily circular, and will not get us anywhere unless at some stage we can point at something visible to everyone, or else say 'You all know what is meant by' such-and-such a term. *Payment* may perhaps be such a term. Payment has been made when a sale has been completed. Payment has been made when the creditor has no further claim. Payment is in some sense final. Those are still only verbal shots. But after all, does not any person know when and whether he has been paid? If we are allowed to take the meaning of *payment* as known we can, for example, define money as the means of payment. Then the quantity of money existing at some moment, the stock of money, can be defined as the means of *strictly simultaneous* payment. That is to say, it is equal to the total of all those payments which could be made without the payers receiving or counting on the payments to be made by others. Simultaneity must be insisted on here, lest we mix up quantity and velocity. A single coin circulating fast enough can carry a payments flow of unlimited size. In thus defining the size of the stock of money, we must require all payments to wait for the gun and each of them to be represented, when the gun goes off, by its value in coins or something equally unconditional. The distinction between *size of stock* and *frequency of turnover* is doubtless best preserved until we see whether we need it. Thus we ought to include in the stock of money (let us call it, at risk of pleonasm, the *momentary* stock of money) everything which can serve to make a payment, and we ought to exclude from it those things which cannot serve to make payments. Coins, notes, bank demand deposits (current accounts) must go in. And so must time deposits. In Britain at least, the distinction of availability between demand and time deposits (current and deposit accounts) is practically negligible. A note to my bank will transfer money at any moment, at a loss of seven day's interest. I cannot write a cheque on my deposit account, but I can write one on my current account which, even if that account is empty, will be honoured if covered by my deposit balance. No holder of accounts in a British bank would make any distinction between the two sorts of account in regard to their readiness of availability, as opposed to the question of loss of interest. Ought we to include, among our simultaneously payable items, money that I may have in a Building Society? No, for this would involve double counting. Building societies keep their money in the bank, so far as it is liquid. If I wish to spend money from my Building Society account, the Building Society must first write a cheque on its bank for me to pay into mine, so that I can write a cheque of my own. But my cheque in this case is waiting on, or counting on, the arrival of the Building Society's cheque, and this does not conform to simultaneity. Only those institutions are *banks* which give their customers cheque books. The money-lender and the pawn-broker are not banks, nor is the 'non-bank lending institution' which merely gathers together a lot of small bank balances (or parts of such) and amalgamates them into one big bank balance, which of course is kept in a real bank.

But there is another item. It is quite obvious (and was pointed out unequivocally forty years ago by Maynard Keynes in the *Treatise on Money*) that a man can just as well make a payment by increasing his overdraft (if he has his banker's permission to do so) as by reducing a credit balance. Unused overdraft permission, 'lines of credit', ought to be included in the stock of money on the same footing as coins, notes and bank deposits, if we are using as our definition of money 'the means of making payments'.

This leads to an obvious further question. If I can pay by increasing my debt to a bank, can I pay by increasing my debt to a shop? The plea that I had paid my debt by creating it will not be accepted. Trade credit is not the *completion* of an exchange, it is merely the postponement of the completion. If we accept the definition that money is a means of making payments, it seems to me plain that we cannot include trade credit. Trade credit, the *process of increasing* trade credit, is the *putting off* of the making of payments. But the evil day will come.

Now let us turn to the question of velocity. Velocity depends upon timing. If, at the opposite extreme from confining payments to those which could be made in disregard of each other, we say that synchronized payments shall be able to count on each other's arrival, so that even if you and I are down to zero in our bank accounts, we can still write cheques to each other for £1,000, provided we exchange them at the same moment, then a society which could synchronize all its payments would need little or no stock of money. With given TP, everyone knows that M depends on V. Synchronicity of payments, or some degree of approach to it, could be achieved by suitable timing. Such a statement is a truism. Now it may well be that *trade credit* is a great help indeed in organizing the timing of payments. If all trade accounts are settled on one particular morning, huge cheques can be written by people who owe and are owed huge amounts, even if they have only £5 in the bank. It is in influencing *velocity* that trade credit plays its part. And it is in influencing velocity that non-bank lenders play their part. Money that, in their absence, might sit in my deposit account at the bank for years on end without moving, may instead, if lent by me to them, and by them to somebody else, go rushing round the country at high speed, without, of course, ever leaving the banking system. It can flit from ledger to ledger, still counting as part of the stock of money, still leaving the *stock of money* unchanged by the vicissitudes of its momentary ownership, but greatly increasing the flow of money, that is, of payments.

We come, then, to two questions: Can we control the stock of money? Can we control the velocity of money? And to a third and fourth question: If we control the stock of money, will this result itself, or the means of attaining it, influence the velocity of money? Will altering the stock alter automatically, for example, the velocity in the opposite sense? And fifthly, if we do succeed in altering the flow, what difference to the effects of this will be made according as we alter the flow by *stock* or by *velocity*? And finally, what *are* the effects of all these manipulations in their various possible associations with each other? This knowledge, I think, is what the New Monetarists are concerned to add to what was so well understood by Alfred Marshall and Irving Fisher.

SUMMARY OF THE GENERAL DISCUSSION

PROFESSOR CLOWER'S views on the definition of money, particularly his insistence on the importance of recognizing 'trade credit'[1] as money, was a major topic of discussion. Clower stood by his argument that the only meaningful way to arrive at a satisfactory definition of money was in terms of the theory of the form and role of payments media in organized markets. He thought that such a definition was now established and led to the recognition of 'trade credit' as money. One discussant observed that one of the difficulties in accepting this kind of definition was that it was not compatible with certain accepted conventions as to what was, and what was not, money. For instance, according to Clower's definition, overdraft facilities were to be regarded as a component of the money supply, but time deposits were not to be so regarded. Clower justified this by pointing to the payments function of 'trade credit'. 'Trade credit' served as a payments media in various markets, while time deposits did not serve as payments media in any markets.

Several discussants saw no objection in principle to accepting Clower's definition of money, but they disagreed with him over the theoretical and practical significance of the advances he claimed would follow from using his definition. They thought that the advances in 'the theoretical understanding of market exchange processes in the real world' (p. 18) that a theoretical definition would lead to, were unlikely to be of great consequence to those engaged on empirical studies of monetary relationships. They also thought it unlikely that the usefulness of the existing body of empirical work on monetary relationships would be altered by acceptance of Clower's definition. Clower, on the other hand, thought that the theoretical understanding gained from using his definition, or one similar, was likely to lead to a reconsideration of the significance of existing empirical studies on monetary relationships, and reveal the importance of studying the role of different components of the money supply in equilibrium *and* disequilibrium states. During the

---

[1] Defined very broadly by Clower to include 'credit card and overdraft facilities, department store credit and travellers' checks, as well as commercial paper and book credits' (p. 18 n. 9 above).

course of the discussion Clower repeatedly stressed the last point. He argued that in disequilibrium states the 'trade credit' component of the money supply would be more volatile than the other components, and this would magnify changes in the supply of money and thus increase the independent influence of money on other economic variables.

Some support for Clower's views on the importance of 'trade credit' was provided by one discussant when he stated the preliminary findings of his empirical work on money, private institutional credit and private expenditure in the United Kingdom. Using constant price data he had obtained good regressions between private institutional credit and private expenditure, both over the whole period covered and over the sub-periods, and in many cases the regressions between private institutional credit and private expenditure were significantly better than the regressions between money and private expenditure.

There was a debate on the significance of work on the technology of money exchange. Clower's view was that part of the weakness of current monetary theory, and current empirical work on monetary relationships, was to be found in the neglect of the nature of the technology of money exchange. He thought the technology of money exchange was important because it had general monetary effects. Against this it was argued that such knowledge was unnecessary for understanding monetary relationships, just as it was unnecessary to describe the technology of pin-making when analysing the price/output behaviour of firms in the pin-making industry. One discussant thought that two important, but distinct, lines of research were being confused by some discussants. One line of research related to the relationships between money and other variables, in connection with which the institutional arrangements of money exchange might be important, and the other related to the explanation of how existing institutional arrangements had evolved. He agreed that there was a relationship between the two, but thought that the best research strategy was to treat them as independent lines of research. Clower agreed that the two could be separated, but thought that the two together would lead to better results, and referred to Patinkin's work as an example of the confusion which resulted from treating the two as being in separate economic boxes.

The issue of the significance of the technology of money exchange was at the root of a discussion of the usefulness of the Walrasian

System for analysing the money economy. Some discussants argued that the Walrasian System was unsuitable for analysing the role of money because it embodied the conception that exchange was a costless process. This view was opposed by other discussants who argued that there was no inherent difficulty in introducing money exchange into the Walrasian System, and that it provided a better framework for analysing monetary relationships than the alternative Keynesian System. Against this Clower argued that it was necessary to introduce the facts of reality into monetary theory. The Walrasian System was unsatisfactory for this purpose because it was a system for analysing equilibrium states, and because it completely neglected the technology of exchange. Disequilibrium states were one aspect of reality, and in disequilibrium states the technology of money exchange was important.

The final topic of the discussion concerned Clower's view that the ways in which new supplies of money were injected into the economy led to different initial results and different final results, a point overlooked by the monetarists. This view was challenged by Professor Friedman. He argued that it was a mistake to concentrate on the first round effects of changes in the supply of money. In his opinion the important effect was the final effect of changes in the supply of money, irrespective of how the change came about. He wanted to know what empirical evidence existed to support Clower's view. Clower claimed support for his view on theoretical grounds and on the basis of various empirical studies. However, the conflict of views remained unresolved at the end of the discussion and reappeared in a later discussion.

III

A MONETARY THEORY OF NOMINAL INCOME

MILTON FRIEDMAN

Discussion Papers
(*a*) SIR ROY HARROD
(*b*) T. WILSON

III

A MONETARY THEORY OF
NOMINAL INCOME*

MILTON FRIEDMAN

(*Professor of Economics, University of Chicago*)

IN a recent paper on 'A Theoretical Framework for Monetary Analysis',[1] I outlined a simple model of six equations in seven variables that was consistent with both the quantity theory of money and the Keynesian income–expenditure theory. The difference between the two theories is in the missing equation—the quantity theory adds an equation stating that real income is determined outside the system (the assumption of 'full employment'); the income–expenditure theory adds an equation stating that the price level is determined outside the system (the assumption of price or wage rigidity).

The present addendum to my earlier paper suggests a third way to supply the missing equation. This third way involves by-passing the breakdown of nominal income between real income and prices and using the quantity theory to derive a theory of nominal income rather than a theory of either prices or real income. While I believe that this third way is implicit in that part of my theoretical and empirical work on money that has been concerned with short-period fluctuations, I have not heretofore stated it explicitly. This third way seems to me superior to the other two ways as a method of closing the theoretical system for the purpose of analysing short-period changes. At the same time, it shares some of the defects

* This paper was published as an article in the *Journal of Political Economy*, Mar./Apr. 1971.
[1] *Journal of Political Economy* 78, no. 2, Mar./Apr. 1970, pp. 193–238.

common to the other two ways that I listed in the earlier paper.

I. THE SIMPLE MODEL

To repeat the model from my earlier paper, it is given by:

$$M^D = P.l\left(\frac{Y}{P}, r\right) \tag{1}$$

$$M^S = h(r) \tag{2}$$

$$M^D = M^S \tag{3}$$

$$\frac{C}{P} = f\left(\frac{Y}{P}, r\right) \tag{4}$$

$$\frac{I}{P} = g(r) \tag{5}$$

$$\frac{Y}{P} = \frac{C}{P} + \frac{I}{P}\left(\text{or, alternatively, } \frac{S}{P} = \frac{Y-C}{P} = \frac{I}{P}\right), \tag{6}$$

where M^D = quantity of money demanded, M^S, quantity of money supplied; Y = nominal income; P = price level; r = interest rate; C = consumption; I = investment are the seven variables to be determined simultaneously.

Equations (1) to (3) summarize the monetary sector; equations (4) to (6), the savings and investment sector.

The simple quantity theory adds the equation

$$\frac{Y}{P} = y_o, \tag{7a}$$

which enables equations (4) to (6) to be solved for the interest rate. Equations (1) to (3) then yield an equation relating the price level to the nominal quantity of money.

The simple income–expenditure theory adds the equation

$$P = P_o, \tag{7b}$$

which enables equations (1) to (3) to define one relation between the interest rate and real income (Hicks's LM curve) and equations

(4) to (6) to define a second such relation (Hicks's *IS* curve).[2] Their simultaneous solution gives the interest rate and real income.

2. A THIRD WAY

The third way that I want to suggest is somewhat more indirect.

(a) Demand for Money

As a first step, assume that the elasticity of the demand for money with respect to real income is unity. We can then write (1) in the equivalent form:

$$M^D = \Upsilon . l(r), \qquad (1a)$$

where I have used the same symbol *l* to designate a different functional form. This enables us to eliminate prices and real income separately from the equations of the monetary sector.

This assumption cannot, so far as I am aware, be justified on theoretical grounds. There is no reason why the elasticity of demand for money with respect to *per capita* real income should not be either less than one or greater than one at any particular level of income, or why it should be the same at all levels of real income. However, we have much empirical evidence that indicates that the income elasticity is not very different from unity. The empirical evidence seems to me to indicate that the elasticity is generally larger than unity, perhaps in the neighbourhood of 1·5 to 2·0 for economies in a period of rapid economic development, and of 1·0 to 1·5 for other circumstances. Other scholars would perhaps set it lower. More important, the present theory is for short-term fluctuations during which the variation in *per capita* real income is fairly small. Given that the elasticity is unlikely to exceed 2·0, no great error can be introduced for such moderate variations in income by approximating it by unity.[3]

[2] Keynes distinguished between the price level of products and the wage rate and allowed for a change in the ratio of the one to the other as output changed, even before the point of full employment. However, this change in relative prices plays no important role in the aspects of his theory that are relevant to our purpose, so I simplified the model by taking prices rather than wages as rigid—a simplification that has been widely used. However, I should have referred explicitly to this simplification in the earlier paper. I am indebted to an unpublished paper by Paul Davidson for my recognition that my earlier exposition on this point may have been misleading.

[3] Of course, considerations such as these can at most be suggestive. The real test of the usefulness of this, and the later assumptions, is in the success of the resulting theory in predicting the behaviour of nominal income.

(b) Savings and Investment Functions

As a second step, it is tempting to make a similar assumption for the savings and investment functions, i.e., to write:

$$C = Y.f(r), \qquad (4a)$$

or

$$C = Y.f(r, Y), \qquad (4b)$$

and

$$I = Y.g(r), \qquad (5a)$$

which would eliminate any separate influence of prices and real income from the savings–investment sector also. However, this is an unattractive simplification on both theoretical and empirical grounds. Theoretically, it dismisses Keynes' central point: the distinction between expenditures that are independent of current income (autonomous expenditures) and expenditures dependent on current income (induced expenditures). Empirically, much evidence suggests that the ratio of consumption to income over short-term periods is not independent of the level of measured income (equation (4a)), or of the division of a change in income between prices and output (equation (4b)). The extensive literature on the consumption function rests on this evidence.

(c) Interest Rates

A more promising route is to combine a key idea of Keynes' with a key idea of Irving Fisher's.

The idea that we take over from Keynes is that the current market interest rate (r) is largely determined by the rate that is expected to prevail over a longer period (r^*). There exists, Keynes argues, a substantial body of asset-owners who have firmly held views about the rate of interest and who force the current rate into conformity with their anticipations. This is the basic idea behind Keynes' short-run liquidity trap.[4]

Carrying this idea to its limit gives:

$$r = r^*. \qquad (8)$$

The idea that we take over from Fisher is the distinction between the nominal and the real rate of interest:

$$r = \rho + \left(\frac{1}{P} \frac{dP}{dt} \right), \qquad (9)$$

---

[4] Friedman, 'A Theoretical Framework', pp. 212–14; Axel Leijonhufvud, *On Keynesian Economics and the Economics of Keynes* (New York: Oxford University Press, 1968), pp. 158, 405, 411.

where ρ is the real rate of interest and $(1/P)\,(dP/dt)$ is the percentage change in the price level. If the terms r and $[(1/P)\,(dP/dt)]$ refer to the observed nominal interest rate and observed rate of price change, ρ is the realized real interest rate. If they refer to 'permanent' or 'anticipated' values, which we shall designate by attaching an asterisk to them, then $\rho*$ is likewise the 'permanent' or 'anticipated' real rate.

Combine (8) and the version of (9) that has asterisks attached to the variables. This gives:

$$r = \rho* + \left(\frac{1}{P}\frac{dP}{dt}\right)^*, \qquad (10)$$

which can be written as:

$$r = \rho* + \left(\frac{1}{Y}\frac{dY}{dt}\right)^* - \left(\frac{1}{y}\frac{dy}{dt}\right)^* = \rho* - g* + \left(\frac{1}{Y}\frac{dY}{dt}\right)^* \qquad (11)$$

where $y = Y/P = $ real income, and $g* = [(1/y)\,(dy/dt)]^* = $ 'permanent' or 'anticipated rate of growth of real income, i.e., the secular or trend rate of growth.

Let us now assume that

$$\rho* - g* = k_o, \qquad\qquad [(7c)] \quad (12)$$

i.e., that the difference between the anticipated real interest rate and the anticipated rate of real growth is determined outside the system. As the designation in square brackets indicates, this equation is the counterpart for the third way of the full employment and rigid price assumptions of the simple quantity theory and the simple Keynesian income–expenditure theory.

There are two ways in which assumption (12) can be rationalized: (1) over a time interval relevant for the analysis of short-period fluctuations, $\rho*$ and $g*$ can separately be regarded as constant; (2) the two can be regarded as moving together, so the difference will vary less than either. Of course, in both cases, what is relevant is not absolute constancy, but changes in $\rho* - g*$ that are small compared to changes in $[(1/P)\,(dP/dt)]^*$, and hence in r.

(1) The stock of physical capital, the stock of human capital, and the body of technological knowledge are all extremely large compared to annual additions. Physical capital is, say, of the order of three to five years' national income; annual net investment is of the order of 1/10 to 1/5 of national income or 2 to 8 per cent of the capital stock. Let the capital *stock* be subject even to very rapidly diminishing returns and the real yield will not be much affected in

a few years time. Similar considerations apply to human capital and technology.

If we interpret g^* as referring to growth potential, then a roughly constant yield on capital, human and non-human, and a slowly changing stock of capital imply a slowly changing value of g^* as well.

Empirically, a number of pieces of evidence fit in with these assumptions. We have interest rate data over very long periods of time, and these indicate that rates are very similar at distant times, if the times compared have similar price behaviour.[5] More recently, the Federal Reserve Bank of St. Louis has been estimating the 'real rate', and their estimates are remarkably stable despite very large changes in nominal rates.

Similarly, average real growth has differed considerably at any one time for different countries—compare Japan in recent decades with Great Britain—but for each country has been rather constant over considerable periods of time.

(2) Let s^* = the fraction of permanent income which is invested. Then the permanent rate of growth of income as a result of this investment alone will be equal to $s^* \rho^*$. Empirically, the actual rate of growth tends to be larger than this product, if s^* refers only to what is recorded as capital formation in the national income accounts. One explanation, frequently suggested, is that recorded capital formation neglects most investment in human capital and in improving technology and that allowance for these would make the relevant s^* much higher than the 10 or 20 per cent that is the fraction estimated in national income accounts, both because it would increase the numerator of the fraction (investment) and decrease the denominator (income) by requiring much of what is commonly treated as income to be treated as expenses of maintaining human capital and the stock of technology. In the limit, as s^* approaches unity, ρ^* approaches g^*, so $\rho^* - g^* = 0$.[6] Without going to this extreme,

$$\rho^* - g^* = (1 - s^*) \rho^*. \tag{13}$$

[5] S. Gupta, 'Expected Rate of Change of Prices and Rates of Interest' (unpublished Ph.D. dissertation, University of Chicago, 1964).

[6] An argument justifying this equality on a purely theoretical level has been developed ingeniously and perceptively by Stephen Friedberg in some unpublished papers that take Frank H. Knight's capital theory as their starting point. This equality is also a key implication of Von Neumann's general equilibrium model (J. Von Neumann, 'A Model of Economic Equilibrium', *Review of Economic Studies* 13 (1), no. 33, 1945–6, p. 7).

The preceding argument suggests that ρ^* is fairly constant, and subtracting g^* decreases the error even further.

Empirically, it does seem to be the case that ρ^* and g^* tend to vary together, though in the present state of evidence, this is hardly more than a rough conjecture.

(d) The Alternative Model

If we substitute equation (1a) for equation (1), keep the original equations (2) and (3), and substitute equation (12) in equation (11) to replace the remaining equations of the initial simple model, we have the following system of four equations:

$$M^D = \Upsilon.l(r) \tag{1a}$$

$$M^S = h(r) \tag{2}$$

$$M^D = M^S \tag{3}$$

$$r = k_o + \left(\frac{1}{\Upsilon}\frac{d\Upsilon}{dt}\right)^*. \tag{14}$$

At any point of time, $[(1/\Upsilon)(d\Upsilon/dt)]^*$, the 'permanent' or 'anticipated' rate of growth of nominal income is a pre-determined variable, presumably based partly on past experience, partly on considerations outside our model. As a result, this is a system of four equations in the four unknowns, M^D, M^S, Υ, and r.

Prices and quantity do not enter separately, so the set of equations constitutes a model of nominal income.

It will help to clarify the essence of this third approach if we simplify it still further by assuming that the nominal money supply can be regarded as completely exogenous, rather than a function of the interest rate,[7] and if we introduce time explicitly into the system. Let $M(t)$ be the exogenously determined supply of money. We then have from (1a), (2), and (3)

$$\Upsilon(t) = \frac{M(t)}{l(r)}, \tag{15}$$

or $$\Upsilon(t) = V(r).M(t), \tag{16}$$

where V stands for velocity of circulation. This puts the equation in standard quantity theory terms, except that it does not try to go

---

[7] Alternatively, we could write (2) as

$$M^S = H.m(r),$$

where H is high-powered money and $m(r)$ is the money multiplier.

behind nominal income to prices and quantities. Equations (14) and (16) then constitute a two-equation system for determining the level of nominal income at any point in time. To determine the path of nominal income over time, there is needed in addition some way to determine the anticipated rate of change of nominal income. I shall return to this below.

Although the symbolism in the demand equation for money (1(a) or (16)) is the same as in the two other specializations of the general model, there is an important difference in substance. Both the simple quantity theory and the income–expenditure theory implicitly define equilibrium in terms of a stable price level, hence real and nominal interest rates are the same. The third approach, based on a synthesis of Keynes and Fisher, abandons this limitation. The equations encompass 'equilibrium' situations in which prices may be rising or falling. The interest rate that enters into the demand schedule for money is the nominal interest rate. So long as we stick to a single interest rate, that rate takes full account of the effect of rising or falling prices on the demand for money.

3. THE SAVING–INVESTMENT SECTOR

What about equations (4) to (6), which we have so far completely by-passed? Here the interest rate that is relevant, if a single rate is used, is clearly the real not the nominal rate. If we replace r by ρ, these equations become

$$\frac{C}{P} = f\left(\frac{Y}{P}, \rho\right) \tag{4'}$$

$$\frac{I}{P} = g(\rho) \tag{5'}$$

$$\frac{Y}{P} = \frac{C}{P} + \frac{I}{P}. \tag{6}$$

If we were to accept a more restricted counterpart of equations (8) and (12), namely

$$\rho = \rho^* = \rho_o, \tag{17}$$

i.e., the realized real rate of interest is a constant, then these equations would be a self-contained consistent set of five equations in the five variables, C/P, I/P, Y/P, ρ, ρ^*. Equations (17) would give the real interest rate. Equation (5') would give real investment, and equations (4') and (6) real income. The price level would then be given by the ratio of the nominal income obtained from equations (14) and (16) to the real income given by equations (4′), (5′), (6), and (17). The two sets of equations combined would be a complete system of seven equations in seven variables determining both real and nominal magnitudes.

Such a combination, if it were acceptable, would be intellectually very appealing. Over a decade ago, during the early stages of our comparison of the predictive accuracy of the quantity theory and the income–expenditure theory, my hopes were aroused that such a combination might correspond with experience. Some of our early results were consistent with the determination of the real variables by the multiplier, and the nominal variables by velocity. However, later results shattered this hope.[8] These empirical findings are reinforced by theoretical considerations.

The major theoretical objections are twofold. First, it seems entirely satisfactory to take the anticipated real interest rate (or the difference between the anticipated real interest rate and the secular rate of growth) as fixed for the demand for money. There, the real interest rate is at best a supporting actor. Inflation and deflation are surely centre stage. Suppressing the variations in the real interest rate (or the deviations of the measured real rate from the anticipated real rate) is unlikely to introduce serious error. The situation is altogether different for saving and investment. Omitting the real interest rate in that process is to leave out Hamlet. Second, the consumption function (4′) seems to be highly unsatisfactory, especially once we take inflation and deflation into account. Wealth, anticipations of inflation, and the difference between permanent and measured income seem to me too important and too central to be pushed off stage completely.

Hence for both empirical and theoretical reasons, I am inclined to reject this way of marrying the real and the nominal variables and to regard the saving–investment sector as unfinished business, even on the highly abstract general level of this paper.

4. SOME DYNAMIC IMPLICATIONS

In equation (14), which determines r, we have so far taken $[(1/Y)(dY/dt)]^*$ as a pre-determined variable at time t and not

[8] M. Friedman and D. Meiselman, 'The Relative Stability of Monetary Velocity and the Investment Multiplier in the United States, 1897–1958' in Commission on Money and Credit, *Stabilization Policies* (Englewood Cliffs, N.J.: Prentice-Hall, 1963).

looked clearly at its antecedents. It is natural to regard it as determined by past history. If it is, we can write (16) as

$$\Upsilon(t) = V[\Upsilon(T)].M(t), \qquad T < t \tag{18}$$

where V is now a functional of the past history of income, $\Upsilon(T)$ for $T < t$. However, the past history of income in its turn is a function of the past history of money, thanks to equation (16) for earlier dates. Hence, we can also write equation (16) as

$$\Upsilon(t) = F[M(T)].M(t), \qquad T < t, \tag{19}$$

where F is a functional of the past history of money. There is also imbedded in these equations the value k_o, i.e., the assumed fixed value of the difference between the anticipated real interest rate and the secular rate of growth of output, so equations (18) and (19) must be interpreted as depicting the movements of nominal income around a long-term trend on which k_o, and its components, ρ^* and g^*, adjust to more basic long-term forces—fundamentally for both, changes in the quantity of resources available (human and non-human) and in technology.

A specific example may help to bring out the dynamic character of this simple model. Take logarithms of both sides of equation (16) and differentiate with respect to time. This gives

$$\frac{1}{\Upsilon}\frac{d\Upsilon}{dt} = \frac{1}{V}\frac{dV}{dt} + \frac{1}{M}\frac{dM}{dt}$$

$$= \frac{1}{V}\frac{dV}{dr}\frac{dr}{dt} + \frac{1}{M}\frac{dM}{dt}. \tag{20}$$

Replace $(1/V)\,(dV/dr)$ by s (to stand for the slope of the regression of $\log V$ on r), and dr/dt by the derivative of the right-hand side of equation (14):

$$\frac{1}{\Upsilon}\frac{d\Upsilon}{dt} = s.\frac{d}{dt}\left[\frac{1}{\Upsilon}\frac{d\Upsilon}{dt}\right]^* + \frac{1}{M}\frac{dM}{dt}. \tag{21}$$

Assume that the anticipated rate of growth of income is determined by a simple adaptive expectations model:

$$\frac{d}{dt}\left[\frac{1}{\Upsilon}\frac{d\Upsilon}{dt}\right]^* = \beta\left[\frac{1}{\Upsilon}\frac{d\Upsilon}{dt} - \left(\frac{1}{\Upsilon}\frac{d\Upsilon}{dt}\right)^*\right]. \tag{22}$$

Substitute equation (22) in equation (21) and solve for $(1/Y)(dY/dt)$. The result is

$$\frac{1}{Y}\frac{dY}{dt} = \left(\frac{1}{Y}\frac{dY}{dt}\right)^* + \frac{1}{1-\beta s}\left[\frac{1}{M}\frac{dM}{dt} - \left(\frac{1}{Y}\frac{dY}{dt}\right)^*\right], \qquad (23)$$

Subtract $(1/M)(dM/dt)$ from both sides, and equation (23) can also be written

$$\frac{1}{V}\frac{dV}{dt} = \frac{\beta s}{1-\beta s}\left[\frac{1}{M}\frac{dM}{dt} - \frac{1}{Y^*}\frac{dY^*}{dt}\right]. \qquad (24)$$

Assume that $0 < \beta s < 1$.[9] Equations (23) and (24) give a very simple and appealing result. If the rate of change of money equals the anticipated rate of change of nominal income, then nominal income changes at the same rate as money—we are in the simple quantity equation world. If the rate of change of money exceeds the anticipated rate of change of nominal income, so will the actual rate of change of nominal income, which will also exceed the rate of change of money—velocity is increasing in a 'boom'. Conversely, for a 'contraction' or 'recession', interpreted as a slower rate of growth in the actual than in the anticipated rate of growth of income.

Note that this way of introducing a pro-cyclical movement in velocity is an alternative or complement to the approach I suggested in an earlier article on 'The Demand for Money'.[10] I there explained the pro-cyclical movement of velocity by the difference between measured and permanent income. The two approaches are not mutually exclusive—as I indicated in 'The Demand for Money', when I left room for interest rate effects on velocity.[11] In the present context, the simplest way to introduce both effects would be to rewrite (1a) as

$$M^D = Y^* l(r), \qquad (1b)$$

where Y^* is permanent nominal income. To complete the system, equation (3) must be replaced with a more sophisticated adjustment

[9] This is the condition for dynamic stability of the system. See P. Cagan, 'The Monetary Dynamics of Hyperinflation', in *Studies in the Quantity Theory of Money*, edited by M. Friedman (Chicago: University of Chicago Press, 1956).

[10] 'The Demand for Money: Some Theoretical and Empirical Results', *Journal of Political Economy*, Aug. 1959, pp. 327–51; reprinted in Milton Friedman, *The Optimum Quantity of Money and Other Essays* (Chicago: Aldine Publishing Company, 1969).

[11] *The Optimum Quantity of Money*, pp. 130–6.

mechanism involving Y—otherwise the system, with Y^* treated as determined by the past history of Y, would be overdetermined. Equation (31) of 'A Theoretical Framework'[12] is just such a more sophisticated mechanism, so that to proceed farther along this line here would simply duplicate part of that paper.

5. COMPARISON OF THE THREE APPROACHES

None of the three simple theories—the simple quantity theory, the simple income–expenditure theory, the simple monetary theory of nominal income—professes to be a complete, fully worked out, analysis of short-term fluctuations in aggregate economic magnitudes. All are to be interpreted rather as frameworks for such analyses, establishing the broad categories within which further elaborations will proceed.

The simple quantity theory puts in the centre of the stage the relation at each point in time between a particular flow—the flow of spending or income—and a particular stock—the quantity of money; the simple income expenditure theory centres on the relation at each point in time between two components of the flow of income—autonomous and induced spending; and the simple monetary theory of nominal income on the relation between the flow of income at each point in time and the past history of the quantity of money.

In 'A Theoretical Framework' I listed six elements that the first two approaches had in common and that indicated the main unresolved problems. The third approach differs significantly in some of these elements:

1. It does not, as they do, 'analyze short-run adjustments in terms of shifts from one static equilibrium position to another' (op. cit., p. 221). It embodies a dynamic adjustment process.

2. It does not, as they do, 'regard each equilibrium position as characterized by a stable *level* of prices or output' (p. 221). It encompasses steady growth in prices or output as long-run equilibrium positions.

3. It does not 'regard interest rates as adjusting instantaneously to a new equilibrium level' (p. 222), because it allows for a change in interest rates along with a change in the anticipated rate of change of prices. However, it does neglect the effect of other factors

[12] Op. cit., p. 226.

on interest rates (the saving–investment process stressed by the quantity theory; the effect of changes in the nominal quantity of money stressed by the income–expenditure theory) except as they affect the course of nominal income and in consequence, the anticipated rate of change of prices.

4. It does, unlike the other approaches, give an 'explicit role to anticipations about economic magnitudes' (p. 222). The differences between anticipated and actual magnitudes are the motive force behind the short-run fluctuations.

5. Like the others, it fills 'in the missing equation by an assumption that is not part of the basic theoretical analysis' (p. 222). The assumption (that speculators determine the interest rate in accord with firmly held anticipations, and that the difference between the permanent real interest rate and the secular growth of output can be taken as a constant for short period fluctuations) is intermediate between the others in its link to economic theory. It is not as clearly linked to a well-developed body of theory as the simple quantity approach is to the Walrasian equations of general equilibrium, yet it has more of a link to theory than does the rigid price assumption of Keynes. Further, like the quantity approach and unlike the income–expenditure approach, there 'is a theoretical link between the short-run model and the long-run model' (p. 222).

6. The chief defect that this model shares in common with the other two is that none of the three 'has anything to say about the factors that determine the proportions in which a change in nominal income will, in the short run, be divided between price change and output change' (p. 222)—the topic with which most of the rest of my prior article deals. The one advantage in this respect of the third approach is that it does not make any assertion about this division as both the others do. It is, as it were, orthogonal to that issue and can therefore be more easily linked to alternative theories about that division.

6. CORRESPONDENCE OF THE MODERN QUANTITY THEORY WITH EXPERIENCE

I have not before this written down explicitly the particular simplification I have labelled the monetary theory of nominal income—though Meltzer has referred to the theory underlying Anna Schwartz's and my *Monetary History* as a 'theory of nominal income'.[13] But once written down, it rings the bell, and seems to me to correspond to the broadest framework implicit in much of the work that I and others have done in analysing monetary experience. It seems to me also to be consistent with many of our findings. I do not propose here to attempt a full catalogue of the findings but I should like to suggest a number, and, more important, to indicate the chief defect that I find with the framework.

One finding that we have observed is that the relation between changes in the nominal quantity of money and changes in nominal income is almost always closer and more dependable than the relation between changes in real income and the real quantity of money or between changes in the quantity of money per unit of output and changes in prices.[14] This result has always seemed to me puzzling, since a stable demand function for money with an income elasticity different from unity led me to expect the opposite. Yet the actual finding would be generated by the approach of this paper, with the division between prices and quantities determined by variables not explicitly contained in it.

Another broad finding is the pro-cyclical pattern of velocity, which can be rationalized either by the distinction between permanent and measured income or, as in the approach of this paper, by the effect of changes in the anticipated rate of change of prices.

On still another level, the approach is consistent with much of the work that Fisher did on interest rates, and also the more recent work by Anna Schwartz and myself, Gibson, Kaufman, Cagan, and others. In particular, the approach provides an interpretation of the empirical generalization that high interest rates mean that money has been easy, in the sense of increasing rapidly, and low

[13] Allen H. Meltzer, 'Monetary Theory and Monetary History', *Schweizerische Zeitschrift für Volkswirtschaft und Statistik*, 1965, pp. 404–22, p. 414. However, he referred to it as a 'long-run theory of nominal income', whereas the theory of this paper is intended to be a short-run theory. I accept much of what Meltzer says about the theory underlying a *Monetary History* but also disagree with much of it; in particular, the way he introduces real income and changes in real income into the analysis. This is strictly *ad hoc* and renders the asserted theory a logically open and under-determined theory.

[14] However, Walters reports a different result for Britain for the period since the end of World War I—a closer relation with prices in the inter-war period and with real output in the post-World War II period (A. A. Walters, 'The Radcliffe Report—Ten Years After: A Survey of Empirical Evidence', in *Money in Britain 1959–1969*, edited by D. R. Croome and H. G. Johnson (London: Oxford University Press, 1970), pp. 39–68).

interest rates, that money has been tight, in the sense of increasing slowly, rather than the reverse.

Again, the approach is consistent with the importance we have been led to attach to *rates of change* in money rather than levels, and, in particular, to changes in the rate of change in explaining short-term fluctuations.

The approach is consistent also with the success of the equations constructed by Anderson and Jordan at St. Louis relating changes in nominal income to current and past changes in the quantity of money.[15]

The chief defect of the approach is that it does not give a satisfactory explanation of the lags in the reaction of velocity and interest rates at turning points in monetary rates of change. We know, for example, that when the rate of growth of the quantity of money declines, the rate of change of income will not show any appreciable effect for something like six to nine months (for the U.S.) on the average. During this interval, interest rates typically continue to rise, indeed generally at an accelerated pace. After the interval, both velocity and interest rates start to decline.

This result is not necessarily inconsistent with the approach of this paper. Suppose that prior to the decline in the rate of monetary growth the system was not in full equilibrium, so that the actual rate of growth of nominal income $[(1/Y)(dy/dt)]$ was higher than the anticipated rate of growth $\{[(1/Y)(dY/dt)]^*\}$. Then, even the new rate of monetary growth could be higher than $[(1/Y)(dY/dt)]^*$, implying from equation (24) a further rise in velocity; from equation (23), a larger actual than anticipated rise in nominal income; from equation (22), a further rise in $[(1/Y)(dY/dt)]^*$; and from equation (14), a further rise in the nominal interest rate. These would continue until $[(1/Y)(dY/dt)]^*$ had risen to equality with the new rate of monetary growth.

However, this reaction would imply a slower rate of rise in velocity and interest rates than prior to the monetary turning point, whereas my impression is that the opposite often occurs. More important, even if the system is not in full equilibrium prior to a decline in the rate of monetary growth, the decline in monetary growth, if large enough, will make the new rate of monetary growth less than $[(1/Y)(dY/dt)]^*$. In that case, equations (24), (23), (22),

[15] Leonall C. Anderson and Jerry L. Jordan, 'Monetary and Fiscal Actions: A Test of their Relative Importance in Economic Stabilization', Federal Reserve Bank of St. Louis *Review*, Nov. 1968, pp. 11–23.

and (14) would produce a decline in velocity and in interest rates contemporaneous with the decline in the rate of monetary growth. Yet the lag in reaction is highly consistent and, in particular, seems to be independent of the size of the change in the rate of monetary growth.

Accordingly, I believe that the movements of velocity and interest rates in the first nine months or so after a distinct change in the rate of monetary growth cannot be satisfactorily explained by the approach of this paper. If these periods were cut out of the historical record, my impression is that the model would fit the rest of the record very well—not of course without error but with errors that are on the modest side as aggregate economic hypotheses go.

Periods just after turning point can, I believe, be explained best by incorporating two elements omitted from the model of this paper. The first is a revision of our equation (3) to allow for a difference between actual and desired money balances, as in equation (31) of 'A Theoretical Framework'. The second is a weakening of equation (8) to permit a stronger liquidity effect on interest rates.

7. CONCLUSION

This paper has neglected completely many important issues—the distinction between short and long interest rates, between different concepts of income, between currency and deposits, and between demand and time deposits, the role of government spending and taxing, and so on and on. It has kept to the high and rarefied, but hopefully not arid, level of $MV = PT$, and $C = a + bY$. On that level it suggests a more satisfactory simple model for analysing short-term economic fluctuations than either the simple quantity theory which takes real output as determined outside the system and regards economic fluctuations as a mirror image of changes in the quantity of money or the simple Keynesian income–expenditure theory which takes prices as determined outside the system and regards economic fluctuations as a mirror image of changes in autonomous expenditures.

That more satisfactory model, which I have labelled a monetary theory of nominal income, is not new. It is implicit and parts of it explicit in much work in the field of money of the past two decades. Its key elements are:

(1) A unit elasticity of the demand for money with respect to real income.

(2) A nominal market interest rate equal to the anticipated real rate plus the anticipated rate of change of prices, kept at that level by speculators with firmly held anticipations.

(3) A difference between the anticipated real interest rate and the real secular rate of growth determined outside the system.

(4) Full and instantaneous adjustment of the amount of money demanded to the amount supplied.

These elements are borrowed mostly from Irving Fisher and John Maynard Keynes. Together they yield a simple two-equation system that determines the time path of nominal income but has nothing to say directly about the division of changes in nominal income between prices and quantity.

Discussion Papers

(a) SIR ROY HARROD

I AM sure that I speak for all in expressing our pride and pleasure in having the renowned Professor Milton Friedman at this conference. He has been a good friend of mine over many years. I think that the first time I met him was at a conference at White Sulphur Springs in West Virginia in March 1951, where there was a large gathering of economists, Congressmen, bankers and other business-men, to discuss whether it was possible to check the inflation then proceeding owing to the Korean war by monetary and fiscal policies and without the use of direct price controls. We did not know that at that same time there was proceeding a little meeting in a studio in Mr. Winn Rieffler's garden in Washington between Treasury and Federal Reserve officials, which led to the famous 'Accord' between the Treasury and the Fed, and released monetary policy for use for the first time since the war.

I was much impressed by the vigorous part played by Professor Friedman at the White Sulphur Springs Conference.

A few days later I was over in Chicago, and he invited me to come into his seminar. It was quite a small class of some eight or ten people, seated around a little oval table. Professor Friedman told me that he had reached a point where he was intending to deal with the velocity of circulation, and invited me to give my views on that subject. After I had done so, he proceeded, by some adroit amendments, of unimpeachable logic I need hardly say, to demonstrate that my views were very near his. I could not refute him, and yet I had an underlying feeling that my views were not in fact as near his as he made them out to be. I thought 'My goodness, this is one of the most agile intellects that I have ever met'. And I have often thought since, how fascinating it would have been to stage a debate between Friedman and Keynes, whose agility was unsurpassed.

I suggest that Friedman's new approach to monetary theory, as presented today, is an extremely interesting one, namely by relating the money supply directly to nominal income and by-passing the problem of how much of the change in nominal income is due to a change in real income and how much to a change in prices. I always hold that to assess the value of a new approach one needs to ponder over it for a considerable length of time. Friedman's idea is certainly a very stimulating one. I would also call your attention to his interweaving of dynamic considerations into the later part of his paper. This strikes me as extremely valuable.

I propose in what follows to deal first with some special points that I find difficult, and then to proceed to some general considerations.

In the early parts of the paper we are presented with two alternative approaches, one based on quantity theory and one based on the income–expenditure theory. The latter, as set out, is not to be identified with Keynesian theory. It can be given a more general significance. I mention this point, not with the idea that our thoughts should be trammelled by a particular master. Nothing could part further from the spirit of Keynes than to treat his works as a sort of sacred text. I mention Keynes only because Friedman himself refers to him in several places. On page 42 above 'the income–expenditure theory' has an equation stating that the price level is determined outside the system. This is an approach worth exploring, but it is not, of course, consistent with the Keynesian system.

I next proceed to a passage where Keynes is mentioned (p. 44):

The idea that we take over from Keynes is that the current market interest rate (r) is largely determined by the rate that is expected to prevail over a longer period (r^*). There exists, Keynes argues, a substantial body of asset-owners who have firmly held views about the rate of interest and who force the current rate into conformity with their expectations. This is the basic idea behind Keynes's idea of the short-run liquidity trap.

This is not acceptable. Keynes doubtless held that there are special occasions when the rate of interest is determined by the views of asset holders about the future. A classic example of this occurred after Keynes's death, when the Chancellor of the Exchequer, Dalton, tried to hold the long-term interest rate at $2\frac{1}{2}$ per cent by the use of monetary policy. If, he argued, we could run a great war at 3 per cent, we ought to be able to run the peace at $2\frac{1}{2}$ per cent. But the asset-holders thought otherwise. The movement into cash was so massive that Dalton could not achieve his objective.

But, apart from some special occasions, Keynes held that the

rate of interest was determined by the relation between the money
supply and the demand for liquidity; by altering the money supply
the authorities could, within certain limits, put the rate of interest
where they wanted it to be. This might almost be said to be the
central core of Keynesian doctrine.

Now, leaving Keynes aside, I find a great difficulty on page 45.
At the top of page 45 we have been given an interesting concept
entitled ρ^*, which is the 'permanent' or 'anticipated' value of the
real rate of interest. Whatever the final value of this concept may
prove to be, it is acceptable in logic. On page 45 we are given another
asterisked term, g^*, the permanent or anticipated growth rate,
which is also logically acceptable. But I do not think that we can
accept an asterisked term for the future rate of increase of prices
or the future rate of increase of nominal income. Surely they must
depend in part at least on policy decisions, which cannot be anticipated.

At the end of the third paragraph there is a reference to the rate
of price increase, where, going back to the right-hand term of
equation (11), I had expected rate of nominal income increase.

On page 46, there is a wrong conjugation in the first paragraph.
I must apologize for thus flatly correcting its distinguished author;
but it has to be. A slowly changing stock of capital should not be
conjugated with a slowly changing value of g^*. It is an acceleration
or deceleration in the rate of change of a stock of capital that should
be conjugated with a changing value of g^*.

I have further difficulties on page 46. Why is the growth of income
equated to $s^* \rho^*$? I should have thought that we had to go back to
the preceding page, where we are given a constant ρ^*. The growth
of income depends on the fraction of national income invested and
on the capital income ratio. I have a further difficulty in that
national income may grow at a different rate from that of income
from capital. There is the question of labour productivity. This may
grow more quickly than national income and more quickly than
income from capital.

I would like to venture a more simple explanation for the lag
between a change in the rate of growth of money and a decline of
the interest rate than that given on page 55. I suggest that this
phenomenon occurs merely because a change in monetary policy
takes some time to change the level of economic activity and of
unemployment.

I will proceed to some more general considerations:

1. It seems anomalous to have what purports to be a system determining the level of nominal income that makes no reference to the degree of wages-push. Some of us think that the wages-push is the primary determinant of an increase of nominal incomes when that occurs. We do not have much knowledge of what determines the degree of pushfulness from time to time; there seem to be cycles of pushfulness. We have with us here Professor Hines who has done important work on this subject.

2. In the system before us the influence of changes in monetary policy on employment does not appear. Yet surely these are important.

3. There is a reference to a view of Irving Fisher that I am shortly about to challenge. But there is no reference to a more helpful view of his as expounded in his Theory of Interest, namely that an equilibrium interest should measure the rate at which the marginal utility of income declines as income grows. Thus the rate of interest is affected by the rate of growth of income per head; it would be equal to that rate of growth only if the elasticity of the marginal income utility schedule were equal to one. We usually suppose that it is lower than one, so that the interest rate should be higher than the growth rate per caput.

4. I now come to my most important point. I am afraid that I shall be challenging a very widely held view, one held by many of you perhaps. It is painful to indulge in a head-on conflict, but it seems to be necessary in me to do so. I do not accept the Irving Fisher view that we should expect the money rate of interest to exceed what that rate would be if there were a prospect of stable prices by an amount equal to the expected rate of inflation. This view goes back beyond Irving Fisher to Alfred Marshall, who expressed it in his evidence before the Gold and Silver Commission in 1886. Keynes gave an outright denial of this doctrine and I am sure that Keynes was right.[1]

Bonds and cash are two forms of asset denominated in money. Neither has a hedge against inflation. Consequently, if after a period in which prices were expected to remain stable there arose a firm belief that prices will rise at a certain rate, the relative value of two kinds of asset neither of which contains a hedge against inflation would not change. The rate of interest represents the rate at which bonds can be exchanged for cash. Since neither contains a hedge

[1] Professor Paul Davidson later supplied chapter and verse for Keynes's rebuttal of Irving Fisher.

against inflation the new-found expectation that inflation will occur cannot change their relative values or therefore the rate of interest.

What the new-found anticipation does is to change the relative values of money-denominated assets on the one side and equities and real estate on the other; to these we should add, antiques, pictures, etc., which have recently become growingly important. As the equities etc. do contain a hedge against inflation which money-denominated assets do not, we should expect their prices to rise and their yields to fall relative to the yields on bonds. This is precisely what has in fact happened in recent years both here and in the U.S.A.

The idea that a new-found expectation can alter the relative value of two money-denominated assets, is logically impossible, and must not be accepted into the corpus of economic theory.

I fear that this flat denial of a theory that is so widely held may set up tension in the minds of some of you. Superficially the theory seems so well borne out by the facts. The fear of inflation has been increasing and interest rates have risen to unprecedented levels. Does it not, you may think, seem obvious that the one is the cause of the other? I hope to be able to relieve your mental tension somewhat.

The occurrence of a new-found belief firmly held, that a certain rate of inflation will occur, cannot affect the rate of interest. But the growth of *uncertainty* about what rate of inflation, if any, is in prospect, can send up the rate of interest. And this growth of uncertainty is, I submit, precisely what has been happening lately. If at a given point of time a man confidently expects a certain rate of inflation, then he will have to make up his mind how to divide his assets between those denominated in money and equities etc. He will hold a proportion of equities even if, owing to the expectation of inflation, they carry a lower yield than bonds. Then he will have to decide how to divide his money-denominated assets between bonds and cash, that depending on convenience. The yield on bonds will be no greater than it would be if stable prices were expected.

But now let us introduce *uncertainty* as regards the future. For instance, at present some may believe that the Government will take manful action to check the rate of inflation that we have recently been experiencing. Alternatively, we may fear that the Government will be weak and feeble, that the rate of inflation will by consequence increase and even in due course develop into a galloping inflation. If a man cannot be certain which way things will go, he may feel that he might have to review his distribution between equities etc., and money-denominated assets, say in a couple of years time. Going into equities means loss of income. He may feel that he has protected himself sufficiently on a reasonable expectation for the time being, but that it is important that he should be free to review the distribution of his assets in the light of how the inflationary situation develops in future. If the prospect gets really bad, he will be prepared to sacrifice even more current income in order to get a larger hedge against inflation.

The idea that he may want to review his distribution in a couple of years time or even sooner will affect the desired distribution of his money-denominated assets between bonds and cash. He will need to stay liquid if he is to be able to go more deeply into equities without loss at a later date. Given the supply of bonds and cash, if more people want to be free to be able to move out of money-denominated assets at a somewhat later date, this will send up the rate of interest on bonds. This is straightforward Keynesian theory of liquidity preference; but I do not recall his citing uncertainty about future inflation as one ingredient in the desire for liquidity.

To recapitulate. Certainty that prices are going to rise in future at a certain rate can have no effect on the rate of interest. Uncertainty about whether they will rise and by how much can send up the rate of interest by making a larger number of people want to remain liquid in respect of a larger proportion of their assets for the time being. I suggest that recent phenomena are fully accounted for by this explanation.

On the side of investment a certain prospect of inflation will tend to stimulate it. If there is initially under-employment the extra investment will be matched by extra saving on the ordinary Keynesian multiplier mechanism. But if there is initially full employment or nearly so, the extra investment may have some tendency to send up prices. This is but another instance of the vicious spiralling that is apt to break out when we have inflation. The prospect of inflation gives rise to extra investment and the extra investment may increase the degree of inflation.

Finally one might raise the question what is the yield of bonds— the yield as recorded or its excess over the time deposit rate? The latter is determined by the Bank of England. The difference between the bond rate and the time deposit rate does not seem to have been increasing markedly recently.

Discussion Papers

(b) T. WILSON

(*Professor of Economics, University of Glasgow*)

As I rise to comment on this paper I feel a little like Rip Van Winkle, for it is some time since I took part in a discussion of the issues before us today. On such an occasion, Rip can scarcely ask for a more invigorating stimulant to his dull enfeebled faculties than a contribution by Professor Friedman.

In the paper before us, as in his recent article in the *Journal of Political Economy*, Professor Friedman combines the quantity theory and the Keynesian income–expenditure theory in half-a-dozen equations in order to provide a means of explaining the determination of money income. We must now ask what can be claimed for this exercise. How much further are we when we have got it? I must confess that one of my difficulties has been to decide how seriously the author himself takes the exercise. In some places he appears to be claiming a good deal; in others he is stressing the limitations of the equations and is retracting much. On the basic issue, however, his position is clear. That is to say, he lays stress on both the desirability and feasibility of providing a set of equations that will explain the determination of money income without it being necessary to specify the extent to which these increases in money income are accompanied by increases in real income. For my part I have serious doubts about this undertaking which I shall mention briefly in a moment.

Meanwhile let us look at some of these functions. Are they adequate and adequately explained? Are they mutually consistent? What empirical assumptions have been made? Professor Friedman himself mentions that his consumption function $[C/P = f(Y/P, r),$ $I/P = g(r)]$ is inadequate, although he does not refer to changes in the distribution of income as one of the omitted factors. The investment function is emphatically non-Schumpeterian in its neglect of innovations in both processes and products; for my part I have long since ceased to believe that the changing flow of investment expenditure can be adequately explained in terms of such aggregates. The terminology also gives some cause for concern. Is it right to use 'permanent' and 'anticipated' as synonyms in some of the contexts? Then there are the empirical questions. We are told for example that it is obviously the real rate of interest (ρ) that is relevant for decisions about saving and investment. How does he know? This is an empirical question the answer to which must be partly affected by the length of period under consideration.

Let us now set the machinery to work by supposing that in a period of depression the investment schedule moves upwards— presumably—in this model—because some fixed capital falls due for replacement. The money rate of interest (r) is pegged at r^* by speculators, so that $r = r^* = \rho + [(1/P)\,(dP/dt)]$. Various questions suggest themselves. Who are these speculators? On what data do they base their anticipations? If the range of determining factors is to be extended on grounds of realism, this last question is one that cannot be pursued very satisfactorily given the assumption of only one rate of interest—as Professor Friedman himself would no doubt concede. An expansion will imply, in Keynesian terms, a transfer from M_2 to M_1 balances. How long then can this go on if it so happens that the total supply of money (assumed to be autonomous) does not rise? There are points that one would wish to see more fully developed but, admittedly, this would carry us beyond the assumptions of the model.[1]

[1] May I insert a postscript at this point? Consider once more a period of expansion. In Professor Friedman's paper, it is only in order to allow for changing prices that speculators will allow r, the money rate, to diverge from ρ, the real rate which equates *ex ante* savings and investment. If, however, we were to start from a period of price stability, and if it were further assumed that prices would rise only when, at 'full employment', there was an element of demand inflation— i.e. no cost inflation—then it would be necessary to ask how a rise in prices *could* occur if r were in fact kept equal to ρ. May be one is inclined to say that the need to allow for a price rise would be present only in so far as r was held *below* ρ. Is there some question of circularity here? Suppose, however, that the autonomously determined money supply were *somehow* raised and all costs and prices were expected to rise by the same proportion, then r^* and r would, on the Friedman assumption, be altered sufficiently to keep savings and investment equal. What is then being described is a demand inflation but it is not apparently, a demand inflation of the kind that reflects any divergence between *ex ante* savings and investment. This does not mean, of course, that such an inflation cannot occur. Moreover, we need not start from a period of price stability. Then, of course, a lagged model with more explicit assumptions about expectations would be desirable.

It is also interesting to ask what happens if M is increased at less than full employment. This, however, would carry us beyond the scope of any reasonable postscript.

Before we leave the question of velocity may I comment on some references to the empirical evidence made by Professor Friedman and also by Professor Laidler? For these also puzzle me. In their comments on the 1929 turning point it is claimed that the rate of growth of the stock of money slowed down before output declined. No one, presumably, would wish to take it for granted without a great deal of additional detailed evidence that a change in the rate of growth of the money stock reflected only a change on the side of supply and not at all on the side of demand. But, in addition to other factors, demand is affected by velocity and, at this time, velocity was increasing. It is surely sensible to infer that the optimistic expectations of the New Era must, in themselves, have tended to move the L_2L_2 curve to the left—if Keynesian language is permitted but equity investment is brought into the picture. Thus the need for additions to total M for the financing of production would be reduced.

Let us now turn to what I regard as the central difficulty. Professor Friedman has offered an explanation of the determinants of money income without specifying the respective contribution of changing output and changing prices. Is this a permissible approach? There are two familiar questions to be asked of any such model. How far does it explain—

(1) the forces that strengthen an expansion or a contraction and tend to make it cumulative, and
(2) the forces that tend to damp it down?

The answers to these questions are surely bound to be much affected by the extent to which changes in money income are accompanied by changes in real income.

Consider two contrasting situations at either extreme:

(a) one where there is a rise in output only with no rise in prices;
(b) one where there is a rise in prices with no rise in output.

In the former case plans to save and to invest may be reconciled in the familiar way by a rise in real income although, with the accelerator at work, neither stability nor stable growth is inevitable. Case (b) corresponds to a situation which interested pre-Keynesian economists and continued to interest some of the Keynesian critics such as Dennis Robertson. It is possible to create a model where savings and investment, *ex ante* are brought into equality not by rising real income but by a change in the distribution of income with corresponding implications for the propensity to save. More recently this line of thought has been developed by Professor Kaldor in his growth model. At the outset, I mentioned that Professor Friedman had omitted an important factor by not allowing for possible changes in distribution. This is what I had in mind. What Professor Friedman has done has been to extend the application of a basically 'Keynesian' function for consumption to cover a 'non-Keynesian' situation. (The word 'Keynesian' needs quotation marks. I do not mean that John Maynard Keynes himself was uninterested in the problems of inflation!)

It is probably still a fair criticism of much that is written about instability that too little attention is given to shifts in the share of profits and too little stress placed on the importance of corporate savings. We must, however, be fair to Professor Friedman by recognizing that a rise in prices is neither a necessary nor a sufficient condition for changes in the share of profits. A non-inflationary cyclical expansion may very well be accompanied by a rise in the share of profits, and this share may similarly decline during a contraction even if prices do not fall. Indeed the position is a good deal more complicated than the pre-Keynesian theory implied. When an inflationary situation has been reached it does not follow that non-profit incomes will lag behind rising prices. Even if we so specify our assumptions as to exclude cost inflation—and this, of course, would be a massive abstraction from reality—it remains quite possible that a demand inflation will make a larger and faster impact on factor prices than on product prices. There is a still more corrosive complication. It is not satisfactory to retain the assumption that changes in the flow of savings have no direct effect on decisions to invest. For there will be a direct effect, and perhaps, an important one, when the savings are business savings. To allow for this effect involves, however, much more than a marginal adjustment to many models as well as Professor Friedman's. My object in mentioning all these difficulties about what has been called theory (b) above is not of course to suggest that the issues with which it is concerned can be neglected but rather to draw attention to the confusing range of possibilities and the paucity of our knowledge. We cannot, therefore, try to push the difficulty aside by assuming that a few modifications of a systematic nature can easily be made in the equations. We scarcely know, nowadays, what form a systematic pattern may realistically be expected to take. I must still, however, contend that *one* of the several factors will be the relationship between the flow of real output and the flow of monetary expenditure. My doubts remain about the wisdom of trying to explain the determination of money income without regard to the extent to which this reflects higher prices and higher output respectively.

Finally I am worried by two omissions. The first is, of course, the omission of government. I do not suppose I shall have any difficulty in persuading you that I am all for simplification—even to the verge of simple-mindedness! But I am not satisfied that the omission of the state is really a simplification. I have in mind not only the general impact on the economy of government expenditure and taxation but also the link between public finance and changes in the supply of money. It is not at all clear how the changes in M assumed by Professor Friedman are brought about in his stateless economy. There have been references in the past to a benevolent helicopter which releases bags of cash. But the manner of distribution is surely bound to have some effect on the response unless, indeed, we are considering a very long period; but then some of the other assumptions in the model could not be expected to hold. One cannot treat the 'length of period' as a handy piece of elastic to be stretched to different lengths for different equations in the same model. The second big omission is, of course, cost inflation which is so clearly an important factor in the present critical situation. It surely will not do to leave out of account pressures on the side of supply in attempting to provide an explanation of changes in the flow of money income.

SUMMARY OF THE GENERAL DISCUSSION

THE discussion opened with a claim that the model presented by Professor Friedman did not reflect the application of a useful methodological approach. One discussant argued that Friedman's approaches were *ad hoc* and exhibited no consistent patterns. The theoretical foundations of his model were implicit rather than explicit and this detracted from the usefulness of the model as a starting point for the analysis of short-period variations in nominal income.

Other discussants questioned the purpose of the model. They argued that the short-run theory of nominal income presented by Friedman was of limited significance because it left unanswered the important short-run question of the price/output breakdown. In his reply to this criticism Friedman recognized the importance of developing an analysis of the short-period price/output breakdown process, but justified his model on the grounds that it provided an important alternative to the quantity and Keynesian income–expenditure theories.

A major topic in the discussion was Sir Roy Harrod's assertion that while the money rate of interest could be affected by the growth of uncertainty about the rate of inflation in the near future, it could never be affected by the certain prospect of inflation in the near future. He claimed support for his view in Keynes's advocacy of the same view in *The General Theory*.[1] In answer to this one discussant referred to Sir Dennis Robertson's comment on this particular passage of Keynes's as 'his curious misunderstanding of Professor Fisher's celebrated proposition'[2] and argued that both Keynes and Harrod were wrong on this issue. He was supported in this belief by most of the discussants.

The argument advanced against Harrod was that the money rate of interest was affected by the *certain* prospect of inflation as a direct consequence of this expectation. A certain prospect of inflation carried with it an equally certain prospect that the amount

[1] pp. 141 ff.
[2] D. H. Robertson, 'Mr. Keynes and the Rate of Interest' in *Essays in Monetary Theory* (Staples Press, London, 1940), p. 21. See also 'Industrial Fluctuation and the Natural Rate of Interest' in the same volume, pp. 89 et seq.

of money paid in dividend per share would also rise by approximately the same proportion as the rise in prices. In this situation it followed that for balance to exist between the expected average yield on bonds in the near future and the expected average yield on equities in the near future, the current yield on equities would have to be below the current yield on bonds. It was then argued that while in principle the required 'reverse yield gap' could arise either through a fall in the yield on equities relative to the money rate of interest, or a rise in the money rate of interest relative to the yield on equities, the former was ruled out by consideration of the required adjustment in terms of equity dividends. If the expected rate of inflation exceeded the 'traditional' yield on bonds, the dividend on equities might have to be negative to leave the money rate of interest unchanged. Hence it was more rational to suppose that the balance between bonds and equities would be maintained by a rise in the money rate of interest relative to the yield on equities.[3] Further, Fisher's real rate of interest reflects the rate of return on capital, allowing for expected price level changes.

It was also argued that Harrod's claim that no equilibrium between bonds and money would be possible if the burden of adjustment was borne by the money rate of interest was wrong. Increases in the money rate of interest would not give rise to a flight from money, but merely, to a reduction in the amount of real money balances held until the increased marginal 'convenience' yield on real money balances had risen by an amount sufficient to re-establish equilibrium.

On Friedman's model, one discussant suggested that a Phillips curve mechanism could be added to the model to explain the short-period price/output breakdown. He argued that by using a Phillips curve mechanism it should be possible to show that in the short-period increases in the supply of money would give rise to increases in real output, but in the longer run they would be absorbed by wage and price increases and not increases in output. Friedman's answer was that this result depended on the existence of stable expectations. If expectations were unstable the relationship would break down. He claimed that the empirical evidence suggested that the Phillips curve was unstable—in reality it was vertical.

Several discussants thought that Friedman neglected the part played by Trade Union pressure in inflationary processes. Their

[3] This part of the summary has benefited from a note provided by Professor Reddaway.

view was that wage-push was not the sole cause of inflation, but that it was an important force in some inflationary processes. Friedman rejected this view. In the historical evidence he had examined Trade Union pressure was unimportant in periods of inflation. The important factor was always increases in the supply of money, irrespective of the reasons for the increases.

A discussant asked Friedman if he stood by his belief that the only way to stop inflation was by reducing the rate of growth of the money supply, even though this would cause output and employment to fall before prices. Friedman replied that he did not think that it was possible to cure inflation without increasing the level of unemployment. He also stated that even attempts merely to hold the rate of inflation constant would still give rise to unemployment. To cure inflation it was necessary to reverse expectations, and in his view the only sure way to reverse expectations was to reduce the rate of monetary growth. Increased unemployment would be the inevitable first consequence of this action, and was essential for bringing about a reduction in the rate of change of prices and a reversal of expectations. It was his view that incomes policy was of no use in trying to reverse expectations.

One discussant claimed that the recent high rate of growth of the supply of money in the United Kingdom was a direct consequence of the failure of incomes policy. This gave rise to a discussion of the exogeneity/endogeneity of the money supply. It was argued that Friedman's views on inflation depended on whether or not the supply of money was exogenous. Friedman accepted that the exogeneity/endogeneity of the money supply was an important issue. His own view was that in reality the money supply was neither wholly endogenous nor wholly exogenous. However, he did not think that this nullified his views on inflation.

At the end of the discussion Friedman gave a statement of his views on the question of the importance of how new money is injected into the system. He stated that he had studied evidence which went back over a long period on increases in the money supply in the United States, and this evidence failed to show that the method of injection was important. Different methods of injection gave rise to different initial results, but he was only interested in the end result, and the end result was not affected by the method and point of injection. He suggested that those theorists who claimed the contrary should stop relying on blind assertion, and present evidence to support their claim.

IV

THE INFLUENCE OF MONEY ON ECONOMIC ACTIVITY—A SURVEY OF SOME CURRENT PROBLEMS

DAVID E. W. LAIDLER

Discussion Papers
(*a*) F. P. R. BRECHLING
(*b*) D. FISHER

A Note on U.S. and U.K. Velocity of Circulation
MILTON FRIEDMAN

IV

THE INFLUENCE OF MONEY ON ECONOMIC ACTIVITY—A SURVEY OF SOME CURRENT PROBLEMS*

D A V I D E. W. L A I D L E R

(Professor of Economics, University of Manchester)

I

THE growth of knowledge about monetary phenomena over the last fifteen years or so has been enormous and recent literature is almost embarrassingly rich in surveys of that knowledge.[1] To write yet another survey paper needs a good reason, and mine is this. Over the past fifteen years, the main task which monetary economists have set themselves has been to convince their, by and large sceptical, colleagues of the importance of the influence of monetary factors not only on real variables, but also upon the variable whose determination was at one time regarded as a purely monetary

* In addition to the official discussants, Frank Brechling and Douglas Fisher, I have received helpful comments on earlier drafts of this paper from Milton Friedman, Charles Goodhart, Richard Harrington, Michael Parkin, David Sheppard, Ian Steedman and John Williamson. Lorne Ellingson provided invaluable help in dealing with the computations whose results are to be found in Section III. A number of important papers appeared while this one was in the course of preparation, leading to a far greater than normal amount of revision and rewriting. Particular thanks are due to my secretary, Mrs. Jane Wild, for coping so patiently with the extra burden of typing this produced. Finally, I am deeply indebted to the Houblon–Norman Fund for the generous financial support without which this paper could not have been written.

Reference to books and articles is by author and date alone; the Bibliography will be found on pp. 132 ff. below.

[1] Among these surveys may be numbered Goodhart and Crockett (1970), especially Appendix 1, Harris (1968), Johnson (1962, 1967, 1970), Laidler (1969a), and Walters (1969, 1970). The Walters references are particularly valuable as guides to work on the British economy.

phenomenon, the price level. The tendency, therefore, whether in research articles or in surveys, has naturally and rightly been to stress what has been learnt rather than to draw attention to what is yet to be found out. Moreover, research strategy has hardly been uniform, and there has been remarkably little debate as to which strategy is likely to be most fruitful. Again, this has been understandable and desirable; had monetary economists permitted themselves to become involved in methodological debate, our stock of positive knowledge about monetary phenomena would be significantly smaller than it now is.

However, it is no longer necessary to be defensive about working in monetary economics. The importance of the field is well established, and it seems worth while to draw attention to those questions which we have not yet answered, and also to look at past work to see whether there is anything to be learnt from it about what particular research strategy is worth following in attempting to deal with these unsettled questions. In this paper, then, there will be more emphasis on what we have not yet learnt about money than on what we know and more explicit attention than usual will be paid to matters of method.

The more important questions at issue are as follows. Is it possible that variations in the quantity of money can have a systematic influence upon the level of real income and prices? Is it the case that there are episodes of economic history that can be interpreted in terms of such influence? Is this influence more predictable than that of variations in autonomous expenditure? If there could, or does, exist such systematic influence, through what channels might, or does, it get transmitted? Are there any significant time lags involved in this transmission mechanism? If there are, are these lags constant? If they are not constant, are they systematically related to any economic variables in a manner that would enable variations in lag effects to be predicted?

In order to organize these questions in a manner that will enable empirical evidence to be brought to bear on them in a systematic way some formal model is required. One cannot have an hypothesis about the answer to any of these questions without a theoretical framework that will yield testable predictions. As we shall see, the greatest difficulties arise in connection with those questions about which we lack formal theories because these are the problems about which we do not yet know which empirical questions to ask. However, a well known and simple theoretical framework will take us quite a long way. The Hicks–Hansen macro model is part of the basic tool kit of every economist and has underlain a great deal of work in monetary economics. The model may be set out as follows, linear in the real variables for simplicity.[2]

E is real expenditure, Y is real output, r is the rate of interest, M is the quantity of nominal balances and P the general price level, and with bars over variables indicating that they are exogenous, we have

$$Y = E = \bar{A} + kY - ar \qquad (1)$$

$$\bar{M} = Md = (mY - lr) P \qquad (2)$$

As it stands, the model is underdetermined. One, though not the only, solution to this problem is to postulate two distinct situations, one characterized by unemployed resources in which the price level is fixed at an historically given value (call it P^*) so that the model determines the level of real income, and the other characterized by fully employed resources which fix the level of income (at Y^*) leaving the model free to determine the equilibrium price level.[3]

It is worth noting explicitly that this model does not enable us to deal with all the questions posed above: the model is static and tells us about the equilibrium relationships between variables. It does not enable us to formulate questions about the time paths whereby endogenous variables approach new equilibrium values when exogenous variables change.

Nevertheless, this model does yield predictions about the relationships between the equilibrium level of income or prices and variables

[2] In equation (1) the aggregation of expenditure into one category is meant to leave open the possibilities that interest rates affect consumption and income affects investment. As Friedman (1970) recently pointed out it is an empirical hypothesis that the borderline between those categories of expenditure largely dependent upon income and those largely independent of it corresponds to the consumer expenditure–investment borderline.

[3] As the reader will notice, this model is a linearized version of the model set out by Alford (1960) and also used by Friedman (1970). The assumption adopted here to deal with the underdetermination of the model is the simplest available way of filling in what Friedman refers to as the 'missing equation' (1970, p. 219). This writer prefers this reverse L-shaped aggregate supply curve to the frequently used upward sloping one whose construction requires the assumption of an aggregate production function in which the capital stock is always fully utilized. This should not be taken as implying that the reverse L is a very satisfactory construction either, however. The relationship between the price level and real income is taken up below in Section IV of this paper.

potentially under government control such as the money stock and the level of government expenditure (subsumed into A in equation (1)) or tax rates (here ignored for simplicity or perhaps subsumed into the parameter k as suits the reader's taste), and, since a great deal of work over the last fifteen years has been devoted to testing predictions yielded by models of this type, any account of unsolved problems in monetary economics is best begun with a brief review of the results achieved by these tests.

II

At the very outset of this survey we are faced with a methodological question. Given that we are interested in finding out about the stability of the relationships between equilibrium levels of income and prices and such variables as the quantity of money and the level of autonomous expenditure, we can proceed in two distinct ways. We may either test hypotheses about the relationships between income, interest rates and expenditure, and those about the relationships between the demand for money and income and interest rates, and then see what the results of these structural tests imply about the relationships that ultimately interest us, or we can take a short cut and attempt to estimate directly the reduced form relationships that exist between the exogenous variables and the target variables such as income and prices.

Now both kinds of study have been carried out, but at least one economist has expressed a preference for reduced form estimates.[4] I will argue in this section that in fact we have learned a good deal less from studying reduced forms than is often supposed because the actual statistical hypotheses tested have been ill-devised to discriminate between the economic hypotheses that were alleged to underly them. The tests in question are supposed to distinguish between simple 'Keynesian' and 'Classical' accounts of the income determination process. The 'Keynesian' hypothesis at stake is that all, or at least most, fluctuations in income and prices are the result of fluctuations in autonomous expenditure while the 'Classical' hypothesis attributes such fluctuations to variations in the quantity of money.[5]

[4] Cf. Walters (1970), p. 51.

[5] Friedman and Meiselman (1963) produced the first comprehensive study of this type for the United States, and their results were challenged by Hester (1964), Mayer and Deprano (1965), and Ando and Modigliani (1965). The latter three

Now if we start from the Hicks–Hansen model, there are three ways to produce a simple 'Keynesian' model. Two of them involve the assumption that the rate of interest is an exogenous variable. This may be justified on the grounds that the demand for money function becomes perfectly elastic with respect to the rate of interest at some positive, exogenously given, value which happens to be ruling in the circumstance being analysed. This assumption is also appropriate if the monetary authorities choose to control the rate of interest and hence permit the nominal stock of money to become determined by the level of nominal income. In either event the supply and demand for money are rendered irrelevant as far as the income determination process is concerned; equation (1) forms a complete income determination model by itself, a model often presented in the form of the famous 'Keynesian cross' diagram. The 'Keynesian' simplification may also be obtained by assuming that expenditure is independent of interest rates. In this case, equation (1) still determines real income, and equation (2) determines the interest rate.

Alternatively, one may make the assumption that the velocity of circulation is independent of the rate of interest, that the parameter l is equal to zero. In that case, income (or the price level in full employment situations) is determined solely by equation (2);

papers were almost solely concerned with showing how changes in the definition of 'autonomous expenditure' could improve the performance of the 'Keynesian' hypothesis. Only Ando and Modigliani touched upon the more fundamental issues, with which I am concerned here, of the ability of the tests to discriminate between the hypotheses at stake. They did so in an appendix to (1965) which apparently was written after their paper was completed (cf. Friedman and Meiselman, 1965, p. 781 for evidence of this) and did not influence the procedures they adopted in the paper. In any event, by failing to distinguish between real and nominal variables in this appendix, they missed some rather serious problems. The research staff of the Federal Reserve Bank of St. Louis have also done work on Multipliers recently (e.g. Anderson and Jordan 1968) but since this work is more aimed at establishing empirical regularities that may be useful for policy purposes than at testing basic propositions about monetary theory, it is less open to criticism than is the earlier work in question; the evidence it provides still cannot be used to distinguish between propositions of economic theory, of course.

For Britain, work on Multiplier has been done by Barrett and Walters (1966), Sheppard (1970), and Artis and Nobay (1969). It is interesting to note that the latter study, modelled on that of Anderson and Jordan was unable to produce the kind of stable empirical relationship between the quantity of money and the level of money income for post-war Britain that Anderson and Jordan found for the United States.

equation (1) determines only the rate of interest. This particular assumption yields a naïve 'Classical' model.[6]

So long as raising the question of which of these simple models has the more empirical content is not read as forbidding one to ask at the same time whether more complicated models do not have more empirical content than either naïve model, and it certainly should not be so read, there can be no objection to the issue being put in this way. Indeed, given the methodological precept that a 'good' theory is one that can predict 'much' from 'little' there is a great deal to be said in favour of this exercise: certainly one would be hard put to it to find two models based on 'less' than these two, and if either of them did prove to be empirically useful, this would be an important discovery. The trouble is that, as I have already indicated, comparing the reduced forms of these two models is not a very useful test of their relative empirical relevance.

The procedure typically followed has been to divide expenditure between an induced (i.e. income dependent) component, usually referred to as 'consumption', and the rest, so that our expenditure function becomes, with C being consumption and I other expenditure, two relationships.[7]

$$C = kY \tag{3}$$

$$I = \bar{A} - ar \tag{4}$$

Regressions of the forms

$$PC = b_0 + b_1 PI + v \tag{5}$$

$$PC = d_0 + d_1 \bar{M} + u \tag{6}$$

are then performed, and the explanatory power of these two equations over time series data is compared, using both R^2 and the consistency of parameter estimates between separate sub-periods as criteria. The use of the money value of the 'consumption' as a

[6] See Additional Note 1 (p. 129 below).

[7] There is, as noted above, an extra empirical hypothesis introduced by this division of expenditure, cf. n. 2 above. There has been quite a lot of dispute as to where in fact this borderline between 'induced' expenditure and the rest ought to be drawn. The bulk of the 'Friedman–Meiselman' debate centred on this issue, but only Friedman and Meiselman themselves noted that consumer expenditure included expenditure on durable goods, which might better be classified as being more closely akin to investment than to consumption of non-durables. I am indebted to Michael Hamburger for drawing my attention to this point. His work on the demand for durable goods (1967) lends substance to this suggestion.

dependent variable rather than the money value of income is of no particular significance. Given that investment is a component of income the use of PY as the dependent variable in equation (5) would lead to spurious correlation between Y and I biasing the outcome of the tests in question in favour of the 'Keynesian' view of the world. Consumer expenditure, which apparently bears a close proportional relationship to income in aggregate time series data, is used as a proxy for income to avoid this problem.[8]

Now we may ask what naïve 'Keynesian' and 'Classical' models might lead us to predict about the empirical performance of equations (5) and (6). The answers we may give will depend upon whether we are dealing with an unemployment situation, in which variations are predominantly in real variables, or with a full employment situation in which it is the price level that is varying. Let us consider the unemployment case first of all.[9]

Our version of the Hicks–Hansen model, modified to make the income determination process independent of the quantity of money, yields either

$$P^*C = \frac{k}{1-k}(A - a\bar{r})P^* \tag{7}$$

if we assume that the interest rate is exogenous, or simply

$$P^*C = \frac{k}{1-k}(A)P^* \tag{8}$$

if we assume that the interest rate is irrelevant to real expenditure. In either event, mere inspection of equations (7) and (8) ought to

[8] But there still remains the problem of expenditure on durables. Cf. n. 7. The reader's attention is also drawn to the fact that the relative prices of consumption and investment goods can shift. To make the assumption that the prices of both groups of commodities may be represented by the general price level is a simplifying assumption that may not hold true.

[9] The * signs attached to the price variable should be read as indicating that this is to be treated as constant. Thus, everything in the discussion that follows applies also to the work of those who have used data cast in real terms in similar tests. (These include Friedman and Meiselman (1963) and Sheppard (1970).) This result follows from the assumption of price rigidity in unemployment situations, and this is really a very unsatisfactory assumption. For example between 1929 and 1933 prices in the U.S. fell by 26·7 per cent while *per capita* income fell by 37·5 per cent. We are faced again with the problem of the missing equation that links output and prices. Cf. n. 3. The full implication of this observation is that the Hicks–Hansen model is inadequate to explain the data with which it is here confronted, but in the absence of a better model it will have to do.

convince the reader that, if the 'Keynesian' model is true, equation (5) ought to provide strong evidence of a close relationship between consumption and 'investment'. The trouble is that, were velocity constant, so that real income was determined solely by the quantity of money, equation (5) would perform equally well, provided only that there was a stable marginal propensity to consume. The equilibrium level of real income, even if a constant velocity of circulation ensures that it is proportional to the quantity of money, must, after all, still satisfy the relationship

$$Y = \frac{1}{1-k} \tag{9}$$

All that is required for equation (5) to provide a good empirical performance is a stable value for k.[10]

Moreover, equation (5) could still perform 'better' than equation (6) even if all systematic variations in real income were attributable to variations in the quantity of money. In the type of model we are considering here, in which there is neither interest elasticity of consumption, nor a 'wealth effect', changes in the quantity of money cause changes in income by way of their effect on interest rates and hence on investment. The quantity of money variable of equation (6) is further removed along the causal chain from income and consumption than is the investment variable of equation (5), and hence might well be found to be less closely related to them even though it was the variable that was solely responsible for determining the latter.

Now we have shown that equation (5) will perform well in unemployment situations as long as the consumption function is stable. What about equation (6)? If the demand for money is independent of the rate of interest, then equation (2) yields

$$P * Y = \frac{1}{m} \bar{M} \tag{10}$$

and, provided that there is a stable average propensity to consume to permit the substitution of consumption for income, equation (6)

[10] Friedman and Meiselman note this point to some extent when they suggest that the good performance of the 'Keynesian' model in the 1930s may reflect effects of the quantity of money working through its influence on investment, but they do not appear to have appreciated its full significance for the appropriateness of their tests. Sheppard similarly recognizes the problem (1970) and tests for the effect. With the money supply lagged he finds it significant for the inter-war period for Britain, and recognizes its importance for the interpretation of his results.

ought clearly to perform well, though not necessarily better than equation (5), as we have already argued.[11] On the other hand, if income is determined independently of the quantity of money whether or not equation (5) will perform well depends upon which version of the 'Keynesian' model it is that is operative. If the level of income were determined independently of the quantity of money because of a 'liquidity trap', then the well-known result that such a 'trap' permits velocity to vary in order to adapt any quantity of money to any level of income implies that only by the most unlikely mischance would equation (6) perform well. Were the level of expenditure altogether independent of the rate of interest, and provided that there was some interest elasticity to the demand for money, equation (2) would yield

$$P* \, \mathit{T} = \frac{\mathrm{I}}{m} \bar{M} + P* \frac{l}{m} r \qquad (11)$$

Since, $P*$, T and $\bar{M}$ would all be determined independently of the demand for money, only the rate of interest could vary to equilibrate this market. Equation (6) would be unlikely to provide a convincing explanation of the observations that would be generated in such circumstances.

Even so, equation (6) is quite capable of producing 'good' results when the 'Keynesian' account of the income determination process is correct. This would happen in a situation in which the monetary authorities were seeking to control the rate of interest, but in which there also existed a stable demand for money function in which the level of income entered as an important argument. In such circumstances a stable relationship between the quantity of money and the level of income might well be observable but the direction of causation involved would be from income to money rather than vice versa.[12]

[11] Given that Friedman's permanent income variable is virtually a linear transformation of consumption (cf. Friedman 1957) and given that Friedman found a close relationship between the quantity of money demanded and permanent income (cf. Friedman 1959) it is arguable that a good performance on the part of equation (6) merely reflects these relationships and adds nothing to what we knew from them already.

[12] This line of argument seems to have been first brought into contemporary debates by Hester (1964), who fully recognized the need to explain the close relationship between money income and the quantity of money in some way if he wished to adopt a largely 'Keynesian' view of the income determination process.

To summarize the last few paragraphs: as far as unemployment situations are concerned, there are circumstances in which the income determination process can be purely 'Keynesian' and in which both equations (5) and (6) will simultaneously produce 'good' results, while equally 'good' results could be obtained with both expressions when the income determination process was purely 'Classical' in nature. Indeed, regardless of what it is that determines income, equation (5), which purports to embody a 'Keynesian' model, will only show up badly if the conventional consumption function is unstable, whereas the 'classical' model will tend to perform well whenever there is a stable relationship between the demand for money and the level of income. A comparison of equations (5) and (6) could actually be misleading, because it is quite possible that equation (5) will produce the better statistical results even when faced with data generated by a world in which income is primarily determined by the quantity of money. Thus, the fact that periods of relatively heavy unemployment, notably the 1930s for the U.S. and 1920s and 1930s for Britain, produce statistical results that show equation (5) to be superior to equation (6) in no sense implies that either economy should be characterized as having been predominantly 'Keynesian'. All such a result shows is that the marginal propensity to consume was reasonably stable over the periods in question. The fact that equation (6), though performing less well on the whole than equation (5), nevertheless gave reasonable results when faced with the same data, is enough to prevent our disqualifying a 'Classical' account of the income determination process during these periods.[13]

This evidence does at least suggest that the 'liquidity trap' was not a phenomenon of any particular importance during the years in question, but, *taken by itself*, it still leaves open the possibility that changes in the quantity of money were the consequence rather than the cause of changes in the level of income. This point will be taken up later.

As far as underemployment situations are concerned then, tests of the relative stability of money and investment multipliers of the

[13] I base this broad generalization of what the results show on evidence produced by Friedman and Meiselman (1963), Ando and Modigliani (1965), Deprano and Mayer (1965), and Hester (1964) for the U.S., and by Barrett and Walters (1966) and Sheppard (1970) for the U.K. Note, though, that both Friedman and Meiselman and Sheppard raised the possibility of causation running from money through 'autonomous' expenditure to income and 'induced' expenditure (cf. n. 10 above).

type described seem to be ill-devised to answer the questions with which they were supposed to deal. None of this evidence tells us anything about cause and effect. The situation is even worse when we come to ask what these same tests might reveal in a situation of full employment. In such circumstances our simple model tells us to treat the level of real income as given, and it becomes a price level determination model.[14] Problems arise the moment we make the 'Keynesian' simplifying assumptions; equation (1) does not permit us to determine the price level. Either aggregate demand is equal to output, in which case the price level will remain at whatever its historically given level might be, or it exceeds it, in which case there will be an 'inflationary gap' which cannot be closed by any mechanism embodied in equation (1); it is nonsensical to treat the simple 'Keynesian model' as having any relevance at all to the determination of the level of *money* income in a fully employed economy.

As Johnson (1967) has pointed out, all this was well enough known during the early post-war period and led many 'Keynesian' economists to superimpose wage cost theories of the price level, and its rate of change, upon this simple macroeconomic model in order to deal with the problem of inflation. However, this problem seems to have been forgotten by their successors who were only too eager to accept the proposition that regression results based on equations implied by an expression like

$$Pk\Upsilon^* = PC = \frac{k}{1 - k}(I)P \qquad (12)$$

would shed some light upon the money income determination process, the only proviso being that the division of national income between 'induced' and 'autonomous' components was done on some basis other than that proposed and adopted by Friedman and Meiselman.

This does not mean, of course, that one cannot get close correlations between the money value of consumption and the money value of 'autonomous' expenditure during periods of full employ-

---

[14] Thus, tests using real variables observed at full employment periods are, in the context of the model I am using here, fundamentally misconceived. Real income, and hence real 'induced' expenditure, is determined by supply side constraints and not by aggregate demand. It must be borne in mind, though, that an unique level of full employment output is more a property of the model we are using than of any actual economy. Again we are faced with the unsolved problem of the interaction of output and the price level.

ment. To begin with the price levels of these two components of national income would tend to move together in inflationary periods, while, to the extent that the economy was growing in real terms, one might expect real consumption and investment to grow together—particularly if the former is indeed proportional to real income.

Now Friedman and Meiselman (1963) found, overall, a poor fit between consumption and 'autonomous' expenditure measured in nominal terms, and the fit was particularly bad in periods of relatively full employment. This result is perhaps a little surprising in view of the foregoing arguments and it is not to be wondered at that different definitions of autonomous expenditure produced closer statistical relationships for the United States, or that similarly close relationships seem easy enough to discover for Great Britain. What is perplexing, however, is that anyone should have suggested that the existence of a well-determined statistical relationship between nominal consumption and the money value of 'autonomous' expenditure, however defined, could tell us anything about the money income determination process in a fully employed economy.

As far as the fully employed economy is concerned, the simple 'Classical' model wins the contest with the simple 'Keynesian' construction by default. Equation (2) implies

$$PY^* = \frac{1}{m}\bar{M} \tag{13}$$

and we need only call $1/m$ by another symbol, V, to realize that we are applying the quantity theory of money in its income velocity form to the very problem with which it was originally designed to deal—namely that of the determination of the price level in a fully employed economy.

This of course is not to say that this model will perform well empirically—only that it is applicable to the explanation of fluctuations in the level of money income in a fully employed economy.[15] An exogenously given level of output is only one condition for this model's success—velocity must be stable and, if

[15] This simple 'quantity theory' approach performs extremely badly for post-war Britain, far worse indeed than for the inter-war years. Cf. Walters (1969) for a summary of this evidence. Note that Laidler and Parkin (1970) have suggested that these difficulties arise from not taking account properly of the lag structure of the economy, rather than from unstable monetary relationships. The question of time lags is taken up in some detail in Section IV of this paper.

in fact the rate of interest is an important variable in the demand for money function, the more variation there is in the rate of interest the less satisfactory will be the performance of equation (6) when faced with evidence drawn from a fully employed economy. Thus, testing equation (6) against such data can reveal inadequacies in the simple 'Classical' model, but since we have no alternative model with which we can compare its results, this does not get us very far. How 'inadequate' we judge the 'Classical' model must always depend upon whether or not it does better than a rival, and we have no rival in this case. At the same time, *taken by themselves*, 'good' statistical results are open to the objection that they tell us nothing about the direction of causation.

As far as a fully employed economy is concerned, then, the tests we are discussing are even less revealing than they are in an unemployment context. The simple 'Keynesian' model should not be applied to such data, since it is not a theory of the determination of the level of money income at full employment. All that 'good' results obtained with equation (5) reveal is that the average propensity to consume is relatively stable and that, over the periods to which the equation has been fitted, the relative price of consumption and investment goods has not varied much. They reveal nothing about the role played by variations in so-called autonomous expenditure in determining the level of money income. What we can learn about equation (6) is also limited. It is reasonable enough to apply it to full employment data, but in the absence of a properly conceived rival theory there is no yardstick by which we may judge the adequacy of its performance. Moreover, even the 'best' statistical fit imaginable would still tell us nothing about cause and effect in the income determination process.

Studies of reduced form equations have not only concerned themselves with asking which of these two simple models is the better approximation to reality. Attempts have also been made to allow for the fact that shifts both in the quantity of money and in autonomous expenditure can contribute to variations in the level of money income. Again using consumption as an income proxy, regressions of the form

$$PC = b_0 + b_1 PI + b_2 \bar{M} + \epsilon \qquad (14)$$

have been run, and the magnitudes and stability (usually as measured by T statistics) of the parameters b_1 and b_2 have been interpreted as yielding information about the relative importance and predictability of monetary and real effects in the income determination process. As far as unemployment situations are concerned, this *appears* to be a reasonable enough procedure, for our version of the Hicks–Hansen model yields, without the simplifying 'Keynesian' or 'Classical' assumptions, the following expression for money income:

$$P* Y = \left[\frac{1}{(1-k) + \frac{a}{l} m} \right] AP* + \left[\frac{1}{(1-k)\frac{l}{a} + m} \right] \bar{M} \qquad (15)$$

It would be easy to confuse this expression with equation (14), for it implies a linear relationship between autonomous expenditure, the money supply, and money income. However, the term 'autonomous' tends to be used ambiguously in macroeconomics. Sometimes it is taken to mean expenditure whose value is determined independently of income (I in equation (14)), and sometimes it is used to describe expenditure that is independent of income *and the interest rate* (A in equation (15)). The empirical studies we are discussing here have used variants of equation (14), and this expression is at best a mis-specified version of equation (15). If monetary policy worked entirely through interest rate effects on investment, as our simple model implies, then to fit equation (14), when I is given by equation (4), would ensure that all monetary effects were already embodied in the so-called 'autonomous expenditure' term; nothing would be left over for variations in the money supply to explain, even if it was in fact the dominant variable in the income determination process. It is small wonder then, for both Britain and the United States, and independently of the exact breakdown of national income made between C and I, variations in autonomous expenditure turned out to be the most important variable when equation (14) was confronted with data from unemployment periods.

When we come to deal with full employment, matters are again worse. With real income fixed exogenously, our simple model yields as an expression for the price level

$$P = \frac{M}{Y* \left[m + \frac{l}{a}(1-k) \right] - \frac{l}{a} A} \cdot \qquad (16)$$

'Autonomous' expenditure clearly effects the level of money income in a positive direction, but once more this is 'autonomous' expenditure in the sense of expenditure that is independent of both income *and the interest rate*. Moreover, it is *real* autonomous expenditure that appears in equation (16). This equation is distinctly non-linear and shows clearly that the effects of changes in the quantity of money and of changes in real autonomous expenditure do not interact in a simple additive way in determining prices and hence money income. Though the relationship between prices and the quantity of money is linear, the 'money multiplier' in this case has a value that depends, among other things, upon the level of real autonomous expenditure. The more unstable is autonomous expenditure, the more unstable will be the money multiplier. The inclusion of the money value of investment as an additive variable in equation (14) represents a considerable mis-specification of the 'true' Hicks–Hansen model as it applies to a fully employed economy, and it is not clear what there is of value to be learnt from fitting equation (14) to such data.

Now the last few pages argue that, in terms of the Hicks–Hansen framework, reduced form studies do not tell us much. They provide some evidence about the stability of a simple aggregate consumption function, thus giving us some information about the structure of the underlying model, while, for most times and places, they also betray signs of a stable relationship between the quantity of money and the level of nominal income. This latter result suggests some sort of presumption in favour of the proposition that changes in the quantity of money could have a stable and predictable effect on the level of income, but they stop far short of establishing it, particularly since the relationship in question is by no means observed consistently, its absence being particularly notable as far as Britain in the 1950s and 1960s is concerned.

If changes in the quantity of money can cause, or have caused, changes in the level of income, then it takes far more than evidence of a statistical association between the two variables to convince anyone of this. First, a plausible transmission mechanism must be demonstrated to exist in order to establish *the possibility* of variations in the quantity of money being able to influence the level of income; second, in order to establish that such influence *has in fact taken place during particular historical episodes*, it must be shown that the variations in the quantity of money that are supposed to have been the cause of variations in the level of income were not rather their consequence.

As far as problems at hand are concerned, then, viewed even in the most favourable light, reduced form studies can only complement

7

an examination of structural relationships and are in no way a substitute for it. In terms of the Hicks–Hansen model, mere inspection of equations (15) and (16) tells one that the parameters of all the behaviour relationships in the model are potentially relevant to the transmission mechanisms whereby both changes in the quantity of money and in autonomous expenditure affect the level of real income and prices; the strict implication of this observation would be that this survey should now branch out to consider in more or less detail the evidence on each of these structural relationships and then go on to ask about the implications of this evidence for the Hicks–Hansen model. Obviously it would take far more than the space of one paper to carry out this task and so, as far as the next section of this paper is concerned, I shall confine the discussion mainly to demand for and supply of money. It is no more justifiable to do this than to concentrate on, say, the investment function. The division of labour is the only viable defence for thus narrowing down the paper's scope at this point.

III

The importance of a stable demand for money function for the workings of monetary policy should be self evident. If the demand for money is a predictable function of a few variables, then changes in the supply of money must result in at least one of those variables changing in order to maintain equilibrium in the money market. Though the demand for money function does not provide the whole transmission mechanism whereby changes in the quantity of money might lead to changes in income, employment and prices, it provides a vital link in that mechanism. Moreover, most of the scepticism concerning the efficiency of monetary policy that is still enshrined in so many textbooks was based on the proposition that the demand for money was highly interest elastic and likely to be unstable. It is not surprising then that a great deal of the work that has gone into re-establishing the importance of the quantity of money as an important economic variable has concentrated on this particular functional relationship.

Most of the work in question has been carried out using United States data, even though two of the earliest modern studies of the demand for money dealt with Britain (Brown (1939) and Khusro (1952)). The American evidence has been surveyed in a fair amount of detail elsewhere (cf. Laidler (1969*a*)), and it will suffice here to summarize the conclusions that have emerged from it. The evidence in favour of the existence of a stable relationship between the aggregate demand for real balances and a few variables is overwhelming. The variables in question appear to be an interest rate, which is interpreted as measuring the opportunity cost of holding money, and 'permanent' real income, or the real value of non-human wealth, either of which variables performs consistently better than current real income.[16] Moreover there is a good deal of evidence that the demand for real balances is independent of the price level. In short there appears to be no empirical basis for the view that the nature of the demand for money function precludes the money stock from having an important and systematic influence on aggregate demand.

Now data for the United States go back a hundred years, and the demand for money function has not remained immutable over so long a period. For example, the elasticity of demand for real balances with respect to permanent income as computed for time series data has fallen from about 1·6 for the pre-First World War period to somewhere in the region of 0·7 over the years since the Second World War. These figures are, of course, but a statistical reflection of the fact that the often noted secular decline in the velocity of circulation was particularly pronounced in the late nineteenth century and has actually reversed itself since 1945. They suggest that there has been a slow shift over time of the demand for money function, a shift that has yet to be explained, but which may well be the result of the increasing financial sophistication of the American economy.[17]

The interest elasticity of demand for money has been more stable, particularly with respect to short rates of interest; this parameter seems to have lain consistently between −0·15 and −0·20 over the period for which data are available, but there is a

[16] Of course the interest rate does not measure the opportunity cost of holding money in the Keynesian theory of the speculative demand for money. However, the absence of evidence for the existence of a liquidity trap or any marked instability in the interest elasticity of demand for money, this theory's two characteristic predictions, seems to justify interpreting the interest rate as measuring the opportunity cost of holding money. A simple discussion of the relevant theoretical arguments and of the relevant empirical evidence will be found in Laidler (1969a), pp. 50–6, 97–8.

[17] Note that results presented below in Table 2 suggest that this falling elasticity *may* be a statistical illusion produced by an inadequate treatment of the price level. The results in question, though, are the product of very preliminary work, and may prove to be quite untrustworthy when investigated further.

growing body of evidence that those assets which are particularly close substitutes for money have changed over time. Since the Second World War, the demand for money appears to have become particularly stably related to the interest rate paid on the liabilities of non-bank financial intermediaries (cf. Lee (1967) and Hamburger (1968)), rather than to rates on such assets as short-term commercial paper.

That there should be some secular shifts in the demand for money function ought not to be too surprising in an economy that has changed as much as that of the United States, and in any event these shifts are largely irrelevant for assessing what are essentially short-run propositions about the interaction of monetary and real phenomena. From this point of view, the demand for money function does indeed appear to be a stable function of a few variables, though it is worth noting that the replacement of current income with permanent income turns out to be of some significance for our assessment of the manner in which monetary policy is likely to work, as we shall see later on in this paper.

Now it is worth asking whether the stability of the demand for money function over such a long period is a fairly general phenomenon or whether it is unique to the United States. No economy has been as thoroughly studied as the United States, but what evidence there is for other economies certainly suggests that a stable demand function for money is far from being a purely American phenomenon.[18] Few countries provide a run of data that is long enough for studies comparable to those done for America to be carried out, but Britain does yield such data. However, as we have seen above, most work done on the British economy has attempted to estimate directly money and autonomous expenditure multipliers; it has not, on the whole, dealt with structural relationships.

An important exception is Walters' (1969) presentation of results on the determinants of the money to income ratio over the period 1878–1961. Walters examined the relationship between the money to income ratio and interest rates and the level of income. He found

---

[18] For example, Cagan's (1956) study of hyperinflation suggests that there existed stable monetary relationships in a number of Central European countries just after the First World War. Breton (1968) has found stable relationships for Canada, as has Hynes (1967) for Chile. Not all work has been successful in finding stable relationships, though. Klein (1956) obtained poor results in studying Germany during the Nazi era, and Friedman's suggestion (1956) that this problem was worthy of further study does not seem to have been taken up as yet.

relationships that are tantalizingly like those that have been well established for the United States. He found a stable negative relationship between this ratio and interest rates, implying a stable negative relationship between the demand for money and the rate of interest, whether he dealt with the levels or the first differences of the data. However he also found that this ratio was positively related to income when he used the levels of the data and negatively related when first differences were employed.

If we postulate for a moment that the variance of both the level of income and the money to income ratio is dominated by their secular trends, and that the variance of their first differences is dominated by cyclical behaviour, then this evidence produced by Walters suggests that, *even when allowance is made for the influence of interest rates*, velocity in Britain has tended to decline secularly but has conformed to the cycle. This, of course, is precisely the characteristic of United States data that caused Friedman (1956, 1959) to formulate his permanent income hypothesis of the demand for money, and Walters' evidence suggests that the same hypothesis ought to deal with British data.[19]

Now a survey paper is not usually the place to present fresh empirical results, but to test the permanent income hypothesis of the demand for money against a long run of British data is straightforward enough, has not (to my knowledge) been done, but ought to be done. I shall therefore digress for a paragraph or so in order to present results which show that this hypothesis does indeed perform well relative to what may be termed the measured income hypothesis when faced with British data. These results are also of interest because they show that, even though the permanent income hypothesis carries over from the United States to Britain, not all American results do so. Hence they present us with problems that would repay further investigation.

The tests whose results are set out in Table 1 (p. 124 below) were not devised to provide the last word on the nature of the demand for money function for Great Britain over the last seventy years. Rather they were designed to generate results as comparable as

---

[19] Tobin and Swan (1969) put the matter as if interest rate variation and the permanent income hypothesis were alternative explanations of the cyclical behaviour of velocity. Surely this evidence of Walters' for Britain, and evidence produced by Laidler (1966) for the United States, shows that both, rather than either, variables are required to provide satisfactory results. This conclusion gains further support from results reported below in Table 1.

possible with those which we already have for the United States, so that any difference between the British and American results could be attributed to differences between the economies rather than to differences in the test procedures used. It is for this reason that, in Table 1B, I give results obtained with identical test procedures over almost identical time periods for the United States. The latter betray the characteristics that one has by now come to expect. Using data in *per capita* real terms, permanent income combined with a short interest rate provides the most stable demand for money function, whether we judge it on the basis of the proportion of the variance in the dependent variable explained over the entire period 1900–65, or on the basis of the consistency of the parameter estimates between sub-periods and their conformity to *a priori* expectations. The slow decline mentioned above in the permanent income elasticity of demand for money over the period is also evident in these results, as is the remarkable stability in the interest elasticity of demand for money.[20]

The British results, given in Table 1A, are different enough from the American ones to raise some interesting problems. To begin with, though the combination of permanent income and a short interest rate provides the best fit overall for the period 1900–65, the superiority of this combination of variables is not confirmed for the sub-periods. For the years 1900–13 the short interest rate takes on an embarrassing positive sign, while for the period 1945–65, its presence causes permanent income to take on a negative coefficient. These problems disappear when the long rate of interest appears in the demand for money function.

My main deduction from Walters' results is confirmed by the results given in Table 1A. Permanent income is clearly a superior variable to measured income for, though a measured income function manages to explain a greater proportion of the variance in the demand for money than one containing permanent income over the period 1948–65, this same functional form is disqualified by having the income variable taking on a significantly negative sign for the 1920–38 sub-period. For consistency between sub-periods, and parameters that conform to *a priori* expectations, the combination of permanent income and a long interest rate is clearly the best

[20] These results differ slightly from those presented in Laidler (1966), Table 2. This is the result of differences in the time periods to which the regressions have been fitted and to minor revisions that have been made to the data since 1966. No substantive issues are in the least affected by these changes, however.

of the four tested for Britain, and in addition to betraying the same moderate decline in the permanent income elasticity of demand for money (from 0·981 for 1900–13 to 0·684 for 1946–65) as the United States it also suggests that the demand for money has become increasingly sensitive to the rate of interest: the elasticity increases from −0·268 for 1900–13 to −0·739 for 1946–65.[21]

Perhaps the aspect of the British results that separates them most strongly from the American is their sensitivity to small changes in the specification of the function fitted. Though there is a definite 'best' formulation for the demand for money function in the United States, departures from it do not produce nonsensical results; apart from the 1900–16 period a long rate of interest still takes a negative sign, while measured income always takes a positive one. This is not the case for Britain and at least one other study (Laidler and Parkin (1970)) has found a similar sensitivity of results to specification, though in that case the problem concerned the specification of lag patterns in the demand for money function when dealing with quarterly data over the period 1956–65. Why the sensitivity of results to specification should be so much more marked for Britain than for the United States is clearly a question worth further investigation.

One particularly noticeable aspect of this sensitivity is the failure of the short interest rate to provide a consistently sensible explanation of variations in the demand for money. Again this echoes results generated by other studies, for both Fisher (1968) and Laidler and Parkin (1970) found the treasury bill rate to be an unsatisfactory variable when dealing with quarterly data generated over the last decade. That this unsatisfactoriness is a characteristic of the Treasury bill rate in particular rather than of short interest rates in general is suggested by the success which Goodhart and Crockett (1970) had in finding a relationship between the demand for money and another short rate, that on local authority debt.[22] Even so,

[21] These results on the relationship between the demand for money and the rate of interest for the U.K. must be treated with great care. Because the particular long rate chosen (the $2\frac{1}{2}\%$ consol rate) performs better than the particular short rate chosen (the three-month Treasury bill rate) does not make it the 'right' rate to use. Thus this increasing interest elasticity may just reflect a mis-specification of the function.

[22] Laidler and Parkin (1970) have suggested that the Bank of England's practice of attempting to stabilize interest rates might have resulted in the Treasury bill rate's becoming a poor measure of the opportunity cost of holding money as far as quarterly post-Second World War data are concerned. However,

though it might be premature to conclude on the basis of the evidence presented here that long interest rates are a better measure of the opportunity cost of holding money in Britain than are short rates, there is nevertheless a problem. As far as the United States has been concerned the choice of a particular interest rate has never been crucial to getting sensible results (though the long rate performs badly in the test reported here for the period 1900–16); as far as Britain is concerned the choice seems much more critical, and it would be nice to know why.[23]

A basic proposition about the demand for money alluded to earlier in this section of the paper is the independence of the demand for real balances of the general price level. This fundamental theorem of monetary economics is embodied in the Hicks–Hansen model discussed earlier, and is not difficult to test. All that is needed is to replace the log. of real balances with the log. of nominal balances as the dependent variable of a regression equation and to add the log. of the price level as an extra independent variable. The latter variable should take a coefficient of unity.

This test was carried out for both the British and the U.S. data, with the results reported in Table 2 (p. 128 below). As will be seen, the hypothesis is strongly confirmed by both sets of data as far as the entire period 1900–65 is concerned, but for sub-periods there are difficulties. The coefficient of the log. of the price level tends to drop significantly below unity for both economies. I am inclined to argue, albeit tentatively, that this problem may be resolved by introducing the 'permanent price level' concept of Friedman and Schwartz. As with income, so with the price level: over the period 1900–65 taken as a whole the variance of the variable would be dominated by its secular trend, while within the sub-periods the data would be more prone to domination by transitory variations.[24]

Table 1 shows that it is only for the 1920–38 sub-period that regressions containing the Treasury bill rate perform adequately. A fully satisfactory resolution of the difficulties to which the use of this interest rate leads must clearly encompass more than just Bank of England behaviour in the 1950s and 1960s. Charles Goodhart has recently suggested to the author that the key to the problem as far as the pre-First World War period is concerned might lie in the fact that Treasury bills were a fairly unimportant asset in those years, to say nothing of the fact that Consols had not yet been robbed of their 'liquid asset' status by post-war fluctuations in the level of interest rates. This suggestion would clearly bear further examination.

[23] See Additional Note 2 (p. 129 below).

[24] It is worth noting here that in his discussion of this paper Frank Brechling suggested that this problem might result from the simultaneous equations bias

Granted these problems, however, over the long run the demand for money function for Britain does not look very different from that for the United States. Whether this conclusion will withstand further investigation of the problems in question is a different matter, but it is worth noting that post-war British data have already been analysed with considerable care and nothing has emerged from the analysis that would lead one to question it. This is a result of considerable importance, because this post-war period is one for which money multiplier studies of the kind dealt with earlier found no stable relationship between the quantity of money and the level of money income.

Three separate studies by Fisher (1968), Laidler and Parkin (1970), and Goodhart and Crockett (1970) found that the key to getting sensible-looking results on the demand for money for post-war Britain with quarterly data was to pay attention to the presence of time lags in the relationship. To use a permanent income variable constructed as a weighted average of past and present levels of income is of course to introduce implicit time lags into the relationship, but what is an adequate procedure when dealing with annual data need not necessarily be adequate when it comes to quarterly observations. As Friedman (1959) suggested, in presenting the earliest results on the permanent income hypothesis of the demand for money, quarterly data might be expected to reflect not only time lags in the adjustment of income expectations to current experience but also lags in the adjustment of actual cash balances to desired balances.[25]

Work on British data certainly seems to bear this suggestion out, for the time lags measured by Goodhart and Crockett seem implausibly long if one interprets them, as they do, as being solely adjustment lags. The results suggest that only just over 10 per cent of any discrepancy between actual and desired cash balances is made

inherent in the use of ordinary least squares for the estimation of a demand for money function being more acute for sub-periods than for the whole period.

[25] It might be thought that the existence of all these lags in the demand for money relationship makes the time lag in the effect of monetary policy too long to be consistent with the relatively high short-run multipliers reported by Anderson and Jordan (1958). This is an erroneous conclusion. Tucker (1966) and Laidler (1968) have both shown that to introduce lags into the demand for money relationship *ceteris paribus* speeds up the money multiplier process. Friedman (1959) also made this point though he carried out no detailed analysis of the matter. These points are discussed below in Section IV of this paper.

good over three months.[26] Laidler and Parkin found similarly long lags and were able to show that the somewhat shorter and *a priori* more plausible lags presented by Fisher were probably the result of biases resulting from the specification of the function he fitted.[27] They were also able to show that much more plausible results were obtainable when the lag effect was shared between an expectations lag and an adjustment lag.

In principle there is no difficulty in sorting out these two types of lags. Feige (1967) successfully did so using annual data for the United States, confirming Friedman's contention that for annual data it was the permanent income lag that was all important. Laidler and Parkin's results for Britain are a good deal less clear-cut than Feige's but, taken at face value, they seem to show that the equilibrium demand for money in Britain depends upon permanent income and that over 80 per cent of any discrepancy between actual and desired cash balances is made up over a three month period.[28] These results are plausible and are quite consistent with those presented in Table 1.

Finally, it is worth noting that these quarterly results for the 1950s and 60s also throw some light on the question of the homogeneity of the demand for money in the general price level. Laidler and Parkin found evidence of a proportional relationship between the demand for nominal balances and the price level, indeed this was the most definite conclusion to emerge from that study, while Goodhart and Crockett, who constrained their functions to produce

[26] Note that DeLeeuw (1965) got a similarly implausible result with U.S. data.

[27] Cf. Laidler and Parkin (1970), Appendix B.

[28] If we have the following model, with all variables in logs and all symbols having their conventional meaning,

$$m^*_d = \alpha + \beta y^e + \gamma r$$
$$y^e = \lambda y + (1 - \lambda) y^e$$
$$m = \theta m^* + (1 - \theta) m_{-1}$$

then successive application of the Koyck transformation yield

$$m = \alpha\theta\lambda + \beta\theta\lambda y + \gamma\theta r - \gamma\theta(1 - \lambda) r_{-1} + (2 - \theta - \lambda) m_{-1} - (1 - \theta)(1 - \lambda) m_{-2}$$

The parameters of this model were estimated, using quarterly data, with a constrained least squares technique by Laidler and Parkin (1970). The relevant results are presented in Laidler and Parkin (1970) Table 2, but are unfortunately based on data into which slight error had crept. Subsequent work with more accurate data suggests that the following, fortunately not substantially different, estimates might be more reliable.

$$\alpha = 0.010, \quad \beta = 0.802, \quad \gamma = -0.008, \quad \lambda = 0.092, \quad \theta = 0.873.$$

It should be noted that these revised results are just as ill-determined statistically as those originally reported.

the same lag in the adjustment of nominal balances to changes in real income, the interest rate, and the price level, nevertheless obtained results consistent with a long run price level elasticity of about unity.[29] These two sets of results are not directly comparable, since Laidler and Parkin did not investigate the question of lagged response to price level change, while Goodhart and Crockett did not attempt to test hypotheses about different speeds of the demand for money's response to changes in different variables, but they do provide evidence in favour of the homogeneity postulate; Goodhart and Crockett's results in particular add weight to the suggestion, made above, that the notion of a 'permanent price level' might well sort out some of the difficulties encountered with annual data.

Now this evidence for Britain certainly points to the existence of a stable demand for money function in that economy. If this matter is not as well established as it is for the United States it is likely that this is the result of less work having been done on the problem for Britain than of there being any fundamental differences between the two economies. At least the evidence seems to be strong enough to warrant my continuing this paper 'as if' the existence of this particular link in the causal chain between the quantity of money and the level of economic activity was well established. For the United States the evidence is overwhelming, and for Britain it is at the very least highly suggestive.

What of the other links? To establish the *possibility* of the quantity of money affecting the level of economic activity we require evidence both of the existence of a demand for money function, and, if we are to stay within the Hicks–Hansen framework, of a relationship between expenditure and interest rates. That there also exists the possibility of a direct wealth effect of changes in the quantity of money on expenditure whenever the money stock does not bear interest at the competitive rate has recently been demonstrated by Pesek and Saving (1967), but in the absence of any evidence as to the empirical significance of such a wealth effect those who want to establish the potential importance of the quantity of money must rely on the expenditure interest rate relationship. Given a stable demand for money relationship, and given that there is evidence enough that changes in the quantity of money have not always been the consequence of changes in the level of income, a matter I shall take up below, then the existence of stable money multiplier relationships provides strong indirect evidence

[29] Cf. Goodhart and Crockett (1970), Table F, p. 195.

that some classes of expenditure at least are interest sensitive. However, direct evidence has always been less easy to come by, and this has been troublesome to monetary economists.

This paper cannot now turn into a survey of theories and evidence on expenditure functions, but it is worth while at least pointing out that this particular gap does now seem to be in the process of being filled. In a series of papers, Jorgensen (cf. (1963) for the most accessible of these papers) has presented a theory of business investment in which the interest rate figures and which copes reasonably well with explaining a good deal of observed behaviour; Hamburger (1967) has produced evidence of the influence of interest rates on consumer demand for durable goods; Wright (1969) reports the existence of a relationship between consumption and interest rates. Less direct evidence comes from Cagan (1969a), who shows that there is a systematic relationship between the lag between economic activity and interest rates at business cycle turning points and the length of the subsequent cycle phase. He interprets this relationship as reflecting the, albeit considerably lagged, influence of interest rates on economic activity. The picture that is beginning to emerge here is one of a widely diffused influence of interest rates on expenditure. If their influence on any one class of expenditure is not great the breadth of the area over which they do have an influence nevertheless makes them a potentially significant determinant of the level of economic activity. The evidence cited here is all for the United States; there appears to be growing up no such systematic body of knowledge about the role of interest rates in expenditure functions in the British economy. Again we have a problem area that requires some work.[30]

Taken all in all, the evidence on the demand for money function, that on the money multipliers, and that on the role of interest rates as an influence on various classes of expenditure, at the very least

[30] Even for the United States, of course, the evidence of the influence of interest rates on expenditure is the weakest link in the case for the importance of the quantity of money. This writer is far from being expert in this literature, but he knows of no study that finds a predominant effect of interest rates on any particular class of expenditure. In the face of this kind of evidence, the case for the existence of a transmission mechanism working through interest rates must rest on the existence of relatively small effects on widely diffused classes of expenditure, as described by Friedman and Schwartz (1963b), rather than on a particularly strong textbook style influence on business investment. Cagan's study (1969a) is, to my knowledge, the only one to approach the empirical evidence from the Friedman–Schwartz point of view, and ought, therefore, to be taken particularly seriously in the present context.

puts the burden of proof firmly upon those who would deny the possibility of the quantity of money having a systematic influence on economic activity. However the question of what *can* happen is not the same question as what *did* happen at any particular moment in time. Before it can be concluded that the quantity of money has had a systematic effect on economic activity it must be shown that variations in the quantity of money to which variations in the level of economic activity are attributed have not come about as a result of the very variations that they are supposed to explain.

This is not a matter about which one can generalize. The very nature of the problem requires careful study of specific cases, and as far as Britain is concerned one of the consequences of the until recently prevailing view among economists of the basic irrelevance of money has been that historical studies of the determination of the quantity of money has been a relatively neglected problem. For the United States, this is far from being the case, and that country's economic history provides us with what have become classic test cases in the shape of the episodes 1929–33 and 1933–41. That there was a close relationship between the quantity of money and the level of money income during both these periods is now well known, but the standard interpretation given to this association until recently has been that it demonstrated conclusively that (a) it was impossible to use monetary policy to offset a downturn (1929–33) and (b) it was impossible to use monetary policy to promote an upturn once the trough was reached. Variations in the quantity of money, in short, were looked on as being the consequences of changes in the level of income during these episodes.

It is now widely accepted that the direction of causation was just the opposite, that the downturn was the consequence of monetary changes, and that lack of sufficiently expansionary monetary policy prolonged the trough, but since Professor Kaldor (1970) has challenged these views, particularly about the 1929–33 episode, in a recent and widely publicized lecture, it is probably worth while going quickly over the sequence of events again.[31] A falling off in the rate of growth of the money supply beginning in mid-1928 preceded a mild cyclical downturn that the National Bureau date as having started in August 1929. October saw the stock market

[31] Kaldor attributes the selection of this period as a test case to Friedman. This is surely to overlook the role that this episode played as *the* example of the ineffectiveness of monetary policy in orthodox post-Keynesian expositions of macroeconomics.

crash which was followed by a contraction in the stock of high powered money and the money stock itself.[32] The former fell by 4·6 per cent of its 1929 value between October 1929 and October 1930, and the latter by 3·3 per cent, while the deposit currency ratio of the public and the deposit reserve ratio of the commercial banks stayed roughly constant, changing from 11·13 to 11·29 and from 12·723 to 12·716 respectively over the same period. The first of a series of banking crises occurred in October 1930 and immediately thereafter both ratios, particularly the deposit currency ratio began to fall steeply setting off a series of further crises, the last of which occurred in January 1933. June 1933 saw the public's deposit currency ratio at 5·08 and the commercial banks' deposit reserve ratio at 8·15, so that although the quantity of high powered money had by that time increased by 10·1 per cent since October 1929 (15·2 per cent since October 1930) the money stock had fallen by 35·3 per cent since October 1929.[33]

The interpretation put upon this sequence of events by Friedman and Schwartz is that a mild downturn was turned into a major catastrophe by the failure of the Central Bank to act as a lender of last resort during the series of banking crises and by its failure to increase the quantity of high powered money sufficiently to offset

[32] All the figures quoted in the following passage are for three-month averages centred on the month referred to. To have simply taken monthly figures would, in this writer's judgement, have unduly exaggerated some of the variations in question, while to have taken longer averages would have tended to obscure important changes in the series that were taking place extremely rapidly. All the results quoted are based on figures given in Friedman and Schwartz (1963a), Table A-1, pp. 712–14 (for the money stock data), and Table B-3, pp. 803–4 (for high powered money, the deposit reserve ratio and the deposit currency ratio).

For a period in which events were happening so rapidly it is difficult indeed to choose summary statistics such as those quoted here without running the risk of being accused of picking particular figures to prove one's case where slightly different data would show matters in a different light. Certainly, by drawing attention to the timing of events within the 1929–33 period, I am presenting here a radically different picture to the one which Kaldor (1970) gives. The reader who wishes to choose between these conflicting views will find time series charts particularly revealing. Charts 31 (p. 333) and 64 (opposite p. 684) of Friedman and Schwartz (1963a) present the relevant data.

[33] Thus Kaldor is correct in picking Friedman up for a slip in his American Economic Association Presidential address (1968). High powered money did indeed increase, not decrease, over the 1929–33 period. That Friedman and Schwartz's interpretation of this period is in no way dependent on a (false) assertion that high powered money decreased should however be quite apparent to anyone who has read Chapter 7 of the *Monetary History*.

the shifts in the deposit currency ratio that was the consequence of the public's loss of faith in the banks' ability to redeem their deposits if asked and the shift in the deposit reserve ratio that reflected the banks' loss of faith in the public's willingness to maintain their deposits. According to Friedman and Schwartz the disturbances originating in the monetary sector were the cause of disturbances in the level of economic activity.

According to Kaldor, on the contrary, the downturn originated in the real sector, and happened despite a monetary expansion, his evidence of this being the increase in the quantity of high powered money between 1929 and 1933 already alluded to. The fall in the public's deposit currency ratio he attributes to the changing pattern of transactions as income fell and in particular to the fall-off in financial transactions after stock-market crash, while the fall in the banks' deposit reserve ratio is put down to their inability to make loans in the face of contracting demand for credit. The public's loss of confidence in the banking system seems to be of little significance for Kaldor, but since he does not explain, or indeed attempt to explain, why a downturn that began in August 1929 and a stock-market crash that occurred in October 1929 should not begin to have any significant effect on either of these ratios until November 1930, which just happens to be the month immediately following a series of important bank failures—a piece of timing he fails to mention—there seems to be no reason to take his interpreparation of the events of 1929–33 very seriously.[34]

Matters are less clear cut when it comes to dealing with events in the years following 1933, for although 1933–7 was the longest peacetime expansion until the 1960s, and although it was accompanied by an increasing money stock, the quantity of high powered money increased more rapidly than did the money stock over the period; much of the effect of its growth was offset by a continued fall in the banks' deposit reserve ratio. The traditional explanation of this is that the recovery originated on the real side of the economy, that the money supply increased in response to the growth in income, but that the ever growing quantity of free reserves held by the banking system were evidence of monetary policy's inability to speed up the expansion. It is not immediately obvious that the growth in the free reserve ratio that continued into 1936 is interpretable as reflecting the banks' response to the shocks of the 1930–3 period, particularly since the public's deposit currency ratio

[34] See Additional Note 3 (p. 130 below), first paragraph.

had stabilized itself by the end of 1934; thus the proposition that monetary policy was 'pushing on a string' over the 1933–7 period has a good deal of superficial appeal.

There are, however, two crucial facts with which this explanation fails to deal. First a slowdown in the rate of growth of the money stock preceded the sharp downturn of 1937 when the 'pushing on a string' argument should have had it following. Second, though the time path of the money supply partly followed that of high powered money, the monetary tightening was greatly accentuated by a series of increases in required reserve ratios which began in 1936 and continued into 1937. These changes should have simply had the effect of turning free reserves into required reserves if the existence of free reserves was due to a lack of investment opportunities for the banks. In fact the changes in question were met by attempts by the banks to restore their free reserve ratios to 1936 levels, attempts that by 1940 had met with success and are only explicable in terms of the free reserves in question performing an economic function for the banks that held them, a function that was sufficiently valuable for those banks to forgo earning opportunities in order to acquire and hold free reserves.[35]

For the United States in the 1930s then, I would argue that the case for variations in the quantity of money as a cause rather than a consequence of variations in economic activity is clear for the 1929–33 episode, and at least plausible, more plausible than the contrary case in my view, for the 1933–40 period.[36] Since this has always been *the* case cited to prove the ineffectiveness of monetary policy, *the* period during which, despite the efforts of the authorities the chain of causation could, allegedly, most clearly be seen to run from changes in the level of economic activity to the money stock rather than vice versa, and since Friedman and Schwartz, in addition to having decisively refuted this view, have been able to show just as decisively for many other episodes that the main line of causation has gone from money to economic activity, it is safe to conclude that as far as that economy is concerned, the *possibility* of money affecting economic activity exists, in the shape of a well-established transmission mechanism, while there is no shortage of

[35] See Additional Note 3 (p. 130 below), second paragraph.

[36] Kaldor largely confines himself to the 1929–33 episode, and in this writer's judgement weakens his own case by doing so. The 1933–7 period would have provided him with more effective ammunition with which to attack Friedman, Morrison's work notwithstanding.

evidence of historical episodes in which the direction of causation *has* gone in that direction.

For Britain, not only is the case of the *possibility* less well established, though it is, as I have argued above, plausible enough, but we do not as yet possess the kind of detailed historical analysis that would enable us to argue that such possibility has turned into actuality in any particular episode. Indeed for one episode at least, namely the years since the revival of 'monetary policy' in the early 1950s, what we know suggests that the quantity of money has had little if any causative role to play, however important a variable it could have been, and whatever role it might have played as an *indicator* of policy. All this is a direct consequence of 'monetary policy' in post-war Britain having been an interest rate policy.

What is being argued here is not just that the quantity of money has been an endogenous variable, in the sense that variations in it are the result of fluctuations elsewhere in the economic system, over the period in question. For example, variations in the quantity of high powered money can be the consequence of balance of payments fluctuations under a fixed exchange rate system, and can still lead on to variations in the quantity of money and hence in the level of economic activity. What is at issue is the special nature of the endogeneity of the money supply when a central bank decides to act in the open market so as to achieve a given interest rate pattern on government securities and hence on securities generally.

A central bank can only carry out such a policy by standing ready to buy and sell securities at a given price, and since it must carry out its transactions in terms of high powered money, it necessarily gives up all control of the money supply when it seeks to peg interest rates. In terms of the Hicks–Hansen model, the quantity of money ceases to be an exogenous variable and the rate of interest takes its place; instead of a causative chain running primarily from the quantity of money through interest rates to aggregate demand, we get a system in which the interest rate directly affects the level of economic activity so that, the two principle determinants of the demand for money being determined, the money supply passively adjusts in order to maintain equilibrium in the money market.[37] In such a system as this, the rate and direction of change of the money supply will usually be reliable indicators of the ease or

---

[37] The distinction between cause and effect here is, to some extent, though by no means entirely, a matter of semantic convenience. See Additional Note 4 (p. 131 below).

8

tightness of monetary policy, they may indeed be more reliable indicators than the level of interest rates that the bank is trying to maintain, but this is a far cry from variations in the money supply causing anything.

That the control of interest rates has been the Bank of England's primary concern over the last twenty years or so seems to be widely recognized by participants on all sides of contemporary monetary debates. Though Mrs. Schwartz (1969) finds some evidence of recognition of the importance of the quantity of money on the Bank's part in its evidence to the Radcliffe Committee she concedes that the publication of the Report of the Committee seems to have finally enshrined the structure of interest rates as the centrepiece of monetary policy. At the same time, some model similar to that which I have sketched out above must surely underlie Kaldor's insistence that the main determinant of variations in the money supply of Britain since the war has been fluctuations in government borrowing. The money supply must fluctuate in tune with such borrowing if the price of government debt is not permitted to vary in order to equilibrate its supply and demand.[38]

None of this means of course that, had the quantity of money been determined independently of the level of economic activity, it could not have exerted an important influence on that activity. Whether or not it would have done so depends upon the existence or otherwise of a stable demand for money function and a relationship between interest rates and aggregate demand.[39] It does,

[38] Bank reserves will also fluctuate in order to accommodate fluctuations in bank deposits in such circumstances. Thus there is no contradiction between the foregoing argument and Crouch's (1967) regression results on the relationship between bank reserves and the volume of bank deposits. The interpretation of these results is different, of course, for Crouch has causation running from reserves to deposits and the foregoing argument would reverse his interpretation of the relationship in question.

It is worth noting that it is precisely when a central bank is supporting interest rates that bank holdings of liquid assets become important in the generation of the money supply since these assets are so readily convertible into high powered money. The debate in Britain over the question of the role of liquid assets in the generating of bank deposits is a complicated one. Coppock and Gibson (1963) provides perhaps the clearest single guide to the issues involved.

[39] Thus, to agree with Kaldor's account of post-war British monetary history in no way implies acceptance of his more general conclusions concerning the futility of attempting to use the quantity of money as a policy variable.

Kaldor seems to regard the level of money income as something that is always determined independently of the quantity of money, and argues as a general proposition that, if there exists an empirical relationship between the two variables,

however, mean that it did not do so during this particular episode, though the recent revival of interest in the quantity of money as an instrument of economic policy still makes it worth while to ask further questions about the way in which this variable might operate if used. The evidence of this and the preceding section of this paper, though there are still formidable gaps in it, is surely strong enough to persuade even quite sceptical readers that the possibility of the quantity of money having a systematic effect on economic activity certainly exists, and that it certainly has in fact had such effects on some, if not all, episodes of recent economic history. However, fundamental to the question of using the quantity of money (or any other variable for that matter) as a policy variable is the question of the time lags involved in the processes whereby it has its effect. It is no use manipulating a policy variable, no matter how sure one may be of its effects, if one does not know when those effects will occur. I will turn to a discussion of these lag effects in Section IV of this paper where I will once more seek to demonstrate the importance of discussing such questions with the help of an explicit model.

IV

The model with which this paper started has not, as we have seen, emerged totally unscathed from empirical investigation. For one thing, there are time lags in the demand for money relationship, and whether one cares to think of them as being mainly adjustment lags or expectation lags is secondary to the general point that their existence, and that of similar lags in the expenditure function, must yield implications about the time path along which the economy adjusts to policy changes. There is of course a substantial literature on the subject, particularly on lag effects in monetary policies (cf. Mayer (1967) for a survey), but the bulk of this work is based on only the most flimsy theoretical foundation.

Some of it (Friedman (1958) is the most famous example) is concerned mainly with comparing the timing of turning points in various time series and the hypothesis underlying such time series comparisons seems to be no more formal than that changes in the

causation always runs from income to money. I cannot resist pointing out, with tongue only partly in cheek, that Kaldor's line of reasoning would lead to the conclusion that the Conquistadores were induced to establish the Spanish Empire and to develop its production of the precious metals by strong inflationary pressures that just happened to be present in Europe during the sixteenth century.

quantity of money (or its rate of change) lead on eventually to changes in the level of economic activity.[40] The transmission mechanism is spelled out clearly enough in more than one place, contrary to what is all too frequently alleged, but there is nothing in the account of this mechanism that tells us explicitly upon what factors the length of the lag depends; there seems to be just a general presumption that in the world, as opposed to in a comparative static economic model, causes take time to have effects.[41] Any length of time lag, and any degree of variability in this lag, seems to be compatible with the transmission mechanism that is described.

Most work subsequent to Friedman's has been prompted by dissatisfaction with one aspect or another of his procedures. The most widely known of this work is that of Kareken and Solow (1963). They produce estimates of lag effects at least as long as those presented by Friedman, despite statements to the contrary in the introduction to their study (cf. Mayer 1967). They broke down the transmission mechanism of monetary policy into component stages—change in reserves to change in quantity of money, change in quantity of money to change in interest rates, changes in interest rates to change in investment—and attempted to measure the time lags involved at each stage. For some reason that is not explained they did not proceed along this sequence to investigate the length of the lag involved in the working out of the multiplier effect of a change in investment on a change in income; they did not therefore have to face up to the difficulties involved in investigating the feedback effects of changing income on interest rates.[42] Their

[40] This is not the place to go into the details of whether the quantity of money or its rate of change is the relevant variable. Suffice it to note here that in (1958) Friedman seems to suggest that the rate of change of the money stock determines the *level* of economic activity but that in Friedman and Schwartz (1963b) and in Friedman (1970) the emphasis seems to shift to relationships between the rate of change of money and the rate of change of income. This writer wonders if he is alone in being somewhat confused by this.

[41] The fullest exposition of this transmission mechanism (until the appearance of Friedman (1970)) is in Friedman and Schwartz (1963b). It is an interest rate mechanism much like that described earlier in this paper, and as Kaldor (1970) p. 9 notes apparently with surprise is not significantly different from that described by Keynes (1936). It is a minor mystery in the recent history of economic thought as to where so many economists have got the impression that Friedman's view of the monetary mechanism is crucially dependent upon some mysterious 'direct' effect of money on expenditure.

[42] Though it is fair to note that the authors in question warned their readers that lack of time had prevented them from completing as thorough a study as they had hoped to carry out.

underlying model, in short, appears to have been a sequential one, in which cause and effect move in a unique direction, rather than being one in which goods and money markets mutually interact: this despite the fact that the analysis of such interaction is central to post-Keynesian macroeconomics, even at the simple level of the Hicks–Hansen type of model set out at the beginning of this paper.

Indeed, most of the work on lag effects seems to suffer from a fundamental methodological defect whether it follows Friedman's example or that of Kareken and Solow. This defect, which probably lies at the root of the dissatisfaction which many—not least those who have carried out the work in question—feel about our current state of knowledge on the question of lag effects is that the work lacks an explicit theoretical basis. It has concerned itself with asking empirical questions about how long are the time lags between changes in variables without first concerning itself with the more basic theoretical questions of why there should be time lags in the first place, and what factors might be expected to determine their length. Thus, at best, this work provides economists with a set of facts. Without an explicit theoretical framework within which these facts may be organized, it is impossible to analyse them, fit them together, or assess their significance.

Those empirical results on structural equations which show that permanent income, rather than measured income, belongs in the demand for money function tell us about one particular lag effect, and they explain its existence in terms of people being slow to adjust their long-run income expectations to current experience. The hypothesis that there are lags in the demand for money function because people find it too costly to adjust their money holdings fast enough to maintain them constantly in equilibrium also provides a theory about the existence of a particular time lag. Such lags have been found to exist elsewhere than in the demand for money function, and analysis of the way in which such lagged functions interact in a model based on the Hicks–Hansen framework seems to me to represent a promising way of investigating the whole leads–lags problem. In principle, this line of work opens up the prospect of an explicit theory of income determination that has time lags between changes in policy variables and changes in the level of income as an integral part of its structure.

A little work along these lines has already been done, on quite a simple level, and it would be wrong to look for much in the way of direct empirical applications for the results so far achieved. However, even when treated as analytic exercises, such models can produce quite startling and counter-intuitive results. They totally undermine the fundamental assumption underlying most measuring exercises that the time path of income towards a new equilibrium after some policy change is smooth and unidirectional. It may not be. They show that the simultaneous interaction of real goods markets and money markets make it just as impossible to treat lag effects of fiscal policy as being independent of money market behaviour as it is to treat monetary policy lags as being independent of real goods market behaviour. Moreover time lags turn out to depend upon the parameters of the underlying static equilibrium relationships as well as upon the parameters of the lag processes themselves, while apparently slight changes in the specification of lag processes turn out to lead to major changes in the behaviour of the complete model.

With expenditure functions and the demand for money function as candidates for the inclusion of lag effects, and with expectations lags and adjustment lags to choose between, or even to use simultaneously, the number of models that could be built and analysed is large. However, what is required here is illustration of the results stated above, rather than a complete and tedious taxonomy, and the results in question can nearly all be derived from a model which was first set out, mainly in geometric terms, in Laidler (1968).[43] The model in question is simply a linear in the real variables version of the Hicks–Hansen model with permanent income replacing measured income in the expenditure and demand for money functions, though later it will be necessary to replace the expectations lag implicit in the use of permanent income in the demand for money function with an adjustment lag in order to derive the final result asserted in the previous paragraph, namely that such an apparently minor change makes an important difference to the model's behaviour.

Since the price level is to be held constant in the following analysis it is notationally convenient to give it a value of unity, and,

---

[43] A model produced by Tucker (1966) concentrated on adjustment rather than expectations lags, and seemed, as far as substantive implications were concerned, to be the same as my own model. Subsequent work has convinced me that this is not the case; expectations and adjustment lags do have importantly different implications for some aspects of the behaviour of Hicks–Hansen type models, as I will show below.

with all other symbols having their usual meaning, the model may be set out as follows.

$$Y_t = E_t = kY_t^e + \bar{A}_t - ar_t \qquad (17)$$

$$\bar{M}_t = M_{d_t} = mY_t^e - l_{r_t} \qquad (18)$$

$$Y_t^e = bY_t + (1 - b) Y_{t-1}^e \qquad (19)$$

It yields, as a reduced form for income,

$$Y_t = \cfrac{1}{1 - kb + \cfrac{amb}{l}} \bar{A}_t + \cfrac{1}{\cfrac{1 - lkb}{a} + mb} \bar{M}_t + \cfrac{(1 - b)\left(k - \cfrac{am}{l}\right)}{1 - kb + \cfrac{amb}{l}} Y_{t-1}^e \quad (20)$$

It is easily shown that the model is stable, that for given values of $\bar{M}_t$ and $\bar{A}_t$, Y_t converges to a steady state solution $\bar{Y}$. Equation (20) may be rewritten as

$$Y_t = \cfrac{1}{1 - kb + \cfrac{amb}{l}} \bar{A}_t + \cfrac{1}{\cfrac{1 - lkb}{a} + mb} \bar{M}_t + \cfrac{b(1 - b)\left(k - \cfrac{am}{l}\right)}{1 - kb + \cfrac{amb}{l}} Y_{t-1}$$

$$+ \cfrac{(1 - b)^2\left(k - \cfrac{am}{l}\right)}{1 - kb + \cfrac{amb}{l}} Y_{t-2}^e \qquad (21)$$

Successively lagging equation (20) one period, multiplying it by $(1 - b)$, subtracting the result from equation (21) and taking first differences yields

$$Y_t - Y_{t-1} = (1 - b) \left[1 + \cfrac{b\left(k - \cfrac{am}{l}\right)}{1 - b\left(k - \cfrac{am}{l}\right)} \right] (Y_{t-1} - Y_{t-2}) \quad (22)$$

which simplifies to

$$Y_t - Y_{t-1} = \cfrac{1 - b}{1 - b\left(k - \cfrac{am}{l}\right)} (Y_{t-1} - Y_{t-2}) \qquad (23)$$

Since $0 < k < 1$ and $0 < b < 1$ it follows that

$$z = \left(k - \frac{am}{l}\right) < 1 \tag{24}$$

$$0 < \frac{1 - b}{1 - b(z)} < 1 \tag{25}$$

A solution for $\overline{Y}$ is easily obtained by substituting $\overline{Y} = Y_t^e = Y_t$ for all t into equations (17), (18), and (19). It is

$$\overline{Y} = \frac{1}{1 - k + \dfrac{am}{l}}\overline{A}_t + \frac{1}{\dfrac{l - k}{a} + m}\,\overline{M}_t \tag{26}$$

Because the model converges smoothly on this steady state solution after any disturbance it is possible to analyse qualitatively the length of the lags involved in the response of income to changes in the money stock and to changes in autonomous expenditure by comparing the 'impact multipliers', the coefficients of A_t and M_t, in equation (20) with the 'steady state multipliers', the coefficients of the same variables in equation (23). The bigger is a steady state multiplier relative to an impact multiplier, the 'longer' will we call the lag effect in the response of the level of income to the variable in question. We may thus treat L_m as an index of the time lag involved in the operation of monetary policy where

$$L_m = \frac{\dfrac{l - lkb}{a} + mb}{\dfrac{l - lk}{a} + m} \tag{27}$$

and we may define a similar index for fiscal policy (inasmuch as this involves changing autonomous expenditure) call it L_a, as

$$L_a = \frac{1 - kb + \dfrac{amb}{l}}{1 - k + \dfrac{am}{l}} \tag{28}$$

Multiplying the top and bottom of (27) through by a/l reduces it to equation (28), so that in effect we need only analyse the one expression. In this model, and it cannot be too much stressed that this property belongs to one particular model rather than to any actual economy, the lag effects of monetary and fiscal policy are identical.[44] Their interdependence is, of course, a more general phenomenon.

Be that as it may, in this model we have

$$L = L_m = L_a = \frac{1 - bz}{1 - z} \tag{29}$$

where, as before,

$$z = \left(k - \frac{am}{l} \right) < 1 \tag{24}$$

Perhaps the first thing to note is that it is only if z is positive that we have an unidirectional time path of income towards its new equilibrium value after a change in the money stock or in autonomous expenditure. If z is negative, the impact multipliers are actually larger than the steady state multipliers. The more sensitive

---

[44] This peculiar result arises because the model contains no time lag between changes in interest rates and changes in expenditure. If we replace the expectations lag in the expenditure function with an adjustment lag, and let G be government expenditure

$$Y_t - G_t = E_t = gkY_t + gA_t - gar_t + (1 - g)E_{t-1}$$

this does introduce such a lag, and has the effect of slowing down the effects of monetary policy relative to fiscal policy. The model thus modified yields

$$Y_t = \frac{1}{1 - gk + \dfrac{amgb}{l}} G_t + \frac{g}{1 - gk + \dfrac{amgb}{l}} \bar{A}_t + \frac{1}{\dfrac{l - lgk}{ga} + mb} \bar{M}_t$$

$$+ \frac{(1 - g)}{1 - gk + \dfrac{amgb}{l}} Y_{t-1} - \frac{m(1 - b)}{\dfrac{l - lgk}{ga} + mb} Y_{t-1}^e.$$

If $g = b$ the money impact multiplier here is unambiguously smaller than that in equation (20) while the autonomous expenditure multiplier is greater. Thus, we reach the hardly novel conclusion that the existence of an adjustment lag in the expenditure function is crucial to the existence of a slower impact for monetary policy than for fiscal policy. It is also worth noting that if we take the foregoing expression for income and treat it in the same manner whereby equation (22) is derived from equation (20), the resulting difference equation will be second order. Preliminary analysis suggests that it is impossible to rule out a cyclical response of income to an exogenous shock in this case so that the very concept of a unique 'lag' which can be measured by the proportion of the distance towards equilibrium which is covered in a given time period is put in question. I hope to be able to deal with this and related issues in much more detail in a future paper.

is the demand for money to income and the less sensitive it is to interest rate (the higher is m and the smaller is l) and the less sensitive is expenditure to income and the more sensitive it is to interest rates (the smaller is k and the larger is a), the more likely is this to happen. Thus at least one important characteristic of the lag pattern with which income responds to a change in an exogenous variable is dependent on the characteristics of the steady state behaviour equations and not on the time lags involved in the short-run versions of those relationships.

It is obvious from (24) and (29) that the length of the lag effect always depends upon the value of the parameters of these basic behaviour relationships, so that if the parameters of the basic steady state relationships of our model vary, then so will the lags we are analysing. For example, if the relationship between expenditure and income is unstable, then so are the lag patterns with which the economy will respond to monetary and fiscal policy. Indeed policy itself might affect the lags: if changes in tax rates alter the propensity to spend out of income, then the lags in the model's behaviour will also be affected.

What about b, the parameter of the expectations formation mechanism, which alone is responsible for introducing lags (as opposed to determining the length of these lags) into the model under analysis? Even here there is not much to be said in general. From equation (29) we can derive

$$\frac{\delta L}{\delta b} = \frac{-z}{(1-z)} \quad \begin{array}{l} < 0 \text{ if } z > 0 \\ = 0 \text{ if } z = 0 \\ > 0 \text{ if } z < 0 \end{array} \tag{30}$$

The sign of this derivative depends upon the sign of z; if the lag is long already, in the sense that the impact multiplier is small relative to the steady state multiplier, then the longer is the expectations formations lag (the smaller is b) the longer will the lag be. This idea is intuitively appealing enough, but it is not so obvious, though equally true, that, if the lag is already so short that the impact multiplier is bigger than the steady state multiplier, then a lower value of b implies a still shorter lag.

Now of course all the foregoing results have been derived in terms of a very special model, in which the only source of time lags is the income expectations formation mechanism of equation (3). We must be particularly careful about generalizing from this special case because it is easy to show that only a slight change to the model is needed to alter its characteristics in an important fashion.

If we replace the expectations lag in the demand for money function with an adjustment lag, so that the demand for money function becomes

$$M_{d_t} = cmY_t - clr_t + (1 - c) M_{t-1} \qquad (18a)$$

we do not alter the steady state solution of the model at all. However, we get as one form of the solution for income at any particular time

$$Y_t = \frac{1}{\dfrac{am}{l} + (1 - kb)} A_t + \frac{1}{mc + \dfrac{cl(1 - kb)}{a}} \bar{M}_t$$

$$- \frac{(1 - c)}{mc + \dfrac{cl(1 - kb)}{a}} \bar{M}_{t-1} + \frac{k(1 - b)}{\dfrac{am}{l} + 1 - kb} Y^e_{t-1} \qquad (20a)$$

The autonomous expenditure multiplier is crucially different from that contained in equation (20). The existence of time lags in the money market now has no effect at all on its value and it is unambiguously smaller than the steady state multiplier. This result suggests that it is of extreme importance to distinguish between adjustment lags and expectations lags in the demand for money function, and, as already noted, it should make us wary indeed of treating the specific results generated in this section of the paper as having any significance other than that which may be attached to them as the outcome of an analytic exercise.

However, even looked at in this rather narrow light, the results in question do seem to yield important lessons for work in the general area of the analysis of the lag effects of policy. First, they suggest that when the interaction of real goods and money markets is taken account of, as surely it should be, the practice of treating the causative mechanism of either monetary or fiscal policy as a purely sequential one, with no feedback effects, comes to appear suspect, to say the very least. They also suggest that to treat the time lags that appear in the world as if they were purely the result of the fact that it 'takes time' to approach a steady state solution, and to treat the analysis of steady state solutions and of time lags as independent problems, is misleading. There is a strong interdependence here. Finally, the fact that apparently relatively small changes in the specification of a model can make an important difference to the time lag patterns implicit in it suggests that we will have to do a great deal of careful empirical work, and not only on the structure of the monetary sector, before we can be even remotely confident that the model which gets pieced together as a result of that work will give us an accurate picture of the lag effects present in any economy.[45]

Not only does the foregoing analysis give us some tentative insight into the empirical questions that need to be asked when considering the length of the lags effects of monetary and fiscal policy. It is equally informative as to where to look when investigating the variability of these lag effects. Movements in the values of the parameters of the structural equations of the model alter not only the amounts by which given policy changes are likely to affect the level of economic activity, but also the speed with which they do so.

Similarly, variations in the parameters governing the behaviour of the expectations formation and adjustment mechanisms will also lead to variation in the length of lag effects in the kind of models with which we are dealing, and the determinants of these parameters are certainly worth investigating. I would conjecture that these parameters are more subject to short period fluctuations than are those of the steady state structural relationships of the economy, and there is already a certain amount of evidence to support the proposition that they do vary importantly.

Consider the expectations lag first of all. This is derived from an error learning mechanism whereby economic units revise their expectations about the value of some economic variable in proportion to the size of the error in their previous prediction. To suggest that the proportion in question tends to fluctuate about some mean value is one thing, but to suggest that it is a constant is quite another. Presumably it is necessary to form expectations about economic variables because there are costs involved in acting in ignorance or in error, and there is no reason to suppose that the costs involved in making an error depend only upon the size of that error and not upon its sign. Furthermore, there is no reason why the relationship between the costs of making errors and the magnitude of the errors in question need to be a simple proportional one.

[45] Grossman and Dolde (1969) represents a pioneering effort at empirically analysing these lag effects in terms of a completely specified macroeconomic model. Their model is similar to, though not the same as, the one set out here.

This line of argument suggests that, when dealing, for example with lags involved in forming income expectations, the parameter b might depend both upon the magnitude and sign of the discrepancy between expected and realized income. Though this matter has not been looked into at all in the context of income expectations, at least as far as this writer is aware, Morrison's (1966) suggestion that commercial banks tend to 'lengthen their memories' when forming expectations about 'permanent deposits' in the wake of heavy unexpected losses of deposits, does amount to applying this kind of analysis to an expectations formation problem.[46] Underlying this suggestion is the by no means unreasonable argument that heavy unexpected losses of deposits are more costly to banks than heavy unexpected gains and are hence more likely to induce them to alter the kind of expectations formation mechanism that led them into error; the specific alteration that Morrison suggests they make is to begin giving less weight to recent experience, to revise their expectations less in the face of current fluctuations in their deposits. This hypothesis, as I note in Additional Note 3, enables Morrison to deal with the question of the slow build up of large amounts of free reserves by United States commercial banks in the post 1933 period, and deserves attention for that reason alone. Probably more important, however, is the fact that it provides a striking example of the way in which the error learning type of expectations formation mechanism can be extended and made more flexible in order to widen the class of phenomena with which it is capable of dealing, an example which would almost certainly be worth following up in other contexts.

The question of the variability of adjustment lags has also been worked on recently, and in the context of the demand for money function. Lags in the adjustment of cash balances to equilibrium arise because, although it is costly to be out of equilibrium, adjustment itself is not a costless process. A potential source of variations in such lags is not hard to find; the cost of adjusting cash balances will depend upon what else it is that must be changed to restore equilibrium. One cannot, after all, have an individual with too few (or many) cash balances without his simultaneously having too much (or little) of something else. For example, if a deficiency in money holdings is matched by too many building society deposits,

---

[46] Though it is worth noting that Friedman (1957) expressed some disquiet about applying an unvarying set of weights to the computation of permanent income in the 1930s. Cf. Friedman (1957), p. 152.

one would expect the restoration of equilibrium to be a good deal cheaper and more rapid than if the matching disequilibrium were too big a house.

This kind of question has been investigated for the household sector in the United States by Motley (1970), who finds that the overall composition of that sector's portfolio does indeed exert an important influence on the speed with which any part of it is brought into equilibrium. The importance of work along these lines should be obvious, and it is intriguing to note the implication that portfolio analysis, far from being an alternative to the demand and supply of money approach to the issues being dealt with in this paper, becomes a necessary complement to this approach once the question of lag effects arises.[47]

Now the analysis of lag effects was carried out above in the context of a model in which the price level is taken as given and all adjustments are in quantities. This is clearly unsatisfactory from any viewpoint but that of an analytic exercise and provides yet another reason for not looking for too much practical significance in its results. This is not to say that the model cannot be extended to deal, in a primitive way, with price level changes. If we postulate, as we did at the outset of this paper, an unique full employment level of income, then permanent income becomes equal to measured income at a level fixed exogenously by supply side factors and the behaviour of the model is then exactly that of the simple Hicks–Hansen framework; or rather it would be, were it not for a factor that I have so far neglected in this section of the paper, namely the whole area of price level expectations.[48]

[47] The basic question is one of degrees of aggregation. Motley's work suggests that vital detail is lost by aggregating into only two categories of assets—money and all others.

[48] There are two distinct, but closely interrelated aspects to the price level expectations problem. First there is the matter of the permanent or expected price level. If it is important to distinguish this variable from the current price level, and evidence presented in Table 2 suggests that it might be, then it has a role to play in the demand for nominal balances function, and also perhaps in the explanation of the determination of the *level* of money wages.

There is also the matter of the expected rate of inflation, which has a theoretical role to play in the demand for real balances function as a component of the opportunity cost of holding them. Evidence recently produced by Gupta (1970) strongly suggests that the expected rate of inflation is a component of observed bond yields so that its failure to appear explicitly in the regression equations dealt with above should not be interpreted as an indication that the variable is not a potentially important determinant of the demand for real balances in either

We do not yet have the kind of knowledge that would enable us to analyse in terms of a variant of the Hicks–Hansen model the time paths of output and the price level, as they interact in response to exogenous shocks. Indeed, our lack of a satisfactory model of this interaction is now widely recognized as perhaps *the* crucial gap in short-run macroeconomic theory. The kind of phenomenon with which any such model would have to deal is the apparently all pervasive inability of economics to meet a contraction in aggregate demand even in the presence of inflation without important contractions in real output.[49] We observe this phenomenon in both contemporary Britain and the United States, where rising unemployment, rather than a falling rate of inflation is the most noticeable short-run response to restrictive policies, and we see it in the history of the inter-war depressions in both countries where rapid price deflations were nevertheless accompanied by massive unemployment.

Exactly how fluctuations in aggregate demand spread their effects over time between prices and output remains mysterious, though it is coming to look increasingly as if the key to these problems

Britain or the United States. Moreover, as far as the money wage bargain is concerned, the existence of an expected rate of inflation of other than zero would presumably turn the bargain into one that set a rate of change as well as a current level of money wages.

Questions arise as to the relationship between these two concepts. If the 'permanent price level' concept turns out to have important empirical content, need it be the case that the expected rate of inflation be measured by the rate of change of that variable? Does it make sense to talk about an expected rate of inflation without also dealing with a permanent price level, or is it possible to measure the latter variable merely by the current price level plus the expected rate of inflation over whatever may be the relevant time period? I do not pretend to have the answers to these questions, but until they are found it is hard to see how much progress can be made in understanding the role that price expectations play in macroeconomics.

[49] The Phillips curve represents an attempt to deal with this interrelationship, as Johnson (1970) has pointed out. Williamson (1970) has used the Phillips curve to produce results showing that initial responses to changes in aggregate demand tend to come in output, with prices being subsequently influenced. The mechanism sketched out below differs crucially from Williamson's in the emphasis it places on the role played by price expectations in the wage bargain. However, it ought to be noted that Williamson's analysis has the merit of being carried out in terms of a growth model. Once the question of the time path of economic variables arises one suspects that the influence of investment on the capital stock, and hence on output, might be an important factor. The fact that this influence is neglected in the foregoing analysis is yet another reason for regarding its likely empirical content as being small.

will be found to lie in the analysis of price expectations. Formal analysis of the type presented earlier is out of the question, given the present state of this writer's grasp of the mechanisms involved, but an informal sketch of the kind of process that might be fruitfully analysed is perhaps an appropriate way to close this discussion of the leads and lags problem.

If it is postulated that the price level that is relevant for the demand for nominal balances is a permanent price level rather than a current one, then it is hard to resist the implication that the same concept ought to be relevant as far as the money wage bargain is concerned.[50] If this is accepted, however, and if the money wage determines the *current* supply price of output, then the scene is set for wages, prices and output to behave asymmetrically depending upon whether goods are in excess demand or excess supply. If we begin with a situation in the region of full employment with stable wages and prices, then an increase in the demand for goods will lead to prices being bid up, and as higher prices feed into price level expectations, to money wages following.[51]

However, if instead we have a fall off in demand, caused by either monetary or fiscal contraction—the source is irrelevant—then the resulting downward pressure on prices will meet with resistance from the supply side. There will be no reason for the labour force to accept money wage cuts unless it anticipates price cuts; to do so

[50] In the discussion that follows I shall deal only with the effects of price level expectations on the wage bargain and hence on the supply side of the economy. The effects of these same expectations on the demand side of the economy, as transmitted through the money market both by the influence of the effect of permanent prices and the expected rate of change of prices on the demand for money will be ignored. Obviously a full analysis of the time path of an inflationary process would have to consider the interaction of its effects on both aggregate demand and aggregate supply and my failure to provide such an analysis here should not be taken to suggest in any way that I do not regard the problem as important.

[51] Phillips curve analysis would suggest that while wages are rising in response to excess demand there might be some fall off in unemployment. When the price and wage levels come to rest again, unemployment would be back to its old level, again according to Phillips curve analysis, and that is why the phenomenon is neglected here. Nevertheless, it is important to note that the asymmetry with which I am dealing here is a product of the price expectations mechanism postulated and not of any assumption that there exists an unique level of 'full employment' output that cannot be exceeded.

When dealing with changes in the rate of change of prices and money wages, rather than in their level, Phillips curve analysis is not so clear on what we might expect to observe. This matter is discussed further in n. 53.

would be to accept a cut in real wages while there was still full employment. To the extent that price expectations are extrapolated from past experience they will not be modified until prices begin to fall; however, to the extent that on the supply side prices are determined by money wages they will not fall until those money wages start to fall. Hence the initial response to a fall in demand is likely to be a fall in output and employment. Moreover, it should be noted that, if we had begun the foregoing analysis in an economy whose past experience led those concerned with the wage bargain to expect a given rate of inflation, then a fall in demand would still lead to a fall in output initially. If real wages were to be maintained stable in such an economy, money wage bargains would be struck for a given rate of change of money wages, and the rate of change of money wages would not fall off until the rate of price inflation began to decline. This in turn would require a slow down in the rate of money wage inflation to set it in motion.[52]

How long a return to full employment would take in such a situation presumably depends upon how fast the real wage responds to the pressure of unemployment, how fast prices (or their rate of change) respond to money wages (or their rate of change), and how fast price level expectations respond to current price level variations.[53] Given some of the rather startling results that the very

[52] The last few paragraphs described a labour market mechanism that is very much in accord with modern interpretations of Keynes (1936). The expectations mechanism permits us to produce relative downward rigidity in money wages (or their rate of change) without having to postulate either trade unions with monopoly power or irrational 'money illusion' on the part of the suppliers of labour. This writer's debt to Leijonhufvud (1968) must be obvious.

[53] If money wage bargains were always struck with the aim of achieving a given real wage, if the price indices relevant for the suppliers of labour were the same as those taken into account by its demanders, and if there were no repercussions from the demand side of the economy, then movement from one rate of inflation to another ought to be no different to movements from one price level to another. In equilibrium, when anticipations have again caught up with what is happening, the real wages will be the same, and, according to the Phillips curve analysis as modified by Phelps (1967) and Friedman (1968), unemployment ought to have returned to its 'natural' rate. Parkin (1970) has recently produced evidence for post-war Britain that suggests that this does not in fact happen, but that a faster rate of inflation reduces unemployment permanently, though not by as much as it does in the short-run. Parkin's result may be due to the price expectations mechanism he postulated (an exponentially weighted average of past rates of inflation to yield the expected rate) being a misspecification of the true mechanism at work, to his failure to allow for demanders and suppliers of labour forming expectations about different price indices and at different rates, or to his neglect

9

simple dynamic model dealt with earlier produced, it would be rash indeed to say anything more specific about the manner in which these factors are likely to interact and the behaviour they are likely to produce without first analysing an explicit model of the processes I have sketched out in the last few paragraphs. The reader will not, I hope, hold it against this writer that he has as yet been unable to work out such a model in a satisfactory manner.[54]

V

A long summary of the issues dealt with in this paper is hardly necessary. First and foremost I have argued that, because the manner in which monetary policy, or fiscal policy for that matter, works involves not just one but all sectors of the economy, some knowledge of the structural relationships that exist in any economy is needed before monetary policy is usefully discussed. However suggestive reduced form relationships may be, and I have argued at some length in Section II of this paper that such relationships tell us quite a lot less than is sometimes supposed, it is impossible to interpret them fully without independent knowledge of the underlying structure of the economy to which they appertain.

A stable relationship between the quantity of money and the level of income taken by itself is open to a variety of interpretations. It is only when we have convincing evidence, as I believe we do for the United States, if not yet for Britain, that variations in the quantity of money took place independently of the variations in the level of income to which they are related, and evidence that a transmission mechanism working through a stable demand for money function and a relationship between interest rates and expenditure can be shown to exist, as once again I think is easier to claim for the United States than for Britain, that such evidence falls into place as one piece in a complex pattern of observations

of the influence of price expectations on the demand for goods. But any empirical study is open to comment that there is more than one interpretation to the results it has produced, and until these suggestions are investigated, Parkin's results ought to make us a little hesitant about accepting too readily the assumption implicit in this paragraph that the economy will, in the long run, always return to a unique level of 'full employment'.

[54] Note that Friedman (1970) pp. 223–34 sketches the outlines of such a model but that he finds the analysis of the time path of money income a more tractable problem than the division of this time path between variations in prices and variations in real income.

that, taken overall, can firmly establish the importance of the quantity of money as a determinant of the level of economic activity.

It is for this reason that the part of this paper that actually presented some new empirical results for the British economy concerned itself with such structural relationships and in particular the demand for money function. Though these results do not give us any reason to suppose that the British economy is any different from the American—apart apparently from producing data that are a bit more sensitive to the precise formulation of the function that is fitted to them—they still quite obviously leave a lot of questions unsettled. Though this writer is on the whole willing to argue that variations in the quantity of money can have just as strong and predictable effects as they do in the United States, there is as yet a great deal of room for scepticism about this conclusion, scepticism which can only be worn down (or justified, depending on the results) by a great deal more empirical work.

However, if we know less about Britain than we do about the United States, there is still a great deal to be learned about the latter economy, particularly on the matter of the time lags involved in the response of the economy to policy measures. Again I have argued that the answers to questions in this area are to be sought in the analysis of models of the structure of the economy. For one thing, the very parameters that determine the static equilibrium properties of the economy also have an important influence on the characteristics of the time path by which static equilibrium is approached, while we do already have some, albeit simple, economic explanations in terms of learning and adjustment mechanisms of the existence of time lags. The work that has been done on measuring lag effects, taken by itself, serves mainly to emphasize our ignorance of these matters; it provides a set of facts that need a model to explain them, and we are only just beginning to build up such models. In particular, our understanding of the factors that determine the way in which variations in money income divide themselves up between variations in real income and variations in prices is imperfect indeed.

However, the main difficulty in any science is knowing which questions to ask, and how to ask them. If this paper has put a sharper focus upon some of the currently unsettled questions in monetary economics and the methods which might usefully be adopted in solving them then it will have served the purpose that prompted its being written.

TABLE I

Log Linear Demand for Money Functions, Per Capita *Real Terms,*
United Kingdom and United States*

A. UNITED KINGDOM

(*i*) 1900–1965 (omitting 1914–18, 1939–45)

Intercept	y^e	y	r_s	r_l	D†	R^2
−1·315 (0·129)	0·663 (0·053)	—	−0·147 (0·013)	—	−0·120 (0·013)	0·942
−1·327 (0·132)	0·795 (0·056)	—	—	−0·570 (0·053)	−0·206 (0·014)	0·939
−1·244 (0·127)	—	0·631 (0·052)	−0·148 (0·014)	—	−0·118 (0·013)	0·939
−1·237 (0·133)	—	0·753 (0·056)	—	−0·569 (0·055)	−0·105 (0·017)	0·933

* y^e is the log of *per capita* real permanent income. For the United Kingdom, this series was constructed by applying Friedman's (1957) weights −0·33, 0·33 (1 − 0·33),... to figures for *per capita* real net national product based on series taken from *Key Statistics of the United Kingdom* and Deane and Cole (1967). These weights sum to unity, and no attempt was made to adjust the data for trend, since they were to be used in log linear regressions in which only the intercept is affected by this omission. It should be stressed that the use of Friedman's weights was prompted solely by the desire to produce tests for the United Kingdom as closely as possible resembling those for the United States and not by any pre-conception that they were particularly appropriate to use for Britain. (I hope that work now in progress will produce a permanent income series based solely on United Kingdom experience.) For the United States the permanent income series used is Friedman's. y is the log of real *per capita* net national product, and for both countries is the measured income series used in constructing permanent income. r_s is the log of a short interest rate, for the United Kingdom the 3-month Treasury bill rate and for the United States the 4–6-month commercial paper rate. r_l is the log of a long interest rate, for the United Kingdom the yield on 2½ per cent consols, and for the United States the yield on 30-year corporate bonds. For both countries the dependent variable is the log of *per capita* real money balances, and in both cases the series include time deposits (deposit accounts) at commercial banks. The decision to include time deposits in the money supply series was dictated by the fact that the only United Kingdom series available includes them. However, it is worth noting that a great deal of empirical work done with United States data has failed to discover any result which hinges upon the inclusion or exclusion of time deposits—moreover theoretical arguments

(*ii*) 1900–1913

Intercept	y^e	y	r_s	r_l	R^2	dw‡
−0·346 (1·061)	0·140 (0·462)	—	0·071 (0·035)	—	0·275	2·085
−2·706 (1·737)	1·241 (0·780)	—	—	−0·268 (0·149)	0·232	2·306
−0·256 (0·512)	—	0·106 (0·223)	0·068 (0·036)	—	0·284	2·137
−0·823 (0·602)	—	0·399 (0·272)	—	−0·165 (0·108)	0·210	2·439

(*iii*) 1920–1938

Intercept	y^e	y	r_s	r_l	R^2	dw‡
−1·964 (0·618)	0·925 (0·260)	—	−0·077 (0·028)	—	0·887	0·588
−1·404 (0·600)	0·793 (0·230)	—	—	−0·448 (0·118)	0·912	0·738
−1·523 (0·484)	—	0·735 (0·202)	−0·087 (0·025)	—	0·889	0·840
−1·003 (0·515)	—	−0·628 (0·193)	—	−0·484 (0·114)	0·907	0·875

seem to lead to no definite conclusion as to whether time deposits ought or ought not to be treated as 'money'. On these issues cf. Laidler (1969*b*) and Friedman and Schwartz (1970), ch. 1. Except for the money supply series, kindly provided by David Sheppard, the source of all the United Kingdom data is *Key Statistics*, while all United States data comes from NBER worksheets kindly made available by Anna Schwartz.

All figures in parentheses are the standard errors of the parameter estimates immediately above them.

† Up till 1919 the British data on the money supply and income include figures for what became the Irish Free State in 1921. A dummy variable taking a value of 1 for years up to 1919 was included in an attempt to deal with any discrepancies arising from this discontinuity. Its negative sign is consistent with the hypothesis that in a predominantly rural economy with a less sophisticated financial sector, the demand for money tends to be less than in a more industrialized society. However, the statistical significance of this variable may well also reflect more general differences between behaviour in the pre- and post-First World War United Kingdom.

(*iv*) 1946–1965

Intercept	y^e	y	r_s	r_l	R^2	$dw\ddagger$
0·576 (0·450)	−0·083 (0·180)	—	−0·124 (0·021)	—	0·875	1·221
−0·931 (0·697)	0·684 (0·306)	—	—	−0·739 (0·129)	0·867	1·047
0·438 (0·412)	—	−0·028 (0·164)	−0·129 (0·021)	—	0·873	1·271
−0·894 (0·589)	—	0·671 (0·260)	—	−0·763 (0·122)	0·877	0·965

B. UNITED STATES

(*i*) 1900–1965 (omitting 1917–18 and 1941–5)

Intercept	y^e	y	r_s	r_l	R^2
−5·901 (0·064)	1·257 (0·022)	—	−0·186 (0·010)	—	0·988
−5·920 (0·143)	1·312 (0·045)	—	—	−0·393 (0·073)	0·946
−5·708 (0·143)	—	1·195 (0·045)	−0·203 (0·022)	—	0·945
−5·766 (0·212)	—	1·250 (0·066)	—	−0·341 (0·108)	0·882

(*ii*) 1900–1916

Intercept	y^e	y	r_s	r_l	R^2	$dw\ddagger$
−6·328 (0·220)	1·393 (0·080)	—	−0·110 (0·040)	—	0·957	0·720
−6·097 (0·522)	1·243 (0·241)	—	—	0·181 (0·253)	0·935	0·924
−6·066 (0·635)	—	1·317 (0·236)	−0·190 (0·106)	—	0·700	1·155
−4·968 (0·359)	—	0·650 (0·148)	—	1·014 (0·140)	0·922	1·320

(*iii*) 1919–1940

Intercept	y^e	y	r_s	r_l	R^2	$dw\ddagger$
−5·978 (−0·326)	1·284 (0·116)	—	−0·156 (0·011)	—	0·939	1·200
−3·982 (0·547)	0·690 (0·189)	—	—	−0·642 (0·078)	0·849	0·584
−3·771 (0·413)	—	0·498 (0·148)	−0·144 (0·024)	—	0·715	0·476
−2·326 (0·452)	—	0·112 (0·151)	—	−0·692 (0·105)	0·751	0·457

(*iv*) 1946–1965

Intercept	y^e	y	r_s	r_l	R^2	$dw\ddagger$
−4·075 (0·853)	0·650 (0·287)	—	−0·168 (0·042)	—	0·565	1·309
−3·232 (1·162)	0·398 (0·405)	—	—	−0·274 (0·133)	0·321	0·559
−3·761 (0·707)	—	0·549 (0·240)	−0·180 (0·046)	—	0·567	1·408
−2·231 (0·719)	—	0·049 (0·254)	—	−0·175 (0·110)	0·284	0·573

‡ *dw* is a Durbin–Watson statistic. Since the series used for the whole period are not continuous, no such statistic is reported for the 1900–65 results. By and large these statistics point to a considerable degree of first order auto-correlation in the residuals of these regressions. One interpretation of this is that there is an omitted variable (or variables), and it is worth noting that when Feige (1967) tested the permanent income hypothesis of the demand for money for the United States in a much more sophisticated manner than that employed here, and when Laidler and Parkin (1970) carried out similar tests which involve using lagged values of several variables as arguments in the function, they all found evidence quite consistent with this hypothesis while finding no sign of first order auto-correlation in the residuals of their regressions. The small Durbin–Watson statistics reported here, therefore, ought not to perturb us too much.

TABLE 2

Log Linear Demand for Money Functions, Per Capita *Terms, United Kingdom and United States**

A. UNITED KINGDOM

Period	Intercept	y^e	r_l	p	D	R^2	dw
1900–1965 (omitting 1914–18 1939–45)	−0·895 (0·190)	0·515 (0·108)	−0·703 (0·066)	1·188 (0·063)	−0·189 (0·014)	0·933	—
1900–1913	−2·566 (1·759)	1·417 (0·811)	−0·108 (0·233)	0·536 (0·516)	—	0·639	2·295
1920–1938	−0·378 (0·305)	0·616 (0·108)	−0·245 (0·060)	0·538 (0·059)	—	0·902	1·395
1946–1965	−0·480 (0·248)	1·036 (0·112)	−0·134 (0·071)	0·109 (0·081)	—	0·975	1·293

* All series as in Table 1. p is the log of a price index, for the United Kingdom a retail price index, and for the United States the NNP deflator.

B. UNITED STATES

Period	Intercept	y^e	r_s	p	R^e	dw
1900–1965 (omitting 1917–18 1941–5)	−5·859 (0·143)	1·229 (0·088)	−0·187 (0·011)	1·020 (0·059)	0·997	—
1900–1916	−6·170 (0·312)	1·243 (0·222)	−0·083 (0·056)	1·131 (0·180)	0·988	0·862
1919–1940	−5·311 (0·246)	1·343 (0·076)	−0·093 (0·014)	0·562 (0·084)	0·957	1·494
1946–1960	−4·581 (0·766)	1·314 (0·358)	−0·070 (0·052)	0·310 (0·268)	0·897	0·982

ADDITIONAL NOTES

1. There is no widely known 'Classical' counterpart of the 'Keynesian Cross' diagram, though one is easily constructed. Holding the price level constant, if we measure real income on the horizontal axis and the real money stock on the vertical, then the intersection of the supply and demand for money determine income. Holding real income constant, plotting nominal money on the vertical axis and the price level on the horizontal would turn the diagram into one which determined the price level. In this case, though, the homogeneity of the demand function in the independent variable would cease to be simply a matter of geometric convenience as it is in the diagram shown and would instead embody a fundamental hypothesis of monetary theory, namely the proportionality of the demand for nominal money to the general price level.

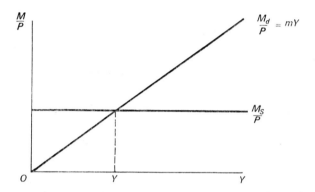

2. There also seems to this writer to be a theoretical issue concerning the relationship between the demand for money and interest rates, which might repay further investigation. In nearly all theoretical treatments of the demand for money, the rate of interest measures the opportunity cost of holding money (the Keynesian speculative demand analysis is an exception). However, as far as empirical studies of the demand for money have been concerned, the choice of which interest rate to use has been dictated as much by what data are available as by any careful consideration of how to measure this opportunity cost.

Now which rate measures the opportunity cost of holding money clearly depends upon how long is the planned holding period of cash balances, upon how long is the horizon over which portfolio compositions are fixed, and this horizon implicitly or explicitly is taken as exogenously given in many studies of the demand for money. However, to the extent that one of the motives for holding money as a means of bridging the gap between the receipt of income and the making of expenditures is to avoid the costs involved in buying and selling other assets as cash is received and is needed for disbursement, this holding period is in fact endogenous. The lower is the rate of return *per annum* on an asset, the longer must it be held before its ownership covers a given cost of acquiring it and disposing of it. To put the same matter another way, as rates of interest fall the opportunity cost of holding money over any time period falls, so that the demand for money increases; however, an essential aspect of increasing the proportion of money in the portfolio is the lengthening of the horizon over which it is planned to hold money.

The foregoing argument suggests that the very idea of using one interest rate as a measure of *the* opportunity cost of holding money is a simplification. What one has in fact is the whole term structure of interest rates measuring the opportunity cost of holding money over various time periods, with the holding period of money itself being a decision variable. In general, the lower are interest rates, the longer is the holding period of money going to be, and hence the longer the rate of interest that measures the opportunity cost of holding money on the margin. This is certainly compatible with the evidence that Cagan (1969b) has recently produced to the effect that longer assets appear to become closer substitutes for money as the level of interest rates falls, and suggests in general that the length of the asset the yield on which measures the opportunity cost of holding money will vary with the level of interest rates in general.

3. Kaldor (1970, p. 13) makes a great deal of the fact that the deposit currency ratio in July 1960 was about the same as it was in July 1932, and that this ratio reached a trough during the Second World War. He seems to think that this is evidence against the view that the behaviour of the ratio in the early 1930s was the consequence of the public's loss of confidence in the commercial banks. Two observations are in order here. First, what is primarily at stake in the 1929–33 episode is the time path of this ratio, not its level at any moment in time. Second, though Kaldor, in looking for reliable sources on the doctrines of 'the new monetarism', specifically singles out Cagan as 'someone who can be relied on to follow the master Friedman closely...' (Kaldor 1970, p. 2), he nevertheless ignores his work on the determinants of the deposit currency ratio. Cagan argues that during the war the disruption of normal banking relations caused by increased population mobility, largely due to the expansion of the armed forces, could be expected to increase greatly the demand for cash in a country where banks do not branch across state lines. Cagan also noted the existence of a strong incentive to carry out black market transactions in terms of currency, and of a related incentive to hide transactions by using currency that arises from high marginal income tax rates. The income tax argument holds for the post-war period as well, of course, while one must not overlook the effects on the deposit currency ratio of the prohibition of interest

payments on demand deposits and the fixing of maximum rates on time deposits. Cf. Cagan (1965).

The most thorough work on the determinants of bank reserves (again ignored by Kaldor) is that of Morrison (1966). The most difficult aspect of bank behaviour to explain for those who argue that the build up of free reserves was the result of purposeful behaviour is the length of time it took. Why was the 'shock' of 1931–3 still causing the banks to build up free reserves in 1937? Morrison's explanation is that banks hold free reserves against what they regard as 'transitory deposits', the difference between 'permanent deposits' and actual deposits. He argues that their estimate of permanent deposits is developed from an error learning mechanism characterized by what is usually a rapid rate of adjustment of expectations to experience; Morrison then suggests that this rate of adjustment is significantly slowed down in the face of large and costly errors such as the banks discovered that they had made in 1931–3. This hypothesis about variability in the error learning mechanism is of potentially much wider application and is discussed in Section IV of this paper.

4. As far as the equilibrium properties of a deterministic static model are concerned it makes no substantive difference if one thinks of a given quantity of money determining a given interest rate and level of income or if one prefers instead to think in terms of a given interest rate determining a given level of income and quantity of money. However, if one introduces a stochastic element into such a model, the distinction in question might be of some importance in designing a regression experiment since it would be crucial in determining where error terms would be found. Furthermore, without introducing a stochastic element, in a dynamic model where the public has less than perfect foresight it is not difficult to conceive of an announced interest rate influencing interest rate expectations in a different way from an announced money supply policy, even when there is no difference between the equilibrium situations to which the policies lead. The time paths of the money supply, the interest rate, and income towards equilibrium could, then, differ depending upon what kind of policy the authorities chose to follow. This could be an important factor in interpreting observed leads and lags in time series data.

Now it is worth noting that control of the interest rate, rather than the money supply, is not necessarily a foolish policy in terms of achieving the traditional goals of full employment and price stability. As Poole (1970) has argued, in terms of the Hicks–Hansen framework the less stable is the demand for money function relative to the expenditure function, the more likely it is that control of the interest rate will be sensible policy, and vice versa.

The Bank of England tends to argue that it is instability in the market for government securities that obliges it to pursue an interest rate policy. Recent work by Parkin (1970) and Parkin, Gray and Barrett (1969) on the portfolio behaviour of both discount houses and commercial banks suggests that these institutions' demand functions for government securities are stable enough, while Norton (1969) goes so far as to suggest that what instability there is in markets for government securities occurs because of, rather than despite, the authorities' activities.

BIBLIOGRAPHY

ALFORD, R. F. G. (1960). 'A Taxonomic Note on the Multiplier and Income Velocity', *Economica* N.S. 26, February, pp. 53–62.

ANDO, A. and MODIGLIANI, F. (1965). 'The Relative Stability of Monetary Velocity and the Investment Multiplier', *American Economic Review* 55, September, pp. 693–728.

ARTIS, M. J. and NOBAY, A. R. (1969). 'Two Aspects of the Monetary Debate', *National Institute Economic Review*, August, pp. 33–51.

BARRETT, C. R. and WALTERS, A. A. (1966). 'The Stability of Keynesian and Monetary Multipliers in the United Kingdom', *Review of Economics and Statistics* 48, November, pp. 395–405.

BRETON, A. (1968). 'A Stable Velocity Function for Canada?', *Economica* N.S. 35, November, pp. 451–3.

BROWN, A. J. (1939). 'Interest, Prices and the Demand for Idle Money', *Oxford Economic Papers* 2, May, pp. 46–69.

CAGAN, P. (1956). 'The Monetary Dynamics of Hyperinflation', in Milton Friedman (ed.), *Studies in the Quantity Theory of Money* (Chicago: University of Chicago Press).

—— (1965). *Determinants and Effects of Changes in the Stock of Money 1870–1960* (New York: Columbia University Press for NBER).

—— (1969a). 'The Influence of Interest Rates on the Duration of Business Cycles', in P. Cagan and J. M. Guttentag (eds.), *Essays on Interest Rates*, Vol. 1 (New York: NBER).

—— (1969b). 'A Study of Liquidity Premiums on Federal and Municipal Government Securities', in P. Cagan and J. M. Guttentag (eds.), *Essays on Interest Rates*, Vol. 1 (New York: NBER).

COPPOCK, D. J. and GIBSON, N. J. (1963). 'The Volume of Deposits and the Cash and Liquid Assets Ratios', *Manchester School* 31, September, pp. 203–22.

CROUCH, R. (1967). 'A Model of the United Kingdom's Monetary Sector', *Econometrica* 35, July–October, pp. 398–418.

DEANE, P. and COLE, W. A. (1967). *British Economic Growth 1688–1959*, 2nd edn. (Cambridge: Cambridge University Press).

DE LEEUW, F. (1965). 'A Model of Financial Behaviour', in J. F. Duesenberry *et al.* (eds.), *The Brookings Quarterly Econometric Model of the United States* (Rand McNally).

DE PRANO, M. and MAYER, T. (1965). 'Tests of the Relative Importance of Autonomous Expenditure and Money', *American Economic Review* 55, September, pp. 729–52.

FEIGE, E. (1967). 'Expectations and Adjustments in the Monetary Sector', *American Economic Review* 57 (papers and proceedings), May, pp. 462–73.

FISHER, D. (1968). 'The Demand for Money in Britain: Quarterly Results 1951 to 1967', *Manchester School* 36, December, pp. 329–44.

FRIEDMAN, M. (1956). 'The Quantity Theory of Money, a Restatement', in M. Friedman (ed.), *Studies in the Quantity Theory of Money* (Chicago: University of Chicago Press).

—— (1957). *A Theory of the Consumption Function* (Princeton, N.J.).

—— (1958). 'The Supply of Money and Changes in Prices and Output', in *The Relationship of Prices to Economic Stability and Growth* (U.S. Congress, Joint Economic Committee, Compendium) pp. 241–56.

—— (1959). 'The Demand for Money—Some Theoretical and Empirical Results', *Journal of Political Economy* 67, June, pp. 327–51.

—— (1968). 'The Role of Monetary Policy', *American Economic Review* 58, March, pp. 1–17.

—— (1970). 'A Theoretical Framework for Monetary Analysis', *Journal of Political Economy* 78, March/April, pp. 193–238.

—— and MEISELMAN, D. (1963). 'The Relative Stability of Monetary Velocity and the Investment Multiplier in the United States, 1897–1958', in Commission on Money and Credit, *Stabilization Policies* (Englewood Cliffs, N.J.: Prentice Hall).

—— —— (1965). 'Reply to Ando and Modigliani and to De Prano and Mayer', *American Economic Review* 55, September, pp. 754–85.

—— and SCHWARTZ, A. J. (1963a). *A Monetary History of the United States 1867–1960* (Princeton N.J.: Princeton University Press for NBER).

—— —— (1963b). 'Money and Business Cycles', *Review of Economics and Statistics* 45, February, supplement pp. 32–64.

—— —— (1970). *Monetary Statistics of the United States* (New York: NBER).

GOODHART, C. A. E. and CROCKETT, A. D. (1970). 'The Importance of Money', *Bank of England Quarterly Bulletin* 10, June, pp. 159–98.

GROSSMAN, H. I. and DOLDE, W. C. (1969). *The Appropriate Timing of Monetary Policy*, mimeo (Brown University).

GUPTA, S. B. (1970). 'The Portfolio Balance Theory of the Expected Rate of Change or Prices', *Review of Economic Studies* 37, April, pp. 187–204.

HAMBURGER, M. (1967). 'Interest Rates and the Demand for Consumer Durable Goods', *American Economic Review* 57, December, pp. 1133–53.

—— (1968). 'Household Demand for Financial Assets', *Econometrica* 36, January, pp. 97–118.

HARRIS, L. (1968). 'Regularities and Irregularities in Monetary Economics', in C. R. Whittlesey and J. S. G. Wilson (eds.), *Essays in Money and Banking in Honour of R. S. Sayers* (Oxford: The Clarendon Press).

HESTER, D. (1964). 'Keynes and the Quantity Theory: Comment on Friedman and Meiselman CMC Paper', *Review of Economics and Statistics* 46, November, pp. 354–86.

HYNES, A. (1967). 'The Demand for Money and Monetary Adjustments in Chile', *Review of Economic Studies* 34, July, pp. 285–94.

JOHNSON, H. G. (1962). 'Monetary Theory and Policy', *American Economic Review* 52, June, pp. 335–84.

—— (1967). 'Recent Developments in Monetary Theory', in H. G. Johnson, *Essays in Monetary Economics* (London: George Allen and Unwin).

—— (1970). 'Recent Developments in Monetary Theory—A Commentary', in D. R. Croome and H. G. Johnson (eds.), *Money in Britain 1959–1969* (London: Oxford University Press).

JORGENSON, D. W. (1963). 'Capital Theory and Investment Behaviour', *American Economic Review* 53 (papers and proceedings), May, pp. 247–59.

KALDOR, N. (1970). 'The New Monetarism', *Lloyds Bank Review*, July, pp. 1–18.

KAREKEN, J. and SOLOW, R. (1963). 'Lags in Monetary Policy', in Commission on Money and Credit: *Stabilisation Policies* (Englewood Cliffs N.J.: Prentice Hall).

KEYNES, J. M. (1936). *The General Theory of Employment, Interest and Money* (London and New York: Macmillan).

KHUSRO, A. M. (1952). 'An Investigation of Liquidity Preference', *Yorkshire Bulletin of Economic and Social Research* 4, January, pp. 1–20.

KLEIN, J. J. (1956). 'German Money and Prices 1932–44', in M. Friedman (ed.), *Studies in the Quantity Theory of Money* (Chicago: University of Chicago Press).

LAIDLER, D. (1966). 'The Rate of Interest and the Demand for Money', *Journal of Political Economy* 74, February, pp. 55–68.

—— (1968). 'The Permanent Income Concept in a Macroeconomic Model', *Oxford Economic Papers* 20, March, pp. 11–23.

—— (1969a). *The Demand for Money—Theories and Evidence* (Scranton Pa.: International Textbook Co.).

—— (1969b). 'The Definition of Money—Theoretical and Empirical Problems', *Journal of Money Credit and Banking* 1, August, pp. 508–25.

—— and PARKIN, J. M. (1970). 'The Demand for Money in the United Kingdom 1956–1967: Preliminary Estimates', *Manchester School* 38, September, pp. 187–208.

LEE, T. H. (1967). 'Alternative Interest Rates and the Demand for Money: The Empirical Evidence', *American Economic Review* 57, December, pp. 1168–81.

LEIJONHUFVUD, A. (1968). *On Keynesian Economics and the Economics of Keynes* (New York: Oxford University Press).

MAYER, T. (1967). 'The Lag Effect in Monetary Policy: Some Criticisms', *Western Economic Journal* 5, September, pp. 324–42.

MORRISON, G. (1966). *Liquidity Preferences of Commercial Banks* (Chicago: University of Chicago Press).

MOTLEY, B. (1970). 'Household Demand for Assets: A Model of Shortrun Adjustments', *Review of Economics and Statistics*, 52, August, pp. 236–241.

NORTON, W. E. (1969). 'Debt Management and Monetary Policy in the United Kingdom', *Economic Journal* 79, September, pp. 475–94.

PARKIN, J. M. (1970a). 'Discount Houses Portfolio and Debt Selection', *Review of Economic Studies* 37, October, pp. 469–99.

—— (1970b). 'Incomes Policy—Some Further Results on the Determination of the Rate of Change of Money Wages', *Economica* N.S. 37, November.

—— GRAY, M. and BARRETT, R. (1970). 'The Portfolio Behaviour of Commercial Banks', in K. Hilton and D. F. Heathfield (eds.), *The Econometric Study of the United Kingdom* (London and Basingstoke: Macmillan).

PESEK, B. and SAVING, T. (1967). *Money, Wealth and Economic Theory* (New York: Macmillan).

PHELPS, E. (1967). 'Phillips Curves, Expectations of Inflation and Optimal Unemployment Over Time', *Economica* N.S. 34, August, pp. 254–81.

POOLE, W. (1970). 'Optimal Choice of Monetary Policy Instruments in a Simple Stochastic Macro Model', *Quarterly Journal of Economics* 84, May, pp. 197–216.

SCHWARTZ, A. J. (1969). 'Short Term Targets of Three Foreign Central Banks', in K. Brunner (ed.), *Targets and Indicators of Monetary Policy* (San Francisco, California: Chandler Publishing Co.).

SHEPPARD, D. (1970). 'Money, Encashable Assets, Private Institutional Credits and Private Expenditure in the UK 1860–1962', mimeo (Graduate Centre for Management Studies, University of Birmingham, University of Aston in Birmingham).

TOBIN, J. and SWAN, C. (1969). 'Money and Permanent Income: Some Empirical Tests', *American Economic Review* 59, May, pp. 285–95.

TUCKER, D. (1966). 'Dynamic Income Adjustment to Money Supply Changes', *American Economic Review* 56, June, pp. 433–49.

WALTERS, A. A. (1969). *Money in Boom and Slump*, Hobart Paper 44 (London: Institute of International Affairs).

—— (1970). 'The Radcliffe Report—Ten Years After: A Survey of Empirical Evidence', in D. R. Croome and H. G. Johnson (eds.), *Money in Britain 1959–1969* (London: Oxford University Press).

WILLIAMSON, J. (1970). 'A Simple Neo-Keynesian Growth Model', *Review of Economic Studies* 37, April, pp. 157–71.

WRIGHT, C. (1969). 'Saving and the Rate of Interest', in A. C. Harberger and M. J. Bailey (eds.), *The Taxation of Income from Capital* (Washington D.C.: The Brooking Institution).

Discussion Papers

(a) FRANK P. R. BRECHLING
(Professor of Economics, Northwestern University)

WE must be grateful to Professor Laidler for having given us such a lucid exposition of his own views of the present state of the 'monetarist' position. His lucidity facilitates the task of evaluating this position and of pointing the way toward further empirical and theoretical analysis in monetary economics.

The most striking point which emerges from Professor Laidler's survey is that the 'monetarist school' has paid relatively little attention to the development of a theoretical model which is essentially different from the conventional models of the influence of money on economic activity.[1] Indeed, Laidler himself uses the Hicks–Hansen type of model which is usually regarded as a formalization of Keynesian theory. This reliance of recent 'monetarists' on simple comparative-static macro-models seems to differ significantly from the position of pre-Keynesian monetarists who placed heavy emphasis on the analysis of sectoral velocities and of the dynamics of the monetary circular flow. To be sure, some studies of sectoral demands for money have recently been undertaken, but the main thrust of the 'monetarist' school has been the assertion that a stable demand function for money exists and that, consequently, an active control of the money supply must affect some (or all) of the endogenous variables of the system (namely, the rate of interest, real income and the price level).

Let me now comment on some of the specific questions raised by Laidler. I quite agree with his first proposition, namely that the reduced form comparisons of the 'monetarist' and the 'expenditure' approaches shed only limited light on the fundamental question of the efficacy of monetary policy.[2] But there is one other problem.

[1] This impression is supported by Professor Friedman's contribution to this seminar and some of Friedman's recent writing.

[2] However, I do not wish to give the impression that the 'reduced form' and 'structural' approaches are mutually exclusive. A properly specified system of structural equations implies reduced forms and there is no reason why both should not be studied.

It seems to me that in the reduced form studies insufficient attention has been paid to the difficult conceptual question of what constitutes 'autonomous' behaviour. Clearly private investment can hardly be regarded as 'autonomous', in the sense of its independence of all economic factors, except possibly in the very short run. Similarly, the supply of money, defined in one of the customary manners, can hardly be regarded as purely autonomous and tightly controlled by the authorities. Suppose, for instance, that the authorities managed to reduce the supply of high-powered money drastically. It seems highly plausible that the reaction of money substitutes would make the effective money supply virtually completely endogenous. Thus, if investment and the money supply are largely endogenous, then a regression of money income (or some other index of economic activity) on investment and the money supply would be a serious mis-specification. Such a regression is bound to perform well, because jointly dependent variables are correlated. But it would shed no light on the efficacy of monetary policy.

Professor Laidler's second major proposition is that there is substantial empirical evidence to suggest that a stable demand function for real money exists. The arguments in this function are the opportunity cost of holding money (approximated by one or other interest rate) and the level of permanent income. Suppose that a strong stable negative relationship between the rate of interest and real expenditure (either consumption or investment) did exist; then, according to Laidler, the existence of a stable demand function for money is both necessary and sufficient for the efficacy of monetary policy. I have the following comments.

First, I think that our ideas of what constitutes stability requires further refinement. We usually look at R^2's, t ratios, and possibly the stability of coefficients across sub-periods. Much less often do we study in detail the nature of the auto-correlation in the residuals. In the present context, this point appears to me to be particularly important. Even if the residuals from the demand for money function are small, so that we have a high R^2, any auto-correlation, if unrecognized by the authorities, may lead to serious errors in monetary management.[3]

---

[3] Some investigators have removed part of the auto-correlation by the so-called rho-transformation. The result is that the residuals will not be highly auto-correlated. From the policy-maker's point of view this result would, of course, be misleading unless he knew how to interpret rho and had an initial value of a

Second, I would like to cast some doubt on the implication that, *given a strong negative relationship between the rate of interest and real expenditure*, the existence of a stable interest-elastic demand for money function is sufficient to make the control of the money supply an effective policy instrument. Suppose, for instance, that the sample period is one in which the supply of money has been infinitely elastic; the monetary authorities have announced discount rates and have supplied whatever amounts of high-powered money the economy has required. Random shocks in the system would be allowed to be absorbed by variations in the supply of money, so that they need not affect interest rates or prices. Suppose that a stable demand functions for money in terms of an interest rate, permanent real income and the price level has been estimated from this sample. Now suppose that the authorities change the mode of their policy and control the money supply vigorously but leaving all rates of interest to be determined by the market. Since a basic institutional aspect of the economy has been changed there is no guarantee whatever that the new aggregate demand for money function should be identical to the one estimated from the sample period. It seems especially plausible to suppose that the demand for money adjusts to its equilibrium position quite rapidly when the supply of money is infinitely elastic and that interest rates, prices and permanent income react sluggishly to exogenous changes in the money stock, thus causing considerable disequilibrium in money holdings. In such a case, the existence of a stable demand function in the sample period may not tell us much about this function in the period of active money supply policy.

Third, let me discuss briefly some statistical problems which arise in the empirical studies mentioned by Professor Laidler. The basic proposition of the 'monetarists' seems to be that the supply of money is exogenous and errorless, and that the demand for money (Md) adjusts to supply $(\bar{M})$ through changes in the rate of interest (i), the price level (P) and permanent income. Let us grant the assumption that $\bar{M}$ is exogenous and, for simplicity of exposition, let us assume initially that neither the price level nor permanent income change, so that a *ceteris paribus* autonomous change in the demand for money must be accompanied by a change

residual. An alternative, possibly better, approach might be for the investigator to examine the entire auto-regressive structure (i.e. not only first-order auto-correlation) of the residuals and to present the results to the policy-maker as his estimate of the unexplained but systematic residuals.

(in the same direction) of the rate of interest. Thus in algebraic terms, the demand for money may be written (linearly) as $Md = \alpha + \beta i + u$ where u is some autonomous disturbance. Since $Md = \bar{M}$, we have $i = (1/\beta)(\bar{M} - \alpha - u)$, which is the correct reduced form for the stated assumptions. Thus i is subject to an error equal to u/β where u is the error in the demand for money function. Now if $\bar{M}$ is regressed on i, then we have a simple case of errors in the independent variable, which, as is well known, must lead to a downward bias in the (absolute value of) regression coefficient of i (namely, of $|\beta|$). Let me take the analysis one step further: Suppose the price level were *not* constant and that the dependent variable was $\bar{M}/p$. With a constant $\bar{M}$, a positive autonomous rise in the demand for money would lead to a rise in i and a fall in P. Consequently $\bar{M}/p$ would be *positively* associated with i, because of this shift in Md. In other words, the errors of the dependent variable $(\bar{M}/p)$ and of the independent variable (i) would be positively correlated and thus might give a serious bias to any existing true negative relationship between the demand for money and the rate of interest.[4]

Although the above biases do not disappear with large samples, they may be particularly severe in sub-samples in which the variance in $\bar{M}$ is relatively small, compared with the error variances and covariances. In other words, for samples in which $\bar{M}$ varies over a wide range, the biases may become small relatively to the underlying relationship, while for samples in which $\bar{M}$ varies over a small range, the regression coefficients may be primarily determined by the error terms.[5] I should like to offer this result as a

[4] I should perhaps emphasize that these biases do *not* arise from a simultaneity in the demand for and supply of money, but rather from an inadequately specified interaction between the exogenous money supply, the rate of interest and the price level.

The problem of the biases may become more severe if a stock adjustment lag model is assumed for the demand for money. I have examined the case in which the disturbance in the demand for money has an instantaneous effect while the influence of the rate of interest is lagged. It is clear that all regression coefficients are likely to be biased, though the direction of the bias cannot always be determined.

[5] The point can be made more clearly in a diagram: Imagine a negative demand for money schedule, i being measured along the vertical and $Md = \bar{M}$ along the horizontal axis. The disturbances cause a band of observations about the true schedule. In a regression of M on i, the horizontal errors will be minimized, thus leading to bias. If, $\bar{M} = Md$ ranges along the entire schedule, the bias may be acceptable. By contrast, if $\bar{M} = Md$ ranges only over a small section of the schedule, the biases may overshadow the underlying negative relationship.

possible explanation for the instability of coefficients across sub-periods to which Professor Laidler refers. It seems to me that, until some of these obvious and potentially highly misleading specification errors have been removed, we should regard our estimates as no more than tentative results.

Let me conclude my comments by mentioning briefly the areas which, in my view, are the most promising for future research. I cannot see that much more can be gained from further empirical investigations of single-equation macro-demand functions for money. Attempts ought to be made to specify clearly the dynamic impact of changes in the supply of high-powered money upon demand and from there upon prices. Specifically, I would like to see more work in the following areas:

(i) More detailed historical and institutional studies on the nature of the determinants of high-powered money appear to be essential as a basis for future econometric work.

(ii) If the monetary impact of the balance-of-payments is invariably neutralized, then high-powered money can be introduced into the economy either by budget deficits or by open-market operations (where the latter is defined to include the rediscounting of Treasury bills). Not much is known about differences in the short-run and long-run effects of these methods of introducing money into the economy. A detailed study of them seems long overdue.

(iii) I feel that our knowledge of the micro-dynamics of monetary behaviour of financial institutions and of the private sector is quite limited. The study of particular sectors or even of institutions (as against macro-economic analyses) seems to me to have, at least, two advantages. First, it is easier to avoid simultaneity problems at the micro-level and, second, any *theoretical* analysis of time lags is likely to be easier if it can be formulated for individual decision units.

Over the past fifteen years the 'monetarists', under the brilliant leadership of Professor Friedman, have been completely successful at convincing their colleagues (as well as bankers, journalists and politicians) that 'money matters'. To quote Professor Laidler: 'it is no longer necessary to be defensive about working in monetary economics'. But where should monetary economics go from here? As the above remarks imply, I feel that the most promising course of action consists of the application and development of more refined theoretical and econometric techniques. Specifically, I would welcome analyses of the micro-dynamics of monetary behaviour. The results of such research would ultimately enable us to obtain a deeper understanding of the role that money plays in modern economies.

Discussion Papers

(b) Douglas Fisher
(*University of Essex*)

Introduction

In the following discussion my comments will fall into three categories: points of agreement, points of illustration, and points of disagreement. The points of agreement concern the general message of Professor Laidler's paper; the points of illustration concern some new evidence of my own which bears on his topic, and the points of disagreement concern Laidler's interpretation of what we can conclude from the data. I will begin with the general comments.

The Process of Monetary Adjustment

To begin with, I heartily endorse Laidler's insistence that the most important task before us is the study of the transmission mechanisms through which the monetary and the real interact. I also agree that this study must be directed towards the special circumstances of the British economy; on the basis of my own investigations, I concur with his judgement that, since the British monetary system is, at present, broadly like the American, the techniques employed successfully in the United States ought to bear fruit when turned to the British data, at least for the post-war data.

I also agree that one should study the lag structure of the system as an economic problem. On the other hand, because I do not see the optimizing behaviour in Laidler's contribution to the lag problem, I am uncertain as to what his arguments tell us other than that the problem is potentially a very complicated one. Perhaps, as Laidler suggests, the portfolio methods will be productive in this area, especially if advantage is taken of embodied expectations, perhaps along the lines suggested by term structure theory.

I think I see what Laidler is saying when he argues in favour of structural estimation, but my own feeling is that a better term to apply to the sort of work we have been doing is *ad hoc* estimation. Indeed, a reduced form equation in which one of the independent variables is the stock of money is simply not sufficiently reduced for my tastes, if it is applied to the British data for any recent period. I shall return to this point in a minute, but let me go on to say that the structural versions of the demand for money which Laidler exhibits do suffer, in their turn, from an 'identification crisis' and that, I suspect, is what Walters had in mind when he offered his criticism.[1]

Let me propose a set of four basic equations with *ad hoc* adjustment mechanisms, which I suggest will tell us more about how the British economy might be characterized, monetarily. I shall present some evidence as I go along. Let me refer to these equations as *short-run* relationships; they appear as Model I.

$$M_t = M_t(M_{t-1}, Y_t, i_t) \qquad (\text{I.1})$$

$$C_t = C_t(Y_t, i_t) \qquad (\text{I.2})$$

$$i_t = i_t(i_{t-1}, B_t, G_t, U_t, \dot{P}_t) \qquad (\text{I.3})$$

$$I_t = I_t(I_{t-1}, i_t, Y_t) \qquad (\text{I.4})$$

Equations (I.1), (I.2) and (I.4) are conventional formulations of the demand for money, consumption, and investment. Equation (I.3) is a reaction function when the interest rate is Bank rate, the arguments are proxies for the balance of payments situation, the growth rate, the level of unemployment, and the rate of change of prices. When the equation has the Treasury bill rate as the dependent variable, it gives us some idea of the influence of monetary policy on the interest rate. When we apply equation (I.3) to British data for the period 1955–68, we find that 73 per cent of the variation in Bank rate and 75 per cent of the variation in the Treasury bill rate can be explained by this equation.[2] Indeed the equation works quite well for B, P, and U, the balance of payments, prices, and the level of unemployment; further, none of these variables works if we put the money stock—any measure of the money stock—in as the dependent variable. I submit that these findings suggest that

[1] A. A. Walters, 'The Radcliffe Report—Ten Years After: A Survey of Empirical Evidence', in *Money in Britain 1959–69*, edited by D. R. Croome and H. G. Johnson (London: Oxford University Press, 1970).

[2] D. Fisher, 'The Instruments of Monetary Policy and the Generalized Trade-Off Function for Britain 1955–1968', *Manchester School*, Sept. 1970.

the burden of proof is on anyone who wishes to treat the money stock as exogenous. If this is Laidler's point, I concur.

Now equation (I.1) is made sensible as a structural relation by the result just cited, but I must hasten to point out that only 75 per cent of the variation in the Treasury bill rate is explained by equation (I.3), so the identification crisis is still unresolved. This problem also exists with respect to equation (I.2). But I have another suggestion to make about the consumption function, and that is that in this form—as a short-run function—one might expect to find evidence of the wealth effect; and so I have. One of the equations tested is here presented as equation (II.2)

$$C_t = C_t(C_{t-1}, Y_t, i_t, i_{t-1}, M_{t-1}, M_{t-2}) \qquad \text{(II.2)}$$

and the result on the British data from 1955 half-way through 1967, a result which survived a battery of transformations of the data,

TABLE I

The Interest Elasticity of the Demand for Real Balances in Britain
(1955–1968)

Equation	Variables	Single equation results		Indirect results	
		Short-run	Long-run	Short-run	Long-run
1	Broad M, Income	0·010	0·021	0·035	0·074
2	Narrow M, Income	0·032	0·093	0·108	0·314
3	Broad M, Perm. Inc.	0·014	0·029	0·043	0·090
4	Narrow M, Perm. Inc.	0·040	0·104	0·121	0·315

was that there was an average short-run wealth effect of between £10 and £18 of real consumption per £100 of undesired money balances and a long-run effect of around £24 per £100.[3] This effect is far from trivial; and it is, of course, the sort of effect which ought to be included if we are seriously concerned with the mis-named 'money multiplier'.

Equations (I.1) and (II.2) are intertwined, of course; to get some idea of the seriousness of the problem, I did a complete (but simple) structural model and solved for the interest elasticity of the demand for real balances by indirect means. The results are briefly summarized in Table 1 for broad and narrow money; also employed

[3] D. Fisher, 'Real Balances and the Demand for Money', *Journal of Political Economy*, Dec. 1970.

was a measure of permanent income. The effects are relatively quite large. They come about, incidentally, because of the effect of the interest rate on consumption; and they result, in these estimates, in tripled interest elasticities of the demand for real money balances. My estimating equations were structural, but there were two of them, so I suppose that puts me somewhere in between Laidler and Walters on the structural/reduced form debate.

Briefly, then, let me add that the demand for money function presented as equation (I.1) is still incomplete in that no account is taken of the speculative demand for money—another adjustment mechanism which we ought to be interested in.

The Significance of ad hoc Specifications

There is one issue which I must take up with Laidler. This is his often repeated claim that certain variables—and certain specifications of the demand for money—perform better than other variables in the demand for money. For example, Laidler claims that the level of income is out-performed by his measure of permanent income in enough cases to warrant the judgement that one ought to use permanent income in general. The evidence offered is statistical and must be evaluated by statistical means. I propose the t-test of the difference between the two coefficients, divided by the square root of the sum of the two standard errors. The results of the comparison of Laidler's own coefficients are gathered in Table 2.

TABLE 2

t-*Values Testing the Differences between Coefficients in Laidler's Tests*

Equation tested	Y_p versus Y	$i_s(Y_p)$ versus $i_s(Y)$
British		
1900–1965	0·099	0·061
1900–1913	0·041	0·012
1920–1938	0·265	0·043
1946–1965	0·094	0·024
American		
1900–1965	0·214	0·095
1900–1916	0·135	0·209
1919–1940	1·529	0·064
1946–1965	0·139	0·040

I submit that these tests do not establish the alleged superiority of permanent income over the level of income. Indeed, this is not surprising since only in the inter-war period did income have a strong enough cycle (especially in the U.S. data) to dominate the trend (i.e., the level of income is a good proxy for permanent income). Furthermore I doubt if Laidler and Parkin's results[4] can be distinguished from either mine or Walter's; and, in particular I doubt that the superiority of the *ad hoc per capita*, logarithmic, expanded money supply, and deflated versions of the demand for money can at present be established. I say all this even though I also believe that the intellectual case for each of these transformations is on a much firmer footing. The statistical case has not, in my judgement, been made.[5]

TABLE 3

t-*Values Comparing the British and American Demand for Money*

Period	Y_p	Y	i_s
1900–1965	2·168		0·256
		1·814	0·289
Pre-War I	1·702		0·660
		1·789	0·686
Inter-War	0·586		0·401
		0·400	0·258
Post-War II	1·073		0·175
		0·907	0·101

Curiously enough, one difference not claimed by Laidler does seem to have some merit on these results, bald as they might be. Table 3 presents the results of repeating the *t*-test of Table 2 for the differences in coefficients between the United States and the United Kingdom. That is, for the entire period, a reasonable *t*-value between the United States and the United Kingdom can be established.[6] But, and here we begin to become alarmed about

[4] D. E. W. Laidler and J. M. Parkin, 'The Demand for Money in the United Kingdom 1956–1967: Preliminary Estimates', *Manchester School*, Sept. 1970.

[5] In the discussion of my paper Milton Friedman has pointed out that, since the six independent tests of Y_p versus Y in Table 2 all favour Y_p, by a simple binomial test, these results are not random. This occurs, no doubt, because Y_p is arrived at by smoothing Y. If, in turn, one examines the R^2 of each equation, as Laidler suggests we do, my conclusion is upheld.

[6] This statement has only one degree of freedom and must be taken as merely suggestive.

Laidler's claim for stability of the demand for money in each case, the *t*-value for the entire period is larger than that for any sub-period; and, in particular from 1920 onwards, no difference can be sustained by these data. Indeed, as you can verify in Laidler's original data, for the United States the inter-war period is strikingly unlike either of the other periods, and for the United Kingdom the post-War II period is unlike either of the earlier periods. Both cases, particularly the former, can be given statistical firmness in the manner of Tables 2 and 3, and, I submit, the evidence of the stability of the demand for money is also under a cloud. But I should also note, in view of the poor identification of the demand model employed in these tests, that I am about as interested in the constancy of the coefficients there as I am in the constancy of velocity.

SUMMARY OF THE GENERAL DISCUSSION

THE main theme of the discussion was the methodological question of the correctness of using reduced form estimating techniques to enhance our knowledge of the nature and stability of the main macro-economic relationships in the economy.

At the outset of this discussion one American economist pointed to the aridity of the reduced form versus structural model debate in the United States, and suggested that the achievement of an efficient use of intellectual resources would be best served by the avoidance of a similar debate in the United Kingdom. This advice was only partially heeded. Professor Laidler and some other discussants argued that he had taken the correct position in his paper and that reduced form estimating techniques led to misleading results and did not answer the relevant questions. Professor Friedman and some other discussants argued against this viewpoint. They argued that structural models were too big to manage, and that for a large class of problems, the limitations imposed by lack of time, lack of information and errors in the data, were such that structural models were no more likely to yield the relevant results than reduced form models. Work based on structural models also suffered from the drawback that using the same information and data it was possible to specify a large number of different structural models so that confusion rather than clarity resulted from such work. Further, Friedman did not accept Laidler's interpretation of the 'Relative Stability Debate' as being relevant to the question. According to Friedman the purpose of the 'Relative Stability Debate' was to convince other economists that money was important, and reduced form models were sufficient for this purpose. It had not been his intention at that time to demonstrate the greater empirical relevance of the 'Classical' model.

This part of the general discussion came to an end when it was generally agreed that the reduced form versus structural models question only had relevance in relation to specific problems and could not be resolved in a vacuum by attempts to establish the correctness of one method over the other. The important question was that of the identification and estimation of control variables, and this required both knowledge of the structural relationships and the reduced form of the relationships. The 'correct' approach was to use all the information gained from work on structural models when using reduced form models.

However, following the above discussion there was a debate over the question of whether or not it was possible to establish the exogeneity of the money supply using reduced form models. One view was that it was not possible. To determine whether or not the money supply was an exogenous variable required the specification of large structural models which allowed for the policy aims and actions of the authorities. Friedman took the opposing view and argued that on the basis of his experience and his study of monetary history he did not think that it was possible to resolve the exogeneity/endogeneity issue using large scale models. He rejected large scale models on the grounds of their complexity and because of the difficulty of obtaining all the information required to construct them correctly. While he did not think that the issue would be solved by regression analysis alone he did think that reduced form models were capable of providing the answer if they were used in conjunction with the information and understanding gained from detailed studies of monetary history.

There was a similar polarization of opinion when it was argued that the final effects of a change in the money supply, as well as the initial impact effects, depended upon the objectives and techniques of the monetary authorities and the initial employment/output state of the economy. It was agreed that, for a given change in the supply of money, you would get different initial impact effects using different techniques of monetary control, and different initial impact effects when using the same techniques of monetary control in different initial states of the economy. Disagreement arose over the question of whether or not the different initial impact effects would also give rise to different final effects. Some discussants thought that different initial effects would give rise to significantly different final effects. For this reason they thought that it was important to know more about the nature of the transmission mechanism whereby changes in the quantity of money lead to changes in other economic variables, and to know more about the time lags inherent in the transmission mechanism. They further believed that this knowledge was only to be obtained by the development of large scale disaggregated structural models. Friedman, on the other hand, argued that the different initial effects did not give rise to different final effects. He made use of an analogy to justify his views on this question. His analogy was that of a lake: information about the inflow/outflow relationship could be obtained by observing what went on in the lake and measuring changes in the water level, but the best way to obtain the required information was to observe the inflow and outflow and to ignore what went on in the lake. In his own work he was not interested in the 'lake' but in the inflow and outflow, that is, changes in the money stock and changes in final expenditure. He agreed that it was useful to know what happened in 'the lake' but that knowledge of the input and output relationship was not altered by what did happen in between. Against this it was argued that knowledge of what happened in 'the lake' was not only important in its own right, but also because it was the lack of this kind of knowledge which had led to the implementation of ineffective and perverse policy measures in the past.

Professor Friedman referred to recent empirical work undertaken by him and Mrs. Anna Schwartz, and a Note by him on the United States and United Kingdom velocity of circulation follows this Summary.

A Note on U.S. and U.K. Velocity of Circulation

MILTON FRIEDMAN

(*Professor of Economics, University of Chicago*)

MRS. ANNA SCHWARTZ and I are currently engaged on a comparison of U.S. and U.K. monetary trends over the past century, interpreting 'trends' to mean movements over periods longer than the usual business cycle. In this analysis, we are using as our basic unit of analysis average values of various magnitudes over a cycle phase—that is, an expansion from trough to peak, or a contraction from peak to trough. Indeed, I had initially hoped to present a paper on this work at this seminar, but unfortunately the research did not go rapidly enough.

The most striking single finding is the extraordinary similarity of velocity in the U.S. and the U.K., particularly from about 1905 to about 1955. In the cycle phase centred on 1906 in both the U.S. and the U.K., velocity was 2·2 turnovers per year in the U.S., 2·1 in the U.K. (velocity defined as the ratio of net national product to money defined as including all commercial bank deposits); in the cycle phase centred on June 1951 in the U.S., and on 1 January 1952, in the U.K., velocity was 1·5 in the U.S., 1·4 in the U.K. In between these dates, plotted curves of velocity follow almost precisely parallel paths, except only for higher velocities in the U.S. during its prosperous twenties than in the U.K. during its depressed twenties.

Before 1905, velocity is highly stable in the U.K., declining sharply in the U.S.; since 1955 or so, velocity has been rising in both countries but much faster in the United Kingdom.

The time plot of the rates of change of velocity—equivalent to the logarithmic derivative of the series showing the levels of velocity—are even more remarkable. The curves are almost identical for the period from about 1905 to 1950, and parallel at somewhat different levels before and since, especially since 1950. On this evidence, there can be no doubt that whatever it is that determines velocity is largely common to the U.S. and the U.K., and that for most of the period no developments peculiar to one country or the other can be regarded as a major source of changes in velocity.

These results have led me to change in one important respect my earlier conclusions for the U.S. I had earlier attributed the sharp decline in U.S. velocity before World War I to the accompanying rapid rise in real income, and this underlay my statistical estimates of the real income elasticity of demand for money as in the neighbourhood of 1·5 to 2·0, say. On this new evidence, that interpretation cannot be fully valid: real income grew more rapidly in the U.S. before 1905 than in the U.K., but so did it thereafter, and any difference between the two periods is not enough to explain the early rapid decline in velocity in the U.S. relative to velocity in the U.K. I am therefore inclined to attribute the early rapid decline in velocity in the U.S. to the growing financial sophistication—spread of banking and the monetary economy—in the U.S. As a result, I am led to reduce my estimate of income elasticity, though I still find it to be well above unity for both the U.S. and the U.K., at least for the longer term movements.

The more rapid rise in velocity in the U.K. than in the U.S. after the 1950s I am inclined to attribute to the much more rapid price rise in the U.K.

One final comment. The velocity series are highly relevant, I believe, to understanding some of the difficulties that have arisen in interpreting monetary experience in both the U.S. and the U.K. for the period since World War II. In both countries, velocity and its rate of change decline drastically during and just after World War II, velocity reaching all time low levels, and then rebounding sharply to the late forties in the U.S., to the early or mid-fifties in the U.K. Velocity then continues to rise in both countries but at a steadily diminishing rate, so that the rate of change of velocity falls. The whole episode judged in the context of the longer period behaviour of velocity, looks like a war-time shock, an over-reaction after the war and then a gradual return to 'normal'. The initial shock to velocity is of about the same magnitude and duration in both countries, but the over-reaction and subsequent return to normal appears both larger and more extended in duration in the U.K. than in the U.S.—as would be entirely consistent with the far greater impact of the War on the U.K. than on the U.S. economy. For both countries, I am now inclined to regard the war-time shock and its aftermath as having lasted much longer than I earlier did and hence as rendering suspect a larger part of post-World War II experience as evidence on 'normal' relationships.

V

MONETARY CONTROL METHODS IN THE UNITED KINGDOM

A. D. BAIN

Discussion Papers

(*a*) A. R. NOBAY
(*b*) W. B. REDDAWAY

Notes

(*a*) B. GRIFFITHS
(*b*) J. S. G. WILSON

V

MONETARY CONTROL METHODS IN THE UNITED KINGDOM

A. D. Bain
(Professor of Economics, University of Stirling)

Introduction

In this discussion of monetary control methods in the U.K. I shall not be concerned solely with the control of the money supply (however broadly or narrowly defined) but shall deal more generally with the means by which the monetary authorities seek to achieve their objectives of economic policy. Nor shall I consider control methods which might appear optimal only if history could be ignored and a new system set up from scratch. I shall assume that policy operates within the present institutional framework and shall confine my attention to changes which may become feasible within the next decade. Thus I shall recognize that policy relates not only to aggregative magnitudes—total output, total flows of credit or stocks of broad categories of assets—or to the general level of interest rates but may also involve discriminatory treatment of some categories of borrowers or types of activities. For example, the authorities may wish to discriminate in favour of fixed investment, to discourage inflows of hot money, or to subsidize exports. I shall not argue the theoretical case for or against such discrimination here, but simply assert that governments are unlikely to give up the power to discriminate in these respects, and that any realistic discussion of methods of monetary control must take account of these practices, even if many economists find them objectionable. Finally, while I realize that the domestic and international aspects of monetary policy are interdependent, I shall be concerned almost entirely with domestic matters.

I shall begin the paper with some preliminaries on the monetary authorities' objectives, and on targets and indicators for monetary policy. Then I shall discuss methods of monetary control in general terms before turning to existing control techniques and considering a number of suggestions which have been made for reforming the system of monetary control in the U.K.

Monetary Policy Objectives

The prime objective of monetary policy in the U.K. should be to create conditions which are conducive to a high rate of economic growth.[1] This implies that the level of investment must be high and, in order to stimulate such investment, that the real rate of interest should be low. Even if the sensitivity of comparatively short-lived industrial investment in plant and equipment to the real rate of interest is debatable there is no question that much of fixed investment, for example in housing and perhaps also in the public sector generally, is sensitive to the long-term rate of interest.

A low real rate of interest is an objective which the monetary authorities may find difficult to accept. After all it may conflict with 'sound money' and their hands are tied, are they not, by the overall configuration of government economic policy? If government policy does not elicit a sufficient supply of savings to warrant high investment, surely it is not the business of the monetary authorities to interfere? I do not find this an adequate reply. The monetary authorities should act as a lobby in favour of low real rates of interest, and while the pursuit of other objectives may require them to vary interest rates in response to fluctuations in the level of demand, they should see to it that government policy allows a low average real rate. This objective has implications for the methods of monetary control in the U.K. because it may make it necessary to try to insulate U.K. financial markets from conditions in other countries.

The second objective of monetary policy is *stable* economic growth. If there are signs that demand will rise (fall) above (below) productive potential the monetary authorities should take counter-measures by raising interest rates and tightening credit during an incipient boom and lowering interest rates and easing credit in the reverse situation.

Monetary *controls* are primarily directed to this end. They are needed to offset the destabilizing effects of sharp changes in export markets, in entrepreneurial expectations or in savings behaviour,

[1] I think it is generally accepted that the pace of economic growth in the U.K. is undesirably slow and that a higher level of investment would help to increase growth. Anyone who believes that 'the market' automatically produces the optimum level of investment will naturally dissent.

or simply on occasions to deal with the aftermath of misguided official measures in earlier periods. If credit flows could be prevented from accommodating these destabilizing influences, which are usually reflected in a considerable change in the relative proportions of private and public sector securities in financial institutions' asset portfolios, a more stable growth of output could be maintained.

The monetary authorities' third objective is price stability, but their power to influence the price level (at a tolerable cost) should not be exaggerated. That high demand generates price inflation is no longer in dispute, and the danger of such inflation is a strong reason for the monetary authorities to seek to balance demand with productive potential. It is questionable, however, whether tight money makes any substantial contribution to counteracting wage inflation, when this is due primarily to imperfections in the labour market. No doubt a sustained restrictive monetary policy would prevent price inflation, but only at the cost of heavy unemployment and widespread bankruptcies amongst firms which would be perfectly sound in more normal conditions. Short of these damaging effects it is doubtful whether the position of employers as a whole will be strengthened by tight credit in the face of large wage increases generally throughout the economy and of strong union pressure. A shortage of funds may even make it harder for employers to face up to the short-run cost of a strike. When the level of activity is low monetary policy should validate wage and price increases which have already occurred, so that the authorities avoid pushing the economy further into recession. At the same time they should set market rates of interest high enough to avoid adding demand inflation to pressures from the cost side.[2]

A fourth objective is the maintenance of a comfortable level of gold and foreign exchange reserves. I shall not discuss exchange rate policy, but shall take some account of the effect of monetary controls on international short-term capital flows.

There should be a fifth objective, which often seems to be over-looked. The monetary authorities should seek to improve the efficiency of the financial system as a mechanism for co-ordinating at low cost the intentions of potential savers and potential investors. If the control methods of recent years in the U.K. are taken as a guide, this objective seems to come rather low in the pecking order.

[2] This prescription differs from that of economists who dispute the existence of independent cost pressure. They attribute much more power to the authorities in influencing prices.

Targets and Indicators

We must now consider what it is that the authorities should try to control. In my view the authorities should attempt to influence real expenditure by aiming their measures at the control of explicit interest rates and credit flows. The mechanism through which these influence real expenditure is broadly that incorporated in the Federal Reserve–MIT econometric model.[3] Changes in rates of interest (including equity yields) affect the demand price of capital goods and hence the level of investment; there are also wealth effects; and there may be availability effects if particular credit flows are restricted. For the analysis of financial structure and for the prediction of the effects of monetary policy it is these variables— not the money supply—which should be considered. Interest rates and the supply of credit are therefore the *targets* of monetary policy.

This still leaves the problem of determining the proper level of interest rates and supply of credit at any time. There are very considerable difficulties in determining what level of interest rates is consistent with stable growth of the economy. How does one judge the effect, for example, of unobserved but possibly substantial erratic shifts in entrepreneurial expectations or in liquidity preference? How does one measure changes which take place in the expected rate of inflation? How does one cope with the fact that knowledge of the structure of the economy—in particular of the relations between financial and real variables—is still inadequate?

In the face of these difficulties it is possible that, notwithstanding the primacy of interest rates as targets of monetary policy, certain asset aggregates including various measures of the money supply could conceivably be better as indicators of the extent to which current policy was adapted to the needs of economic stability. Suppose, for example, that the factors affecting the demand for money were well established, so that it was possible to predict with some confidence the level of money holdings consistent with smooth growth of income. Any substantial discrepancy between the observed level of money holdings and the amount predicted would be a sign that some corrective action was required. If the observed holdings exceeded the predicted by a considerable amount action should be taken to raise interest rates and restrict credit, and vice versa in the opposite situation. Even if the characteristics of the demand for money are not known precisely it should be possible

[3] F. de Leeuw and E. M. Gramlich, 'The Channels of Monetary Policy', *Federal Reserve Bulletin*, June 1969, pp. 472–91.

to define limits within which desired money holdings could be expected to lie; if experience showed that monetary growth was falling outside the limits consistent with the predicted growth of output at current interest rates one could be reasonably confident that output was not conforming to what had been expected. Similar possibilities exist with Domestic Credit Expansion. Although I do not think it has yet been done, it might be possible to determine the normal rate of growth of DCE consistent with a steady growth of income, with deviations from this pattern again acting as warning signals. These asset or liability totals might therefore be useful as indicators for monetary policy.

It seems to me most probable that in future the monetary authorities will use some combination of indicators as guidelines for their policy: it is extremely unlikely that they will base their policy entirely on the movement of any single indicator. Monetary measures may be employed to lower interest rates from 'too high' levels provided that other indicators do not flatly contradict the impression that interest rates are indeed too high. The monetary authorities will, no doubt, feel justified in departing from their guidelines when they believe they can detect special circumstances which seem likely to distort normal relationships. For example, they might wish to permit more rapid monetary growth if there were signs of paralysis in the long-term capital market, due perhaps to differing price expectations on the parts of lenders and borrowers.

General and Specific Methods of Control

The instruments of monetary control fall into two groups. On the one hand the authorities can make use of general instruments which affect certain key interest rates, or they may engage in transactions in certain key markets. These instruments and transactions have a wide-ranging impact on flows of credit generally, affecting the cost and availability of capital funds throughout the economy. On the other hand the authorities may employ specific instruments of control which apply to the business of particular groups of financial institutions. Their primary impact is restricted to the institutions immediately affected, although they often produce secondary repercussions in other institutions which may sometimes go a long way towards negating the primary effect of the control.

Specific controls on particular financial institutions will be frustrated to the extent that they lead merely to a diversion in the flow of credit. The larger the proportion of customary credit flows which are included in the controlled sector the more effective the controls will be, because as they become more pervasive, it becomes progressively less easy and more costly to bypass them. Since new financial institutions can grow rapidly and weaken the initial impact of specific controls, monetary authorities which rely heavily on such controls may be compelled to spread the net of controls ever more widely.

There are two types of general control, both of which are intended to influence interest rates. The authorities may intervene in security markets, usually the markets for Government securities but also if they wish the markets for private securities. And the authorities can set the nominal rates of interest on certain types of public sector debt.

The authorities have very little control over the total nominal value of public sector debt; it is determined by past debt issues, by current refinancing, and by new government borrowing. But through open-market operations in either public or private sector securities the authorities can change the *relative* volume of different types of debt. In practice operations are confined almost entirely to government securities—although the authorities may also vary the size of their commercial bill portfolio—because no large official portfolio of private sector securities is available for this purpose.

Open-market operations give the authorities some control over the relative yields on securities of different types and maturities. How much control depends upon the degree to which there is segmentation in the market amongst private borrowers and lenders and on the speed of response to changes in relative yields. Because the authorities' portfolio is large it is unlikely that changes in the supply of private sector securities will offset their actions rapidly. It should be noted that this power to influence relative yields does not depend on the observance of particular asset ratios by certain financial institutions (e.g. the clearing banks) and it does not depend on a rigid control of the supply of cash: such control together with the rigid observance of a fixed ratio by the clearing banks (i.e. a fractional reserve system based upon the cash ratio) might increase the short-run impact on interest rates of a given scale of open-market operation, but it is not a necessary condition for some impact to occur, and the impact of controls of this type could be gradually weakened by the growth of financial intermediaries offering liabilities which are closely competitive with bank deposits.

The authorities also influence the level of interest rates by setting the nominal yield on certain official liabilities. For example, Bank rate determines the rate of interest charged on Bank of England advances to the discount market, and this is closely linked with the rates of interest on a wide variety of short-term liabilities. The nominal interest rates on non-marketable Government debt of varying maturities also influences the yields on marketable securities.

General measures of monetary control are non-discriminatory. Of course, particular measures affect some financial institutions and some categories of borrower more than others, e.g. changes in long-term yields have a greater impact on those financial institutions which specialize in long-term borrowing and lending than on those which specialize in shorter dated securities. The opposite is true of changes in Bank rate. But this differential impact reflects the inherent nature of the institutions' business, and is not due to any external constraints imposed upon them.

The essence of specific controls is that they are discriminatory. They interfere with the business of some financial institutions and consequently reduce their profits or impose financial losses on them. The most important forms of specific control are asset ratios, interest rate ceilings, lending ceilings, request, and controls on instalment lending.

Before discussing the details of particular control schemes it is worth looking at the case for having any specific controls at all. Why not simply rely on open-market operations, and allow financial institutions of all kinds to react quite freely to the changes in the market situations facing them? This might, of course, need open market operations on a massive scale and involve very large changes in interest rates to obtain the desired response, but if that is what is required what is the objection to it? I think the objection is that it would throw almost the entire burden of adjustment on to explicit interest rates, with very little taking place through credit rationing. There would naturally be some short-run quantity adjustments: the building societies, for example, would probably prefer to ration loans rather than change their interest rates quickly. However, I have no doubt that sharp short-run changes in interest rates would be needed.

I think it is worth while noting how industry and commerce reacts to an erratic shift in demand for products. Typically, rationing is preferred to auctioning, and erratic pricing is to say the least unusual. Indeed, the temporary profiteering which would result from an erratic increase in demand in the event of inelastic supply would usually be frowned upon. Even people who are left behind in a bus queue may very well prefer a queueing system to the alternative of auctioning tickets at the bus stop.

It seems to me that sharp changes in rates of interest in financial markets may be just as disruptive as sharp changes in the markets for goods and services.[4] If supply and demand schedules in financial markets are inelastic in the short-run, the changes in short-run equilibrium interest rates could indeed be sharp—so sharp as to weaken existing financial institutions. To avoid this it may be desirable to constrain credit flows so that substantial increases in demand are choked off by rationing rather than by changes in explicit interest rates. I am aware that this procedure is open to the objection that it fails to maximize welfare in the usual Pareto sense, but suggest that conventional social welfare functions omit some of the costs of changes which are important in reality.

The Present Control System

I turn now to consider alternative methods of applying specific controls to the monetary system, and to provide a background I shall begin by outlining the main features of the present system, both to point out what it achieves and to examine some of the objections to it. Briefly, the present system consists of fixed minimum asset ratios applied to the composition of the portfolios of clearing banks; of additional variable asset requirements—namely Special Deposits for the clearing banks and Cash Deposits for the other banks; of ceilings on the level of total private sector lending by individual banks or groups of banks, and of guidance on priorities between different categories of borrower; of arrangements to provide cheap finance to certain privileged borrowers; of guidance on changes which might be permitted in the structure of financial institutions and in the financial instruments which exist; and of hire purchase controls.

The clearing banks' cash ratio, which compels them to hold cash amounting to 8 per cent of their deposit liabilities, is important because it is an essential part of the mechanism adopted for the control of short-term interest rates. It is not used as a fulcrum for a credit multiplier process.[5] Nor is the clearing banks' liquidity ratio

[4] This does not imply that rationing is an appropriate response to a change in the supply/demand situation which is likely to persist.

[5] As will become evident later, this categorical statement is not universally accepted. The view that the authorities can influence equilibrium short-term interest rates by first creating a shortage of cash and then subsequently providing

really any more suitable as a fulcrum for a credit multiplier process, because it is not rigid in the short-run and because the authorities do not usually control the supply to the clearing banks of all the assets which are treated as liquid. However, by narrowing the definition of liquid assets or otherwise restricting their supply, the liquidity ratio could be used as the basis of a fractional reserve system. In that case, special deposits would act in the same way as a variable reserve ratio and a call for special deposits would compel the clearing banks to cut back on any expansion in their lending. In practice up till now calls for special deposits have not worked in this way but have usually been associated with guidance on the changes in clearing bank asset portfolios desired by the authorities.

The Cash Deposits scheme, which applies to the non-clearing banks, is a strange creature. Since these banks are flexible in their liquidity practices, it can have little effect through constraining liquidity, and since interest is to be paid on cash deposits the effect on banks' profitability will also be minimal. Moreover, by competing more actively for deposits from the public these banks could undoubtedly expand their liabilities and assets to make good any resources tied up in cash deposits. A call for cash deposits would therefore, on its own, have little effect on their lending behaviour. However, the scheme does provide the authorities with a stick to back up any guidance given to the banks upon the scale or direction of their lending. The authorities can, if they wish, call for cash

---

it again (by buying or discounting bills at market rates) is often contested. It is asserted that the short-term rate of interest will return to its initial level after the cash shortage has been relieved. This would be true if the demand function for treasury bills included only the current rates of interest on these and other securities, but if the demand function also includes expected future rates of interest it is difficult to see why this should be so. Provided that by their actions in the market the authorities are able to influence expected future interest rates they would have an effect on the equilibrium volume of treasury bills demanded at any given level of current rates. The notion that the authorities use their ability to create a shortage of cash as a device to inform the market of the direction in which they would like, and expect, future interest rates to move is consistent with the notion that demand will reflect future expected interest rates. Indeed, in a market in which many holders of treasury bills finance their portfolios through short-term borrowing, the behaviour of short-term interest rates in the near future is likely to be of paramount importance in determining the demand for treasury bills. If expectations are determined autonomously (by the authorities) the fact that the same level of demand for treasury bills exists at different interest rates does not necessarily imply that either situation is a disequilibrium one; such differences are the predictable result of a change in market expectations of future short-term rates.

deposits of different sizes against different types of liability, for example Euro-dollars switched into sterling and domestic sterling deposits, and they may also in certain circumstances refrain (as a penalty) from the payment of interest on the cash deposits they receive. In that event they would have a real sanction to enforce their wishes, particularly if the penalty was imposed on an individual bank and not upon these banks as a group.

Ceilings on the private sector lending of individual banks or groups of banks appear to have been moderately effective in achieving their proximate objective of curtailing such lending. Whether they have been so successful in curtailing real expenditure flows is more doubtful, since some credit flows must have arisen which bypass the banking system. However, the severe restraints on private lending which have persisted for a substantial period do appear to have had a significant influence on company liquidity and on the housing market, and may be partly responsible for the relatively low level of real investment now. Measures of this sort, when maintained for a considerable period certainly have a severe effect upon competition between lending institutions. They prevent the more efficient banks from expanding at the expense of less efficient and tend to drive credit flows through less efficient channels of financial intermediation. It is hard to reconcile the existence of this type of control with the authorities' objective of creating an efficient financial mechanism.

There seems to be clear evidence that some of the authorities' requests on the direction of their lending have been observed, e.g. the request to discriminate against lending to persons, and this may have helped to free resources for purposes other than consumption. Subsidized financial arrangements have also been effective, though one is entitled to ask why the banks should be expected to bear the cost of subsidizing particularly favoured groups of borrowers. One may also question whether the informal pressure which inhibited until recently the introduction of new financial instruments (such as sterling certificates of deposit) or mergers between banks was altogether desirable.

It is clear that hire purchase controls restrain consumption demand, although they must be used with care because the time path of their effect is anything but smooth and their impact falls upon a narrow range of industries. The latter is, however, an almost inevitable result of any measures to restrain consumer demand.

What does the present system achieve? The authorities can influence interest rates, primarily through open-market operations and control of the nominal rates of interest on some debt instruments. Alternatively, they can control the supply of money or DCE, but to do so they have generally to resort to requests and lending ceilings. They are able to encourage discrimination in lending. And in spite of all the leakages and the incentives to circumvent normal channels, they appear to have exerted some influence on real expenditure flows. But I think it is fair to say that the response to any set of measures, even if predictable perhaps in qualitative terms, is of an extremely uncertain magnitude.

It is difficult to defend the present system. It seems to consist of a hotch-potch of controls, mixed in with some large dashes of moral suasion. The performance of the U.K. economy in the last two decades does not suggest that it is an outstandingly successful system. It is easy therefore to make out a case for reform. What are the suggestions?

Control Through the Cash Ratio

The latest proposal that the money supply in the U.K. should be controlled via the cash ratio comes from B. Griffiths.[6] He regards the present system of regulations as irrelevant to 'what should be the authorities' main responsibility: control of the money supply or of Domestic Credit Expansion'. His proposals are directed towards establishing a more competitive banking system. While by no means agreeing with his view of the authorities' main responsibility, I share his concern to increase competition in this sphere. Mr. Griffiths proposes a six point plan for banking reform of which the relevant features are:

  (a) the rates of interest on advances, deposit and current accounts should be fixed without reference to Bank rate,
  (b) savings banks, building societies and foreign banks should be encouraged to enter retail banking,
  (c) the Government should not force the banks to lend a certain proportion of their assets to the public sector,
  (d) minimum liquidity ratio and special deposit requirements for the clearing banks should be abolished,
  (e) the banks should receive interest on their cash holdings.

[6] B. Griffiths, 'British Banking: A Plan for Competition', *The Banker*, May 1970, pp. 491–9. For a Note by Mr. Griffiths see pp. 186–9 below.

Mr. Griffiths also discusses the role of Bank rate in a more competitive system, but since one of the possibilities which he envisages is a continuation of the present practice, we do not need to discuss his alternative suggestions further here.

Some of these proposals are rather surprising. It seems unrealistic to suggest that rates of interest on advances and deposits should be fixed without reference to Bank rate, when changes in Bank rate affect the costs of other short-term financial assets and liabilities which are good substitutes for deposits and advances. Surely in a competitive system a change in one key market rate would lead to similar changes in the rates of interest of close substitutes? The practice of quoting interest rates in relation to Bank rate is not confined to the clearing banks' cartel. It applies also to many short-term deposits with local authorities and finance houses, which compete in a market which is a close approximation to a freely competitive market. The link with Bank rate is simply an administrative practice which reflects the high degree of substitutability amongst certain financial assets. It is not rigid, particularly on bank advances, since borrowers are able to negotiate more or less favourable terms according to the funds which the bank has available to lend.

I am inclined to agree with Mr. Griffiths' suggestion that some other financial institutions should be encouraged to enter retail banking; at least they should not be actively discouraged from doing so. But I must contest Mr. Griffiths' view that this would not involve any change in the technique of monetary control, which depends critically on his assertion that 'the monetary authorities would continue to exercise their legitimate and necessary control over DCE by varying the total of bank cash reserves via open-market operations.' If this was a correct and full description of how monetary control operates at present, and if any other institutions entering retail banking were compelled to keep cash reserves to the same extent as the clearing banks, then there need be no change in actual technique.[7] However, in my opinion the assertion that the authorities control DCE via the cash ratio at present is wrong, and the incursion of other financial institutions into retail banking

---

[7] The authorities would have some difficulty in deciding how much DCE should be allowed to expand, if the assets of other financial institutions which entered retail banking became part of DCE. One of the difficulties in applying the money supply or DCE as a guide for monetary policy is that its value must depend on stability in the structure of the banking industry.

would require the extension to them of the specific controls applied to the clearing banks now.

The present arrangements by which certain banks may be forced to lend a proportion of their assets to the public sector is undoubtedly inequitable so long as other closely competitive financial institutions are not subject to similar constraints. In so far as Mr. Griffiths' proposal is designed to ensure equity between institutions I would go along with it, though as will be seen my own proposals include equal constraints on asset holdings rather than no constraints at all. The proposal to abolish the minimum liquidity ratio and the special deposits requirement follows from the view that monetary control should be exerted through the cash ratio: without this they would have to be replaced by something else. Finally, there seems little doubt that the present 8 per cent cash ratio compels the banks to hold more of a non-interest bearing asset than they require for the proper working of their business. It does not seem to me obvious that they should be paid interest on those working balances of cash which they require, but if the authorities compel them to hold more than this, the proposal that they should be paid interest on the excess seems just.

Before leaving the Griffiths' proposals it is worth enquiring whether a system of monetary control through a cash ratio would in fact be desirable in the U.K. It seems to me that, while not impossible, it would be difficult to work in practice and would have some undesirable side-effects. First of all, we should notice that the reaction to a change in the supply of cash would be very large if a normal multiplier model applied and the cash ratio were set at a reasonable level of, say, 4 per cent. One must observe too that the supply of cash in the U.K. varies very substantially from day to day, partly because the Bank of England are bankers to the Government and there are large erratic changes in central government receipts and payments, partly from activities in the foreign exchange market, and partly as a result of transactions by the authorities in the gilt-edged market. While the authorities try to forecast these movements in cash and to offset them, they cannot do so with great precision. Some people would assert that gilt-edged transactions cannot be regarded as a source of 'disturbance'; in reply one can only point out that if all official gilt-edged transactions were geared towards controlling the supply of cash in the short-run, there would be significant implications for the marketability of government debt and substantial problems in the refinancing of maturing issues.

These difficulties do not rule out the use of the cash base for control-ling the money supply; they simply ensure that there would be considerable costs of doing so in terms of failure to achieve other objectives. In particular, if the authorities were not able to smoothe out erratic changes in the supply of cash there might be very sharp fluctuations in short-term interest rates (such as were deliberately allowed to arise immediately after the devaluation of the pound sterling in 1967).

In my view a cash ratio system would be unlikely to operate successfully so long as the Bank of England continue to manage the national debt. This is one institutional arrangement which is unlikely to change within the next decade. Nor would Mr. Griffiths' system give the authorities those powers to discriminate which they are unlikely to give up. My conclusion on his scheme is there-fore that his desire both to increase competition in the British banking system and to do away with some aspects of the present system of control is laudable, but that this is not the best way of achieving his objective.

Control of Interest Rates

In an article[8] discussing the regulation of the U.K. banking and financial structure, Professor J. S. G. Wilson made a number of proposals. The objectives of new legislation would be twofold: to block leakages in the present system of monetary control and to re-integrate the clearing banks and other components of the secondary banking system. I shall be concerned only with the former objective here, and in this connection Professor Wilson proposed that the authorities should have the power to specify the maximum rates of interest payable on the liabilities of certain financial institutions.

He takes the point that it is in some ways desirable that the main impact of restrictive monetary measures should fall upon the commercial banks, because these institutions are *general* lenders. In this way 'the particular needs of the general run of commercial and industrial firms may, at least to some extent, be safeguarded'. He contrasts the effects of control on the banks with the 'harsh and damaging' effects of hire purchase controls which have a highly

[8] J. S. G. Wilson, 'Regulation and Control of the United Kingdom Banking and Financial Structure', Banca Nazionale Del Lavoro, *Quarterly Review*, June 1969, pp. 128–45. For a Note by Professor Wilson see pp. 190–1 below.

concentrated impact. He therefore suggests that monetary controls should attempt to regulate only the rate of growth of non-bank financial intermediaries (which specialize in specific activities) 'with the general lenders (like banks) still being expected to absorb the primary impact of monetary policy measures'. Any restrictions would be reinforced by open-market operations to influence the general level of interest rates.

It is not absolutely clear what sort of control system Professor Wilson envisages for the commercial banks in future. He makes the point that the appearance of 'unfair competition' must be avoided if the central bank is to secure the cooperation necessary for success-ful implementation of its policies. This suggests that a continuation of the existing system is envisaged. But although he does not see other financial institutions as credit-creating Professor Wilson acknowledges their potential influence on economic activity and, in contrast with the Radcliffe Committee, believes that an extension of controls to cover these institutions is desirable.

As mentioned earlier, his proposal[9] is that the maximum rates of interest payable on some institutions' liabilities should be controlled, so that by denying them the funds they desire the authorities are able to check the expansion of their lending. I have a number of doubts about the desirability and efficacy of such a system. First of all, I am not certain where this leaves the banks, especially those which are not subject to the cash and liquidity ratios at present. How are they to be controlled, and in particular, are they too to be subject to interest rate regulations? Secondly, although control of the interest rates offered by some financial institutions, such as building societies and trustee savings banks, would be comparatively easy, since their liabilities are standardized, more difficulty would be experienced with other institutions such as hire purchase finance houses and the 'secondary' banks if these were included in this part of the control system. These institutions borrow on a very wide variety of terms, and it would presumably be necessary to stipulate a correspondingly wide range of interest rates. Thirdly the proposal seems to assume that financial institutions will continue to be specialized. What would happen if re-integration or other changes in the structure of the banking system took place? Would it be possible to maintain such a control system if the building societies

[9] It should be pointed out that this is only one amongst a number of propoals for the registration and regulation of financial institutions contained in the article.

entered retail banking, as for example Mr. Griffiths suggested? In my opinion, the proposals depend very much upon the continuation of something like the existing structure of financial institutions, and might not stand up well to institutional change. Finally, U.S. experience suggests that interest rate controls applied to some major financial institutions may simply lead to dis-intermediation: the rapid growth of the commercial paper market must have partially offset monetary stringency in the U.S.A. during 1969 and early 1970.

It is difficult to see how far this system of control would permit the authorities to achieve their objectives, partly because the control system for the commercial banks has not been specified in detail. It would probably give the authorities a firmer control of credit creation in the economy, and it would still permit discrimination between particular categories of borrower. There would, however, almost certainly be great practical difficulties, especially if the 'secondary' banks were covered by the interest rate regulations. For example, if these applied to Euro-dollar borrowing by the banks they would seriously damage the international competitive position of City institutions; and if they did not apply to Euro-dollars, how would it be possible to control switching of Euro-dollars into sterling to provide funds for potential borrowers? Finally, interest rate controls would distort the normal structure of interest rates and alter the pattern of credit flows in the economy, thus leaving the authorities without any means of assessing the probable impact of their measures on the economy.

Control Through Asset Ratios

Like Mr. Griffiths' suggestions my own proposal for reforming the system of monetary control in the U.K. is designed to increase competition between financial institutions and to eliminate discriminatory controls on them. I therefore place considerable weight upon open-market operations in gilt-edged securities and on the control of key interest rates such as Bank rate as the main techniques for influencing the level and structure of interest rates. But since I do not give any *special* importance to the money supply I am not in favour of control schemes geared specifically towards bank deposits. In my opinion open-market operations should be supplemented by a set of asset ratios applied to a wide range of financial institutions.

It seems to me important to cover a wide range for a number of reasons. First, as Tobin[10] has forcefully argued, credit creation is not the prerogative of banks: if the peculiarities of the techniques of control which are applied to banks were removed, their ability to create credit would be on a par with that of other financial institutions. Moreover, restricting banks, and not other institutions, is inequitable. The arguments concerning efficiency are tangled, but it is not obvious that more widespread controls would be less efficient than controls concentrated on a narrow sector. Secondly, most financial institutions work to certain asset ratio guidelines, although usually these are by no means rigid or uniform. Basing a control system upon asset ratios may then be seen as a development from the existing system, rather than the imposition of something entirely new upon it. Thirdly, I believe that some formal controls are needed in addition to open-market operations in order to deal with sharp changes in the credit markets. As I have argued above, reliance upon open-market operations alone could lead to very severe interest rate movements which may be unacceptable for other reasons. Changes in asset ratios would help to avoid sharp changes in explicit interest rates—substituting credit rationing or changes in the other terms on which credit is provided—in response to a large increase in the demand for funds or a diminution in the supply.

I envisage a system in which financial institutions would be required to hold in their asset portfolios public sector debt (or the equivalent) equal to some specified minimum proportion of their liabilities, the proportion varying with the category of liability. Before going into details it is important to understand the principles on which such a system might operate.

In general the authorities would attempt to maintain balance in credit markets through open-market operations and changes in key administered interest rates; they would attempt by these means to avoid any undue expansion or contraction of credit. I have already observed (p. 160 above) that their power to do this does not depend on ratio controls or the use of some fractional reserve mechanism. However, consider a situation in which the demand for credit rises sharply and, for one reason or another, the authorities are unwilling to choke it off by raising interest rates sufficiently.

[10] J. Tobin, 'Commercial Banks as Creators of "Money"', *Banking and Monetary Studies*, edited by D. Carson (Irwin 1963), pp. 408–19.

In the absence of official restraints, financial institutions generally would seek to alter the balance of their asset portfolios to take advantage of this high demand, and would set up a process of credit expansion terminated only when the marginal return from additional assets equalled the marginal cost of increasing their liabilities.

In the conventional cash ratio model of the determination of the volume of bank deposits, the banks are fully loaned up and the authorities control the supply of cash so the cost (to the banking system) of additional deposits is infinite. An increase in the marginal return on assets is therefore unable to cause an expansion of credit. And in reality, if the authorities did control the supply of cash, any expansion of credit would be small because the marginal cost of deposits would rise rapidly to match any increase in marginal asset earnings. In this model, however, credit expansion in response to a rise in demand will take place if the banks have any spare cash, since the marginal cost of deposits does not rise appreciably until the spare cash has been absorbed into required reserves: to avoid credit expansion in these conditions the authorities must either reduce the supply of cash (through open-market operations) or raise the required cash ratio.

The same principles can be applied to any group of financial institutions holding any class of 'reserve' assets. To increase their liabilities they must persuade the public to shift out of other assets, and this can only be done at increasing cost. Assuming that 'reserve' assets are lower yielding than other assets the constraint on their asset portfolios prevents them increasing the marginal return by altering the balance of their portfolios. And an increase in the asset ratio will either absorb surplus 'reserve' assets or, if sufficiently large, cause a contraction in portfolios because the marginal return from assets now falls below the marginal cost of liabilities. Thus, in addition to open-market operations to influence interest rates generally, I envisage that the authorities might wish occasionally to alter asset ratios as an additional means of controlling credit expansion.

In my opinion, the asset ratios should apply to categories of liability rather than to types of institution. The range of financial institutions is much wider than the types of business in which they engage. A system of control based upon types of liability and types of asset—irrespective of the name of the institution concerned—would eliminate discrimination between institutions whilst still giving the authorities the power to discriminate in favour of or against certain types of business. Such a system would be much less sensitive than the present one to the detailed structure of the financial system, and could probably remain substantially unaltered in the face of considerable changes in the activities of particular financial institutions. It would avoid the need to recognize the changing nature of the business of individual institutions or groups of institutions, with the implied necessity for a complicated re-negotiation of the control system.

The specified assets in the proposed control system would consist of public sector debt and certain private sector assets which are essentially indirect holdings of such debt. The ratios would differ according to the maturity of the deposit or period of notice required, with base levels reflecting prudential liquidity considerations, and could be varied to encourage or discourage credit expansion generally—as a supplement to market operations—or for some specified purpose.

There are two reasons for suggesting that the scheme should employ public sector debt ratios rather than cash ratios or more broadly based liquidity ratios. The first is that stabilization policy is often concerned with the division of resources between the public and private sectors: controls on financial institutions based upon either only one type of public sector debt (e.g. cash) or including substantial amounts of private sector debt might be easily frustrated. The degree of substitutability between different types of public sector debt is typically greater than between public sector and private sector debt as a whole. Unless the authorities controlled the supply of the specified assets in the hands of the financial institutions they could probably increase their holdings relatively easily by selling to the public assets not included in the ratio and buying in exchange the specified assets: the greater the similarity between specified and other assets the more likely is this to occur.

The second reason for preferring public sector debt ratios is that a restricted range of institutions (e.g. the clearing banks) might continue to observe cash ratios—the cash being included in their holdings of public sector debt—set at a level which reflected their normal cash requirements. This would allow the authorities to retain their present degree of control over short-term interest rates, which have important implications for international short-term money flows.

Sterling deposits would be grouped into a small number of

classes, with asset ratios applied to each class. For example, the normal ratios *might* be:

Term	Ratio
Sight and up to 7 days' notice	30%
8 days' to 91 days' notice	15%
92 days' to 364 days' notice	5%
365 days' notice and over	Nil

It is emphasized that these numbers are purely *illustrative*. Rules would be required to cover certificates of deposit and term deposits taken initially for a fixed term (e.g. 1 year) and thereafter with a short period of notice (e.g. 7 days); these might be classified according to the minimum period which must elapse before the institution could be called upon to encash the deposit. Building society shares would be treated as if they were deposits with some fixed period of notice. Net switching of foreign currency deposits into sterling would be treated as if it were a sterling deposit, with an asset ratio fixed by the authorities at a level which would reflect the extent to which they wished to encourage this activity.[11] Asset ratios would not be applied to foreign currency deposits, other than those switched into sterling.

Account would have to be taken of the special position of the discount houses and certain other borrowers of money at call. It is suggested that *secured* lending to a restricted group of institutions, which would include the discount houses, running brokers and gilt-edged jobbers, would count as public sector debt to the extent that such lending was secured by public sector debt.

Incentives (or disincentives) in relation to certain identifiable categories of private sector lending could easily be incorporated in such a scheme. For example, if the authorities wished to discourage lending to persons (other than for house purchase) they might require that holdings of public sector debt should be increased by an amount equal to such lending in excess of, say, 5 per cent of total assets. Conversely, lending on special terms to exporters might be associated with a reduction in the required level of public sector debt holdings.

[11] Some control on borrowing from abroad is essential to any successful monetary control scheme in the U.K. One way of achieving this, which seems to appeal particularly to advocates of control schemes based upon a cash ratio, is to adopt a floating exchange rate.

If a system of asset ratios was introduced, with the authorities having the power to vary the required ratios, the special deposits and cash deposits schemes would be superfluous. It would also be unnecessary to set credit ceilings, which depended upon the voluntary cooperation of the institutions. In my view arrangements of this sort would be well-suited to present-day conditions in which credit markets involve a large number of highly varied financial institutions; they contrast with the existing system which grew up from arrangements more suited to a time when a small compact group of banks dominated the supply of credit to domestic borrowers in the U.K.

Conclusion

In conclusion, it seems to me clear that some revision of the monetary control methods in the U.K. is required, and that the present system ought not to be allowed to persist for longer than is necessary to devise something better. Any new system should stimulate competition between financial institutions at the same time as giving the authorities a better chance of attaining their objectives. I believe that the alternative system which I have outlined would allow the authorities this opportunity. They would certainly be no less able to seek a low real rate of interest. Through their control of Bank rate and other administered interest rates and through open-market operations they would be able to operate monetary policy so as to maintain balance in credit markets. In the face of any strong destabilizing tendencies these conventional means of control could be supplemented by changes in asset ratios to ensure that the supply of credit grew steadily. Compared with the present system, they would have the possibility of a firmer and more predictable control over the supply of credit and of the rate of growth of any relevant financial aggregates, and this would improve their power to ensure stability of economic growth and of the price level. Differential asset ratios on sterling liabilities would enable them to influence the net switching of foreign exchange into sterling and thus to influence in the short-term the gold and foreign exchange reserves, while at the same time the asset ratios would in no way impede foreign currency borrowing and lending by U.K. financial institutions. Finally, by eliminating many of the present controls which severely distort competition between financial institutions, the authorities could make a substantial contribution to improving the efficiency of the financial system.

Discussion Papers

(a) A. R. NOBAY
(University of Southampton)

PROFESSOR BAIN has provided us with a wide-ranging and controversial paper, and indeed, some of the fundamental issues in this area have already been discussed in previous sessions at this conference, e.g. demand for money characteristics, prices and monetary policy, etc. Here I propose to limit my comments to the first half of the paper.

In addition to the somewhat more conventional objectives of monetary policy, such as income and price stabilization, and efficiency of the financial system, Bain proposes as his primary objective the 'conditions which are conducive to a high rate of economic growth', and this requires that the 'real rate of interest should be low'. How do we achieve this?—clearly, not by operating through monetary policy on prices, as in his view we should not exaggerate the authorities' power to influence the price level (at a tolerable cost), and so we are essentially left to controlling nominal interest rates. Bain is clear that to influence real expenditure flows, the authorities should attempt to control explicit interest rates and credit flows—it is these variables and not money supply which are the proximate targets of monetary policy. We now come to the fundamental problem of the paper, and that is the appropriate level of interest rates and credit flows at any time. Here, Bain suggests that money supply could act as an indicator of the stance of monetary policy for economic stabilization.

Interest rates and credit flows conducive to such economic stabilization are achieved through the familiar instruments of open-market operations, rate setting, and altering the maturity classification of government debt. All this might sound very much like the control of money supply, but this is not the case—indeed, the cash ratio is seen more as an essential mechanism for the control of short-term current and expected interest rates (see p. 162 n. 5 above), than fulfilling a conventional fractional reserve role. An important proviso of the paper with respect to interest rates is the undesirability for these to fluctuate too widely because of disruptive effects on the financial markets.

My main observations on Bain's paper are as follows:

I am not too happy about an objective function including a growth rate, let alone a 'high growth rate' argument. Besides the obvious 'what rate' and 'for how long?' objections, one would prefer to see a usual objective function minimizing some loss function with conventional arguments, i.e. unemployment, prices, balance of payments, etc., which then yields the relevant 'ex-post' growth rate. Note that the real rate of interest is not quite synonomous with Tobin's S.P.C.—in a mixed economy such as the U.K., it is feasible for these two concepts to go in opposite directions. The real rate objective in the paper, though, is somewhat short-lived— we are essentially back to the familiar nominal interest rate setting game. Bain's sobering observations on the considerable difficulties in setting that rate (p. 158, second paragraph), if extended, opens up the possibility of the authorities inducing greater instability. In any event, it is clear that Bain's model would not allow wide fluctuations in interest rates because of disruptive effects on financial markets, so in reality the centrepiece of the paper is the typical money market/defensive operation central banking system.

I must confess to being quite unclear and somewhat puzzled by the whole paragraph (p. 158, final paragraph) of the paper dealing with the indicator problem. No doubt this is a thoroughly condensed version of Bain's view on the issue, and this will be clarified in our subsequent discussions. As I understand it, if 'the factors affecting the demand for money were well-established' can be taken to mean a demand function for money which is econometrically satisfactory, and ignoring Brechling's earlier comments on the identification problem, a large residual outside the sample period surely must be interpreted as being stochastic, and so any policy move would be clearly inappropriate. Interpreted as a conventional demand for money function, I would have thought that one would clearly be faced with the modern quantity theory *prescriptions* of changes in nominal money supply, and this is rejected as a proximate target of monetary policy. Actually, given Bain's assumption that a stable and well specified LM function exists, together with 'possibly substantial' shifts in entrepreneurial expectations, i.e. an IS function subject to stochastic shocks, it is clear that the authorities' control over the money supply will yield less fluctuations in income, than would an interest rate policy.[1]

The proposition that the term structure of interest rates is influenced by the maturity classification of debt has to my knowledge not been demonstrated empirically in the literature on the subject. The contention that the authorities are able to determine autonomously interest rate expectations (cf. p. 162, n. 2) is clearly far reaching—one is tempted to ask, given this facility, if conventional textbook methods of control, which Bain clearly rejects because of potential interest rate fluctuations, do not now become operative and preferable to the various ceilings controls. Indeed, if as Bain notes, it is the interest rates and 'credit' and not the supply of money that should form the main stream of monetary policy, why consider at some lengths the alternative techniques of controlling the money supply. This surely becomes a 'non-issue' with money supply passively adjusting to maintain equilibrium in the money market.

I agree entirely with Bain that there ought to be a serious objective of seeking to improve the efficiency of the financial system, and that this has often been overlooked. Regrettably, amongst other things, Radcliffe neglected this issue. We often hear the view that in the pursuance of short-term monetary policy inevitable distortions occur and are of tolerable magnitudes. However, these short term expediencies taking place continuously over a long period do matter. They inevitably tend to perpetuate and extend inefficiency (in the Pareto sense) in the financial system. In this respect, it seems to me that if we are agreed that the imposition of an asset structure on the clearing banks is both inequitable and inefficient, it would be somewhat inappropriate to extend such methods to a broader range of intermediaries. What we need for monetary policy in the 1970s then is the evolution of anonymous central banking operations in a Tobin world of 'Commercial Banks as Creators of "Money"' etc., where the authorities control aggregates or pursue monetary policy on the basis of the predictable way in which financial intermediaries react.

[1] Cf. W. Poole, 'Optimal Choice of Monetary Policy Instruments in a Simple Stochastic Macro Model', *Quarterly Journal of Economics* 84, May 1970, pp. 197–216.

Discussion Papers

(b) W. B. REDDAWAY
(Professor of Political Economy, University of Cambridge)

WE all know that when it is a matter of drawing up regulations, including taxation regulations, we have to proceed on the *assumption* that you can draw dividing lines between what is covered (or covered at particular rates) and what is not—but that this is difficult to achieve, because there are usually no convenient 'discontinuities' through which the lines can be drawn: as the holder of a Chair previously held by Alfred Marshall, I might well quote his traditional statement 'Natura non facit saltum'. In the field of monetary regulation, the problem is made particularly difficult by the fact that money serves many different purposes, and the functions of money for one man may not be the same as for another: 'near-money' may be a good substitute for money in some of its aspects, but not in others.

Consequently, the first point which I would like to make is that any system of control in the monetary field will not be perfect, largely because of the absence of convenient discontinuities. Professor Bain has said—and I agree with him—that one does not want to have control only of the public banks, and that it would be logical to regulate the activity of 'deposit-creation' by any institution which took part in that process, whatever it might be called, rather than to concentrate on regulating the affairs of the banks or other particular institutions. This immediately raises, however, all sorts of problems of definition, and these are very far from being academic niceties—and they will become much more tricky if an institution can escape from a restrictive regulation by changing the legal nature of some practice which it follows.

Objectives

Logically, of course, one should start by examining the question why we should wish to control or influence the creation of deposits in any way, but on that fundamental point I will confine myself to two very brief remarks:

(a) In view of the great disturbance which is caused if a bank fails, there is a need for regulations of one kind or another to minimize the risk that the illiquid assets which it holds will 'go bad', and also to ensure that it has sufficient cash to meet demands from the depositors (which means, of course, that it must hold *more* than it would 'normally' require, either in cash or in a very liquid form, so as to meet some degree of 'abnormal' transactions). This is *not*, however, what we are discussing today—although it is very important!

(b) To my old-fashioned mind, the activity whereby 'non-financiers' can go into a bank or other financial institution, and exchange an illiquid asset (e.g. their own IOU) for something which is effectively money—without thereby producing an equal reduction in the liquidity of the bank—is one which cannot be left free of any public regulation as to the *scale* on which it is conducted.

Professor Bain says that he 'does not give any special importance to the money supply', and it may be that his system of prescribing that deposits shall be backed by a minimum percentage of public sector debt will be adequate, as part of a general system; alternatively, it may be that no more effective system can in practice be operated, so long as the Bank of England manages the public debt. But we should be under no illusion on one point: since there is plenty of public sector debt held outside the financial institutions, by people who are quite prepared to sell some of it to the financial institutions, Professor Bain's system does not in itself impose any limit on the extent to which the banks as a class can create deposits by buying securities; moreover, having raised their percentage of public sector debt to deposits above the minimum in this way, they can then create further deposits by granting advances.

The Administrative Problems

It is, however, the administrative side which I want primarily to discuss. I am sympathetic to the idea that one should regulate a certain *activity*, no matter who conducts it, rather than regulating certain institutions: I have been up against this same sort of problem in connection with our investigation of the effects of the Selective Employment Tax, which is charged basically on the 'establishment' principle, rather than the 'activity' principle. But I cannot help being a bit puzzled about how Professor Bain's proposed regulations would work out in practice.

Fundamentally, Professor Bain suggests that 'categories of liability' should be defined, against which the debtor would have to hold at least certain minimum percentages of assets in the form of public sector debt. But he is almost completely silent about what kind of liabilities should be covered, apart from a general reference to 'sterling deposits' and a statement that building society shares would be treated as if they were deposits with some fixed period of notice. Moreover, he emphasizes, with two underlinings, that the percentages which he proposes for deposits of different terms are purely *illustrative*—but that does not, of course, get over the problems which would inevitably arise if one tried to fix *actual* figures, especially as the people and institutions concerned could then adjust their practices to take advantage of arbitrary dividing-lines.

Let me illustrate this problem with a few examples:

(a) *Coverage.* Since the definition is supposed to be by type of liability, rather than by the business of the borrower, one would like to know whether the definition would be aimed at covering things such as the following:

(i) Loans obtained by a big company in the inter-company market.

(ii) 'Savings banks' run by big companies for their employees (e.g. the old railway companies).

(iii) 'Deposits' obtained by Local Authorities to cover their capital expenditure.

In general, these 'deposits' constitute near-money from the point of view of the lenders, so that it would be perfectly logical to regulate them in some way but it would not be too easy to draw a definition which would include what was wanted, without including other forms of credit, and whatever definition was drawn, the operators could adjust their practices so as to escape its real intentions. Moreover, one must note the very differing effect which regulations of the Bain kind would have on different types of business, although he is ostensibly seeking to secure 'non-discriminatory' treatment. Thus it would obviously be no hardship to the Local Authority, which received the deposit, to have to hold x per cent of it in the form of public sector debt: very possibly the 'borrowing' section of the authority would be allowed to count the IOU of the (say) housing department as a 'public sector debt' for the purpose of the regulations, in which case it would automatically have 100 per cent of the deposits invested in public sector debt; but if this was excluded each local authority could pair up with its neighbour, and arrange to invest reciprocally in the debt of the other to give the required percentage. But to compel the company which borrowed in the inter-company market to hold *x* per cent of the proceeds in public sector debt would seem very queer indeed.

(b) *Effects on the Borrower.* Quite generally, the effects of the provision on different types of intermediary will be very different. Thus the savings bank which anyhow uses all its funds to buy public sector debt will not be affected at all; banks which traditionally hold public sector debt may also be unaffected, if the percentages come to less than their normal holdings of Treasury bills, *plus* government securities, etc.—but the impact may differ from bank to bank quite substantially for no obvious reason; and those cooperative societies which have been using all their deposits in their own business will be seriously upset, whilst others which have been less active on the trading front (or more active in seeking saving deposits) will be unaffected, because they normally invest funds which are surplus to the requirements of their business in public sector debt anyhow. The rule may be non-discriminatory in form, but highly discriminatory in its effects, for no good reason.

(c) *New Types of 'Liability'.* Until an actual scheme is produced, it is hard to judge its workability; but I feel bound to express the view that the ingenuity which has been shown in the past at circumventing the Bank's regulation of institutions will find no difficulty in inventing ways of getting round definitions of 'regulated liabilities'. If the minimum percentage is a serious handicap on the borrower, then in terms of Professor Bain's scheme one would expect to find that all sorts of deposits were exempt because they were legally for 365 days, but incorporated 'in practice' facilities for getting the money back sooner: and new 'instruments' would be likely to appear which just excaped from the control.

My conclusion is that whilst, as indicated above, one cannot possibly expect *perfection*, the scheme put forward by Professor Bain needs a lot more detail before it can be properly considered. One cannot get very far on the basis of broad principles and 'purely illustrative' figures.

SUMMARY OF THE GENERAL DISCUSSION

THE twin issues of the efficiency of monetary control methods, and the efficiency of the financial system in general, constituted the main theme of the discussion. A large number of the discussants expressed the view that too little attention had been paid in the past to the question of the influence on the competitive efficiency of the financial system of the control techniques used by the authorities, and to the related issue of the overall competitive efficiency of the financial sector.

The distributive efficiency of the present system of monetary control methods was questioned on several grounds. One line of argument related to the fact that the commercial banks existed to provide banking facilities for the public and not a convenient control mechanism for the Government. It was felt that inefficiency was promoted by the use of control methods, such as directives, which placed a disproportionate burden of adjustment on the commercial banks. A second line of argument stressed the inefficiency caused by the implicit tax imposed on the commercial banks through the requirement that they hold minimum reserve holdings of non-interest earning and relatively low interest earning assets, requirements which no longer reflect liquidity considerations on the part of the commercial banks but the control techniques used by the authorities. In this case it was thought that efficiency would be increased if the authorities paid the commercial banks interest, at the market rate on these reserve holdings. Lastly, in connection with this aspect of the efficiency issue, several discussants pointed to the need for the authorities to have at their disposal an efficient monetary control technique, in the sense of a technique which yielded predictable control. Here it was argued that predictable control was unlikely to result from the spread of the control net and the proliferation of new control techniques. According to the pure theory of monetary policy, the authorities only need to control one nominal monetary magnitude (high-powered money) and the nominal interest rate paid on this (zero in the U.K.), to give them predictable control of the financial system.

On the question of the overall efficiency (Pareto efficiency) of the financial system, the virtual cartel arrangement amongst the commercial banks which served to limit interest rate competition between the banks, and the acceptance by the authorities of this cartel, was strongly condemned as one of the prime sources of inefficiency in the financial system. The general view of the discussants was that the efficiency of the financial system could be increased, and that with this in view the commercial banks' cartel should be broken, and the authorities should abandon discretionary techniques of monetary control in favour of techniques which rely more on market forces and have a more equitable impact on the various institutions which make up the financial system.

The other themes of the discussion related directly to some of the proposals and arguments in Professor Bain's paper.

Bain's argument in favour of discriminatory rationing control techniques on the grounds that market allocation through interest rate charges would probably give rise to interest rate instability, was contested by several discussants. They doubted whether greater reliance on market allocation through interest rate changes would give rise to interest rate instability (no empirical evidence supporting this belief) and thought that the efficiency loss imposed on the system by discriminatory rationing was too high a price to pay for the avoidance of interest rate instability. It was further argued that if interest rate instability did manifest itself in the system, speculators would enter the market to smooth out fluctuations.

Similarly, Bain's proposal that the monetary authorities should take as their main policy objective the achievement and maintenance of a low real rate of interest in the belief that this would stimulate investment and thus the rate of economic growth, provided another topic of discussion. One discussant took objection to the value judgement implicit in this proposal and suggested that the level of the real rate of interest and the rate of economic growth were best determined by market forces. Against this it was argued that the desirability of a higher rate of economic growth was not an unacceptable social value judgement, and therefore the monetary authorities should adopt such an interest rate policy. The difficulty with this proposal was the specification of the desired level of the real rate of interest and the feasible rate of economic growth.

In like fashion another topic of discussion was Bain's proposal for reforming the system of monetary control in the United Kingdom by use of public sector debt asset ratios applied to a wide range of financial institutions. Several discussants reaffirmed Professor Reddaway's observation that this method of monetary control was unlikely to be very effective in practice because of the large volume of public sector debt outstanding in the private sector. They also reaffirmed Reddaway's other contention that in theory the proposal was unsound in that not only would the financial institutions subject to this form of control be able to acquire the necessary holdings of public sector debt from the non-financial sector, but that they would be able to acquire these assets through expansion of their own liabilities. In theory the proposal not only failed to provide a mechanism of monetary control, but would also give rise to the reverse of what it was intended to achieve. Doubt was cast on the technical feasibility of implementing the proposal. Bain remained convinced that his proposal was worthy of serious consideration. It was pointed out that Bain's proposal was sound if within the required holding of public sector debt there was a fixed percentage of high-powered money.

Lastly, Professor J. S. G. Wilson commented on what Bain said about his control proposals for non-bank financial intermediaries. He emphasized that control of the interest rates at which they borrowed was only one of a number of his proposals. He argued that the growth of non-bank financial intermediaries should be regulated both by controlling the interest rates they offered and charged, and by liquidity controls. Wilson argued with Bain on the importance of the problem of the 'control net' and the 'slipping-away effect': as non-bank financial intermediaries were brought within the control net, new financial intermediaries developed beyond the net. However, Wilson was not as much afraid of this possibility as the Radcliffe Committee, although it was one of the problems with which the authorities had to deal. Further, there was the problem of the growth of financial conglomerates for which conventional techniques were inadequate. Admittedly, interest rate control caused distortions, but this was intended.

Notes

(*a*) BRIAN GRIFFITHS
(*London School of Economics*)

THE essential features of the proposals which I put forward for reforming the U.K. banking system[1] were (i) by abolishing the interest rate agreements of the banks and prohibiting any price discrimination against new members of the bankers' clearing house, to create conditions of free entry into retail banking, and (ii) by removing all restrictions on the banks' portfolio of assets, to ensure that government regulation of banking was minimal, so that the authorities simply fixed the nominal stock and nominal price of high-powered money.

The implementation of the above set of proposals would result not only in a redistribution of existing income, but also in an increase in real income. There would be a redistribution of income from (i) the Treasury and the Bank of England to the clearing banks, (ii) the clearing banks' shareholders to bank depositors, (iii) bank lenders to bank depositors, (iv) those for whom bank services are performed and who do not have a credit balance to those for whom bank services are performed and who do have a credit balance. There would be an increase in real income from (i) the gain in consumers' surplus as a result of the public holding an increased stock of bank deposits in real terms, (ii) the increased real output which could be got by bank credit being used to finance expenditures yielding higher rates of return than at present, (iii) with existing inputs of labour and capital, an increase in the output of banking services (based on the Monopolies Commission assessment of the productive inefficiency of the existing system), and (iv) the reduction in the number of bank branches and in the number of services supplied, releasing resources from the banking industry for use in other industries where they would be more highly valued by society.

Professor Bain's criticisms of these reforms and their implications for monetary policy are (a) that the link between clearing banks'

[1] See p. 165 n. 6 above.

interest rates and Bank rate is simply an administrative arrangement which reflects the high degree of substitutability among certain financial assets, (b) that they would involve a change in the technique of monetary control, and (c) that it would be difficult to work in practice and would have undesirable side effects, in particular, greater fluctuation in short-term interest rates.

It is certainly true that in a competitive financial system a change in one market rate would lead to changes in the rates on close substitutes. But this can hardly be an adequate explanation of the fact that in the U.K. no explicit interest is paid on current accounts and that the rate paid on deposit accounts is rigidly fixed at 2 per cent below Bank rate. Similarly, the fact that building societies tend to tie their deposit rates to the level of Bank rate is simply an indication of the lack of competition among them. In the competitive market for short-term deposits, namely deposits at merchant banks and overseas banks, the relationship between the rates they pay on deposits and the level of Bank rate has broken down completely in the sixties, the rate being particularly influenced by external factors. Rather the present relationship between the cartel rates and Bank rate gives the Bank of England a similar control over interest rates as the U.S. monetary authorities derive from Regulation Q. The reason banks should pay rates on deposits without reference to Bank rate or previous rate-fixing with other banks is an attempt both to break the cartel and also to change the present discretionary monetary policy, which derives its power from the level of the re-discount rate being fixed only marginally above certain market rates and in fact below other short-term rates.

The extent to which the implementation of these proposals would involve a change in the technique of monetary policy can be easily overestimated. The main problem seems to be the way in which the central bank could influence interest rates if the cartel were abolished. Even if we ignore the fact that in an open economy on a dollar standard the level of Bank rate may well be effectively determined by monetary policy in the U.S., the existence of the cartel is neither a necessary nor a sufficient condition to influence the level of domestic interest rates. The rate of interest can be fixed at any desired level, simply by the monetary authorities pegging the price of marketable government debt. The choice for monetary policy between a competitive or cartelized banking system is not that in a competitive system the authorities cannot influence the level of interest rates whereas under a cartel they can, but simply that at present a change in Bank rate has a direct effect on a small number of administered rates immediately whereas under a competitive system a change in the stock of money would change the market rate of gilts and by the process of substitution the whole spectrum of financial and real assets.

The most undesirable side effect of these proposals is, according to Professor Bain, the resulting very sharp fluctuations in interest rates. Given the existence of private speculation, the extent of the variation in the level of interest rates is by no means obvious. Even if there were the variation which is alleged, presumably its most important side effect would be to reduce in the long run, the demand for public sector debt. However, existing holders of gilts will tolerate wider short-run variations in their prices, provided they are compensated with a higher average return. If this is so, then the alleged greater variation in the level of rates is not an argument against open market operations, but the reluctance of the authorities to pay a higher rate of interest on public sector debt.

Although Professor Bain's proposals recognize the need for increased competition in the financial sector, the desirability of the Bank controlling certain aggregates and the need for an explicit set of rules within which the financial sector can operate rather than an informal system of moral suasion, they suffer from two main defects. Firstly, although Professor Bain seems to suggest that the Bank should control the total lending of financial institutions to the private sector via the technique of reserve requirements, there is no explicit mention of what determines the total of both private and public sector lending to these institutions and in particular a subset of them, the banks, whose liabilities form an important part of the money supply. While reserve requirements can be used as a method of allocating credit between the public and private sectors of the economy, they are not in themselves an adequate method of controlling an aggregate such as domestic credit (DCE) or the money supply, unless the stock of high powered money is already determined. In his proposals, this problem is ignored.

Secondly, the use of reserve requirements is simply a method by which the government imposes an implicit tax on financial institutions ensuring that, at the existing rates of interest on the various types of reserves, they supply more credit to the public sector than they otherwise would. While Professor Bain attempts to ensure more equity between financial institutions, he is increasing the inequity between the public and private sectors. Any control over the distribution of the earning assets of banks and of the rates they earn via a system of reserve requirements, is an attempt to subsidize various sectors of the economy and ultimately to control the composition of output. In general, it is more efficient to effect a given subsidy by a lump-sum transfer rather than by fixing a price, either explicitly or in this case implicitly. Government's attempts to change the composition of GNP would be better achieved by a direct fiscal transfer rather than by implicit subsidies and taxes.

Notes

(b) J. S. G. WILSON

(*Professor of Economics, University of Hull*)

IN my article on 'Regulation and Control of the United Kingdom Banking and Financial Structure' in Banca Nazionale del Lavoro, *Quarterly Review*, June 1969,[1] I gave priority to regulation of the rate of growth of the non-bank financial institutions, which I sought to maintain effectively over the long term (see p. 138). The first step was the compilation and maintenance of a register, which could be combined with the licensing of the relevant institutions. On the basis of this register, 'the authorities could then require the observance of certain minimum standards of behaviour (e.g. minimum capital, reserve and liquidity requirements; possibly also some regulation of the distribution of earning assets as between categories and/or in terms of geographic spread) in order to provide the bases for avoiding insolvency and maintaining sound growth. Furthermore, in the case of finance houses, for each class of durable good concerned, they might be required at all times to insist upon a specified minimum percentage of the total purchase price as deposit or down-payment; and contracts might be similarly regulated with respect to the relevant pay-out period. And for all non-bank financial intermediaries, the requirement of minimum liquidity ratios would provide depositors with a margin of safety (what constitutes liquid assets would also need definition); borrowing potential could be restricted (e.g. by limiting the attraction of deposits to a certain multiple of own capital and free reserves); there could be insistence on a minimum of paid-up capital; a minimum provision for reserves; and so on.' (pp. 138–9.)

My second priority was to regulate 'the rate of growth both of deposits and of the related provision of loan finance' (p. 139). I then went on to say that the availability of these moneys can be attacked, if something can be done to stem the inflow of funds to the non-bank financial institutions themselves. 'Hence, if the

[1] Cf. p. 168 above.

maximum rates that might be offered on deposits could be regulated (on all categories of deposits—with the possibility of some discrimination, since there may develop a number of channels through which funds can be secured and one would wish to avoid the "slipping away" effect that the Radcliffe Committee feared so much), the relevant institutions can be controlled and the growth of their business regulated in the short-run as well, simply by varying the terms they are permitted to offer for the moneys basic to the undertaking of enlarged lending' (p. 139). Further on (at p. 140), I say that 'it is important that the regulation of rates should be extended to the whole structure, because it is relative rates that matter and a level established in one part of the structure will certainly give rise to repercussions elsewhere, until a degree of consistency obtains.'

VI

THE NATURE AND USES OF BANK LIQUIDITY

J. E. WADSWORTH

Discussion Papers

(a) R. F. G. ALFORD
(b) J. M. PARKIN

VI

THE NATURE AND USES OF
BANK LIQUIDITY

J. E. WADSWORTH
(*Economic Consultant, Midland Bank Limited*)

A DISCUSSION on 'Monetary Theory and Monetary Policy in the 1970s' is soon involved in aspects of bank liquidity, particularly now that greater emphasis is being placed upon money supply. As money arises and is distributed to the public through the banking system, institutional arrangements and developments are of first importance, not least as they bear upon liquidity. In Britain, as elsewhere, liquidity continues to provide the key to the structure of bank balance sheets, but for the clearing banks it has altogether changed in character and purpose, especially by becoming part of the mechanics of economic regulation. This aspect has been further developed in recent years, as the authorities have sought to rely more heavily upon bank liquidity ratios in influencing credit conditions, even though such levers have, so far, proved uncertain in action and hard to find, since the money market environment has changed, with a tide of funds rising through other financial intermediaries and flooding into parallel markets. Of course it is not ratios alone that have impinged upon bank liquidity: for example, restrictions on advances and medium-term lending for exports upon official requests and terms have played a part, as also, and more weightily, has the policy of the authorities towards long- and short-term interest rates. Yet as bank liquidity is now renewed in monetary action, it is interesting to look more closely at the background in financial history to assist in peering into prospects for the 1970s.

Liquidity in banking is not simply, nor even mainly dependent upon the observance of precise ratios, whether imposed by convention or statute. It rests essentially upon the judgement and practices of bankers in the selection and disposition of their assets; it is powerfully influenced by the structure of the banking system, and by financial institutions, markets and instruments; and bound up with such matters as postal and transport facilities. With these in mind, bank managements, now as in the past, work to ensure liquidity, so that cash is always available on demand and funds are not locked up in frozen advances or other assets. When the authorities take a hand by defining which assets may be counted as liquid, by making these more readily available, or less, and by applying ratios in which they are to be held, the task becomes more complex. So also when advances are subject to directives of the authorities and other official pressures, and when prices of bank holdings of gilt-edged stocks respond to movements in interest rates.

Well over a century ago hundreds of country banks in Britain issued their own notes, gaining thereby a source of funds and furnishing local liquidity. But cash consisted of gold, and banks maintained a store of gold and other coins in their tills. Many would also keep a holding of Consols, 'in the Funds', as the usual phrase had it, as well as a balance with their London agents, to call upon as needed. In those days Consols recorded steady prices over considerable periods and could be readily turned into cash. Hence they enjoyed a high place among liquid assets of the banks, though with slow and difficult transport facilities only gold in safes and in tills could be relied upon should a run develop.

The importance of the distribution of bank assets had still to be recognized, for some early bankers lent by way of advances and discounts a total exceeding deposits, notes issued, and even capital as well. Frequently joint stock banks offered loans to investors against the security of the bank's own shares and extended their resources by re-discounts and loans from other banks. Before the days of published accounts the position was not known outside the bank itself, and in later years publication did much to improve practices and liquidity. The crises of last century showed the need for reform, and an early proponent of closer attention to the assets structure in banking was George Rae who, as general manager of the North and South Wales Bank, in 1878 instituted the submission of weekly financial statements to his directors, setting out the proportions in which the assets of the bank were distributed, 'with a view to raising the standard of liquidity'.[1]

[1] W. F. Crick and J. E. Wadsworth, *A Hundred Years of Joint Stock Banking* (London: Hodder and Stoughton, 1936), p. 190.

As with the progress of the amalgamation movement banks became large units, liquidity was generally improved. True, it was diminished as local note issues dwindled away under the Bank Charter Act of 1844, and when re-discounting became less common as overdrafts replaced bills. But liquidity gained much more from the improvements in communications; from the spread of risks; from economies resulting from the simplified, country-wide banking structure, and as cheques drawn on bank accounts moved to the forefront in monetary transactions. Still more important, the Bank of England was operating as a central bank, acting as lender of last resort and as support under the pressure of financial difficulties. Besides gold, bank liquidity came to rest upon the limitless resources of the central bank tapped through the pipeline of the discount houses and money market assets of the banks.

Stability in Britain's banking system was firmly established by the early years of this century, as witness the way in which banks withstood the upheavals of wartime finance and subsequent financial disorders. It was in this period that changes in the nature and uses of bank liquidity were marked, especially so after the close of the Second World War. It is, in fact, barely twenty years since the authorities officially imposed a liquidity ratio in banking arrangements, and they did so when, in the fifties, the use of interest rates was being resumed, likewise for regulating monetary conditions. By 1955 the Bank of England was insisting upon 'the 30 per cent liquid assets ratio in the London clearing banks—a device of control whose existence had never been officially admitted before that date'.[2] In 1963 the ratio was reduced to 28 per cent of gross deposits, and so it remains, though it has never been closely observed like the cash ratio, but rises from the floor to meet seasonal needs.

The liquidity ratio was, however, the second liquidity percentage to be devised for Britain's banks. The cash ratio, that other principal working ratio in banking, was in being long before the liquidity ratio became an official requirement. Following the difficulties of the Baring crisis in 1890 and the admonitory speeches of Mr. (later Lord) Goschen, attention was directed to the level of banking reserves, and the leading banks thereafter began to publish monthly statements of account. Hence a sufficient proportion of cash to deposits had to be shown as evidence of banking strength, and banks and public became manifestly ratio-conscious. By the end of

[2] Committee on the Working of the Monetary System (*Radcliffe Report*), Cmnd. 827, para. 429.

the First World War comprehensive information about banking figures became available, since the amalgamation movement had resulted in the emergence of a handful of large banks, all publishing monthly figures based on weekly averages.

A further consequence of regular publication was that this showed month by month movements in bank cash, and the analysis then accepted by the authorities regarded the level of bank cash as determining the volume of bank deposits and providing the source of credit.[3] Open market operations on bank cash influenced the level of deposits, but this called for the observance of cash ratios by the banks. Shortly before the outbreak of the First World War the banks were building up these cash holdings, then comprising gold bullion, gold and other coins, and Bank of England notes and balances, and the proportion of bank cash to deposits stood at around 15 per cent for the leading banks, though definitions of banking assets and liabilities were by no means uniform, nor was the ratio the same for all. Indeed, for individual banks cash holdings were adjusted to suit the requirements of their situation and business, for example, to meet the needs of the type of customer they served, to take into consideration the proportion of current to deposit accounts and to allow for the extent of foreign business. In the banking system generally, a further lack of precision resulted from the widespread practice of 'window dressing' that was wittily condemned by the Macmillan Committee.[4]

Thus during the inter-war years the cash ratio operated somewhat loosely; although it was generally shown at around 11 per cent, a level at which it had settled down, in fact it was rather lower, a situation reflected in arrangements eliminating window dressing introduced after the Second World War. The banks then agreed to establish the existing method, whereby the accounts for all clearing banks are struck on the same day, usually the third Wednesday in each month, and all keep to a cash ratio as near as possible to 8 per cent of gross deposits as in the monthly statements. Here, then, was confirmed the first firm working ratio in Britain's banking system, providing formalization of a self-imposed liquidity, but improved primarily to aid the mechanics of monetary control. It did not, however, remain a regulator after the fashion of the Macmillan analysis, for during the Second World War bank cash was provided to meet the rising volume of deposits, and this practice

[3] Committee on Finance and Industry (*Macmillan Report*), Cmd. 3897, para. 71.
[4] Ibid., para. 368.

continued: as a consequence, the role of regulator was left to the liquidity ratio, a requirement that, although officially recognized in the mid-fifties, has still to prove effective when unsupported by restrictions on advances. Views on liquidity were changing, and a year or two later the Radcliffe Committee looked at the liquidity of the whole financial system, of which notes and bank deposits are only a part.[5] The banks, however, are directly concerned with their own liquidity, and in this narrower aspect noteworthy developments have occurred.

In bank cash gold was of special significance until 1914. Inevitably the tendency to work with low central gold holdings had gained ground in Britain, where the banking approach in monetary affairs had found early expression. This was, indeed, a practice held responsible for inconveniently frequent changes in Bank rate[6] but also, in the distribution of these reserves, distinctions were far from clear between home and overseas requirements, or between the responsibilities of government and the banks. Early this century the large banks were being officially enjoined to build up their liquidity, including holdings of gold, partly to strengthen the nation's financial situation, and they did so to an extent that enabled them to lend substantial sums to the central bank on occasions of pressure. One large joint stock bank offered gold to the Bank of England, though, at the price asked, this was refused.[7] With the outbreak of the First World War, gold disappeared from circulation and from bank safes and tills, and Treasury notes took over the task of providing currency: Treasury notes were replaced by Bank of England notes in 1928. Today bank cash comprises, besides token coins, notes of the Bank of England and balances with it (excluding special deposits), the balances accounting for one-quarter to one-third of the total.

Other liquid assets have also experienced far-reaching changes following sweeping innovations in money markets and in government finance. Reference has been made to the practice of early country banks of holding currency, including their own notes, as first line defence, and balances with London bankers and discount

[5] *Radcliffe Report*, para. 389.

[6] R. H. I. Palgrave, *Bank Rate and the Money Market* (London: John Murray, 1903).

[7] L. S. Pressnell, 'Gold Reserves, Banking Reserves, and the Baring Crisis of 1890', in *Essays in Money and Banking Presented to R. S. Sayers*, edited by C. R. Whittlesey and J. S. G. Wilson (Oxford: Clarendon Press, 1968), p. 220.

houses, as well as investments in Consols, as second line support. Commercial bills held in portfolio by the banks could also be re-discounted. However, there were no firm conventions governing the proportions of liquid assets to liabilities, nor as to the items that were defined as liquid, and occasional references to holdings of liquid assets to the extent of one-third of liabilities cannot be regarded as representative.[8] A century ago, an early attempt to assemble and interpret banking statistics[9] provides no justification for supposing such a rule to be of general application, and similar uncertainties surround efforts to analyse the tables of statistics published regularly in *The Economist* from 1877 onwards. In general, it can be said that bankers were reluctant to keep their funds idle in cash or as balances with the Bank of England or other banks, and found remunerative employment for these in various directions. As Walter Bagehot noted a century ago, the banks were placing their reserves to work as to a 'main part...on deposit with the bill-brokers, or in good and convertible interest bearing securities. From these they obtain a large income.'[10]

By then, the leading banks were moving towards orthodox practices, and besides adopting a sounder assets structure they were favouring short-term self-liquidating advances, with the commercial bill as a typical example, pointing the path to be so well trodden in British banking. In the choice of liquid assets, however, the banks were aided by a widening of components, notably in modern times. The customary loans to the money market, overnight or for a few days, were made against commercial bills, but to ensure access to central bank funds the bills had to conform with Bank of England rules of eligibility. A great extension in available liquidity followed upon the invention and introduction of Treasury bills in the seventies; they not only provided substantial funds for government, especially during and after the First World War, but also replaced commercial bills among liquid assets when these declined in general use. Moreover, Treasury bills came to provide the usual repository for spare funds of government departments as well as financial institutions, and their volume swiftly increased when Bank of England notes replaced the Treasury issue and when the Exchange Equalisation Account was established in 1932. Thus Treasury bills moved up along with cash to first place

[8] Pressnell, op. cit., p. 230.
[9] John Dun, *British Banking Statistics* (1876), pp. 80–5.
[10] *Lombard Street* (London: John Murray, 1870), 14th edn., pp. 240–1.

among liquid assets of the banking system and came to constitute a main vehicle for monetary regulation.

Meanwhile, liquid assets had been diminished by the removal of Consols from among them after a decline in market prices of government securities in the early years of this century. Then, too, cheques in course of collection and other transmission items ceased to be included among liquid assets, but in other directions the range of components was enlarged considerably, for money market transactions and for banks. A notable addition to liquidity potential followed upon the inclusion of a growing proportion of short-term government bonds in the securities supporting central bank loans to discount houses when these took over jobbing in short-dated gilts. In the early fifties the Bank of England had specifically called for the liquidity ratio to be maintained, and it has defined precisely and since widened the components of the liquid assets of the clearing banks. These have been extended by embracing other quick assets, such as local authority bills, the banks' own holdings of Tax Reserve Certificates, money at call other than to discount houses and, for the past decade, the refinanceable portion of medium-term export credits.

Of monetary significance has been the change in use, whereby liquidity ratios have added to their old functions of providing for cash replenishment and acting as safeguards for the system generally. Nowadays, the stability of the clearing banks is never in question, though for ordinary banking activities they still have to take good care of their liquidity positions. Cash has to be received wherever offered, held in safety and made available for pockets and purses in every part of the country, and this is essential to public confidence.[11] It is moved around for business and personal requirements through the banking system, a costly and sometimes dangerous service. Currency ebbs and flows, for seasonal and other reasons, involve cash holdings at strategic points as well as at the centre, so that a substantial volume of currency must always be on hand, though banks would be comfortable with a ratio somewhat below 8 per cent. Similarly, the settlement of clearing balances, with all the swings in personal and business affairs, renders necessary the holding of liquid assets to refresh Bank of England balances as

---

[11] *Select Committee on Nationalised Industries*, 1969–70. Bank of England No. 258. Evidence of the Governor of the Bank of England: 'The whole purpose of the cash ratio is that cash has got to be seen there constantly. This is part of the confidence in banks.' (para. 65 (Q 375)).

14

required, though, here again, 28 per cent is regarded as unnecessarily high for banking reasons alone.[12]

It is not, however, the purse-filling functions of the clearing banks that have been in the minds of the authorities when they have imposed working ratios. The cash ratio clarified an existing practice, so as to make more effective official influence on the cash base, even though wartime finance had then moved the source of credit from cash to the liquidity ratio. This, in turn, was therefore brought into the armoury of monetary weapons, but it was at a time when directives, comprising selective and quantitative controls, or 'ceilings' on bank lending, had long held sway for damping down credit. The Radcliffe Committee believed that the case for retaining both the cash and liquidity ratios was 'overwhelming', but neither for reasons of cash requirements nor for the regulation of the level of deposits. It was because the authorities would not be able to conduct a satisfactory interest rate policy unless banking activities were restrained by observing the ratios, which, therefore, the Committee believed, should be made 'absolutely explicit'.[13] The cash ratio, in particular, serves to support regulation of the short-term rate and the interchangeability of Treasury bills for cash, a situation that suits the authorities and is of first importance to the banks in ensuring liquidity.

The liquidity ratio remains as a restrictive device for bank credit, but it has still to become fully effective in monetary arrangements if the banks are ever to escape from the hobble of direct restrictions on lending. Unfortunately, in recent years the efforts of the authorities to substitute ratios for directives have failed one after another. When in 1958 restrictions on advances were suspended for a time, a new form of regulation was announced, to buttress, if necessary, the restraining effect of the liquidity ratio. This was the system of special deposits, whereby the banks were required to place with the Bank of England special deposits at a proportion of their total deposits, as determined by the authorities from time to time. Such special deposits receive interest at a level just below the rate of discount for Treasury bills,[14] but they are not counted among liquid assets for calculating the ratio, still less can they be treated as cash,

[12] *Select Committee on Nationalised Industries*, 1969–70. Bank of England No. 258, para. 65 (Q 659–67).

[13] *Radcliffe Report*, para. 505.

[14] The rate was halved in June 1969, when the clearing banks failed to bring advances down to the required level, and restored in Apr. 1970.

as are other balances with the Bank of England. The effect is to withdraw lending power from the banking system by freezing resources for arbitrary periods in an unavailable asset. Notwithstanding this deprivation of resources and liquidity, special deposits might well have been preferred by the banks to direct restrictions on lending, but it soon turned out to be no choice at all. Special deposits were originally requested in April 1960, and just over a year later directives on advances returned as well.

This was the first breakdown in post-war efforts to regulate bank credit by liquidity pressures alone, for the Chancellor of the Exchequer had spoken of the original call for special deposits as an 'alternative to making a request to the banks'. A second attempt to escape from directives formed part of the Budget of 1967, and once more reliance was placed upon special deposits. The ceiling on bank advances was removed—at that time bank advances to the private sector were restricted to 105 per cent of the level at March 1956— and, the Chancellor said, 'the special deposits system will be used in future in a new and more flexible manner...as a routine adjustment to conditions as they develop. The object will be to maintain a continuous control over bank lending.'[15] But, with devaluation in the following November, ceilings were re-imposed on bank advances and special deposits remained at the level of 1966, namely 2 per cent for banks in England and 1 per cent in Scotland. The rates were raised to $2\frac{1}{2}$ and $1\frac{1}{4}$ per cent when a third attempt to establish regulation by special deposits was anounced in the Budget speech of April 1970 in words close to those of three years earlier. Two reasons were given: first, that quantitative restrictions on lending, though effective in the short-run, gave rise to 'rigidities and distortions which...intensify with the passage of time'. Secondly, the liquidity of the banks had now 'come under pressure',...and... 'the use of the special deposit mechanism will allow us to exert a continuing influence over the liquidity and lending capacity of the banks'.

Both observations are justified in banking experience, but it is the second reason, the new-found pressures on bank liquidity, upon which hopes for success are centred, buoyed up by expectations of closer attention by the authorities to fiscal patterns and to the money supply. One troublesome inconsistency in the aims of government during most of the post-war years has been the growth in the volume of Treasury bills at times when the authorities were

[15] *Hansard*, 1 Apr. 1967, col. 100.

seeking to restrain bank credit. Although it was sought to expand sales of marketable government securities, funding policy was not pressed and an over-all Budget deficit, with the poor market for gilt-edged securities, led to growth in the Treasury bill issue and hence the further availability of liquid assets to the banking system. In recent years, and especially since 1967, the volume of Treasury bills has fallen sharply, as Table I shows. This is not simply because of funding operations, nor by reason of increased savings, nor because of borrowing from abroad. It is attributable to the fact

TABLE I

Treasury Bill Holdings in £m.

	London clearing banks	Discount market	Other	Total
March 1960	941	446	1,880	3,267
1961	790	328	1,790	2,908
1962	794	371	1,594	2,759
1963	667	366	1,462	2,495
1964	667	363	1,564	2,594
1965	559	215	1,320	2,094
1966	656	400	1,249	2,305
1967	403	219	1,100	1,722
1968	371	255	2,452*	3,078
1969	310	261	2,637*	3,218
1970	77	198	1,169*	1,444

* The sharp increase in 'other holdings' in 1967–8 and the decline in 1969–70 were largely accounted for by overseas central monetary institutions and reflect the sterling counterpart of U.K. drawings on swap and other central bank credits made available to support sterling, and their subsequent repayment.

that with increased taxation and a buoyant revenue the government borrowing requirement moved sharply into reverse, from borrowing £1,335 m. in 1967/8 to repaying £273 m. in the following year and £1,119 m. in 1969/70, a tremendous swing into a massive credit position. Over the period, the rate of growth in money supply was also reduced considerably, but the effect on bank liquidity is noteworthy. Treasury bill holdings of the clearing banks had dwindled by March 1970 to well below the level of one-twelfth of that of ten years previously, and for the discount market to below one-half of the earlier figure.

With all that has been said of the main part played by Treasury bills in bank liquidity, such large-scale and rapid withdrawals might have been expected to result in unendurable strains. But as one component of liquid assets diminished, others were expanded, and the net effect has been simply to bring the banking situation more closely subject to liquidity pressures. The growth of bank

TABLE 2

London Clearing Banks

(averages of monthly figures, £m.)

	1960	1966	1967	1968	1969	Latest* available 1970 Jan.–July
Current and deposit accounts	6,722	8,491	8,853	9,511	9,612	9,659
Other	513	885	919	920	998	283
Gross deposits	7,236	9,376	9,772	10,431	10,610	9,942
			Liquid Assets			
Cash	588	767	798	851	879	816
As per cent of gross deposits	*8·1*	*8·2*	*8·2*	*8·2*	*8·3*	*8·2*
As per cent of current and deposit accounts	*8·75*	*9·03*	*9·01*	*8·95*	*9·15*	*8·45*
Money at call and short notice to money market	490	731	806	896	981	946
As per cent of gross deposits	*6·8*	*7·7*	*8·2*	*8·6*	*9·1*	*9·5*
Treasury bills	1,007	689	564	468	294	163
As per cent of gross deposits	*13·9*	*7·3*	*5·8*	*4·5*	*2·8*	*1·6*
Money at call, etc. other than to money market	72	275	330	439	469	463
As per cent of gross deposits	*1·0*	*2·9*	*3·4*	*4·4*	*4·2*	*4·7*
Other bills	143	446	492	527	568	691
As per cent of gross deposits	*2·0*	*4·8*	*5·0*	*5·1*	*5·4*	*7·0*
Total Liquid Assets	2,300	2,908	2,990	3,182	3,191	3,078
As per cent of gross deposits	*31·8*	*31·0*	*30·6*	*30·5*	*30·1*	*31·0*
As per cent of current and deposit accounts	*34·22*	*34·25*	*33·77*	*33·46*	*33·20*	*31·87*

* Figures for deposits and ratios are not strictly comparable with earlier figures because of accounting changes.

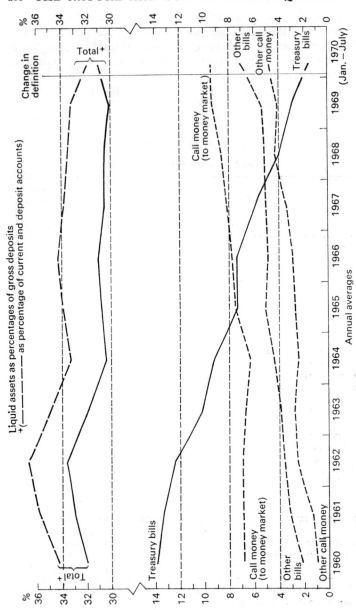

Liquid assets as percentages of gross deposits
+(———— as percentage of current and deposit accounts)

LONDON CLEARING BANKS

Annual averages

deposits slackened in 1967 and the total has fallen somewhat for the past two years. Meanwhile, the restoration of liquid assets has been made through several channels. A marked revival in the use of commercial bills occurred—and by lending in this form banks contribute to their own liquidity—notwithstanding the fact that bills, too, came to be subject to the ceiling. Money at call to the discount market also grew rapidly as the use of funds in short bonds was developed and call loans in other directions were likewise extended. A further supply of qualifying assets came from the growing volume of the refinanceable portion of medium-term export credits made under the guarantee of the Export Credits Guarantee Department. This is set out in Table 2 and illustrated by the accompanying chart showing the huge switches brought about in the composition of the liquid assets item in bank balance sheets, switches that demonstrated the adaptability of banks and money market to an extent that is surprising today and that would have astonished members of the Radcliffe Committee.[16] The substitution of other items for Treasury bills, that nonpareil among liquid assets, was aided by the wider official definition of liquid assets.

Bank liquidity was further influenced by pressures affecting the other principal asset items: advances and investments. Bank lending has been restrained and re-directed by the authorities over so long a period that a mix of advances different from that to be expected without regulation has resulted. Official restrictions are not likely to favour advances supporting new initiatives, and tend towards increased circumspection in bank lending. This does not necessarily result in more liquid banking conditions, since official priorities have to be followed and the judgement of bankers is thereby inhibited. In one area, moreover, lending funds have been diverted into medium-term commitments. At the request of the authorities clearing banks provide medium-term finance for exports and shipbuilding at fixed concessionary rates, and, as an indication of orders of magnitude, at the end of 1969 for one of the large banking groups the total so lent was over four times as big as its special deposit with the Bank of England, and the further sum

---

[16] The *Radcliffe Report* referred to the 'irreversible shrinkage in the relative supply of commercial bills' (para. 584), and thought that the 'funding of Treasury bills beyond a certain (not very remote) point would cause a major upheaval in our financial institutions' (para. 543). For components of call money, see *Midland Bank Review*, Aug. 1969, p. 4.

committed was only a little below the amount then outstanding.[17] The arrangements whereby the Bank of England is to take over part of further increases in this lending will help to relieve this pre-emption of banking resources and deviation from the short-term principle.

Bank holdings of investments have also changed in status and volume, having plunged from standing high among liquid assets to be counted eventually as, like advances, a risk asset. The days when Consols—not just gilt-edged, but gilts without a redemption date—ranked virtually as cash were being left far behind with the decline in market prices in the early years of this century. Nevertheless, the banks with money liabilities continued to hold money stocks and these holdings of gilts were of assistance to the authorities in war and post-war years. The clearing banks emerged after the Second World War with over four-fifths of their resources lent to the government, largely by way of Treasury Deposit Receipts. In time these were converted into bills and government securities, and the clearing banks, with ample liquidity, began to expand advances.

Further changes followed the nose-dive in market prices of gilts with the resumption of the use of interest rates in the fifties. Then the fall was such that holdings of the clearing banks showed declines below cost of tens of millions of pounds[18] and banks turned to quoting cost rather than market prices of investments in published accounts, with footnotes recording the discrepancy. Last year when, with the advent of disclosure, several reforms were made in banking figures, a new and uniform method of valuing investments was introduced whereby premiums or discounts on purchase prices were passed to profit and loss account over the years remaining to maturity.

A further consequence of sharp price movements was the change in the composition of bank investment portfolios. Banks turned to gilts with few years to run, commonly from five to ten, and to selecting bonds maturing in successive years, as evenly as could be arranged. By this means the banks were better protected from declines in market values and set up defences against the blows of credit policy, since by holding bonds in echelon, as the method came to be known, a periodic reinforcement of cash provided cushions to blunt the edge of official monetary policy. Meanwhile,

---

[17] *Midland Bank Report and Accounts*, Dec. 1969. Special deposit £46·3 m.; special medium-term finance lent £186 m., committed £168 m.

[18] *Company Law Committee* evidence, question 3082, p. 94.

investments have continued to act as the residual item in bank balance sheets, rising or falling inversely with the level of advances. No regular proportion to deposits has been observed and, significantly, the banks did not regard themselves as 'locked in' by falling market values. Indeed, during post-war years lending has grown in spite of restrictions and advances have moved up to 58 per cent of deposits, while investments have fallen to below 12 per cent. Plainly the scope for further reduction is limited if investments are to hold their place in liquidity arrangements.

In the near future bank liquidity will probably have to operate in swiftly changing conditions, with the further development of new forms of business and institutional arrangements in the money market and a somewhat different emphasis in banking activities. Nowadays, large funds seek high rates in the parallel markets, and do so through specialized institutions centred at home or abroad. 'Wholesale' banking of this kind is conducted usually on a single-office basis, sometimes through subsidiaries of the clearing and other banks, or by other money market institutions, or by branches of banks with head offices abroad. Many United States banks have opened in London recently, and now about thirty are in operation. Table 3 shows the further swift growth since 1966 in the various groups of banks of the totals for current and deposit accounts, in sterling and currencies. The long-established style of 'retail' business conducted through the extensive branch systems of the clearing banks thus tends to lose its supremacy in the financial system, though remaining of great importance in providing services and cash on demand throughout the country. So far, it is the development of parallel market institutions and not the sluggish progress of the national giro that presents the challenge. Then, too, the clearing banks are finding that the needs of large business units are extending, in particular with the growth of multi-national companies, and hence the considerable development of bank activities abroad and associations between home and overseas banks. The modern banking groups, with all their subsidiaries and connected undertakings, are far different from the relatively simple deposit banks of a generation ago. When restrictions on lending and on capital transfers overseas are relaxed, a further surge forward may be expected.

In recent years the new institutions and developing activities of established ones have brought into being a different pattern of interest rates at substantially higher levels and additional financial

TABLE 3

Banking Groups—end-March figures in £ millions

	Accepting Houses	British O'seas and Common-wealth	American	Foreign banks and affili-ates	Other O'seas	Other
Current and Deposit Accounts in sterling and currency:						
1966	1,108	1,638	1,657	462	588	314
1970	2,514	4,447	9,820	1,775	1,331	2,625
Selected Assets						
Cash and Bank of England:						
1966	0·8	1·6	0·3	0·2	0·2	0·1
1970	1·3	1·6	0·6	0·3	0·1	0·1
Balances with other U.K. banks:						
1966	245	377	216	187	74	53
1970	660	1,727	1,918	771	161	837
Money at call and short notice:						
1966	76	103	30	29	27	4
1970	94	58	36	20	14	26
Loans to local authorities:						
1966	258	119	26	57	12	85
1970	356	385	123	75	10	578
Treasury bills:						
1966	29	34	—	4	2·4	10
1970	17	8	—	6	—	18
Other bills:						
1966	21	87	8	5	7	1
1970	16	64	7	7	6	11
Total of above assets:						
1966	629	720	280	282	121	153
1970	1,145	2,243	2,085	880	192	1,469
Total as per cent of Current and Deposit Accounts:						
1966	*57*	*44*	*17*	*61*	*21*	*49*
1970	*46*	*50*	*21*	*50*	*14*	*56*

instruments, such as 'yearling' bonds of local authorities and negotiable certificates of deposit of the banks. Large funds now move through the local authority and finance houses, the inter-bank[19] and the Euro-dollar markets[19] and, as transactions are conducted mainly through existing institutions, including sub-sidiaries of the clearing banks themselves, a full awareness of liquidity needs may be taken for granted. To a large extent these needs are satisfied by matching, where appropriate, of the periods for which deposits are accepted with those for which loans are made, assisted by the facilities of the inter-bank market.[20]

Among parallel market institutions liquidity can be provided for subsidiaries of the clearing and other large banks through the resources of parents or head offices. Local authorities have to observe official limitations on the proportion of total borrowing that may be raised at short-term,[21] and under ordinary banking arrangements overdraft facilities may well be available. Movements of funds within these markets commonly represent changes in ownership of balances at the clearing banks. In the Euro-dollar markets operators are usually large institutions, and commitments are market knowledge, while 'suasion' by the Bank of England plays a major role here, as elsewhere.[22] Liquidity questions may arise because, on the one hand, surpluses on the United States balance of payments might reduce sharply the supply of Euro-dollars, while, on the other, a continuing and growing deficit might bring the dollar into disfavour.

Methods of regulation, other than 'suasion', present difficulties because the banks operating in the parallel markets—there are about 175 in all—vary widely in the character of their business and do not observe fixed or uniform liquidity conventions as do the clearing banks. From the figures in Table 3 it might be supposed that the distribution of assets within the various groups of banks

[19] As illustrating the pace of change, the *Radcliffe Report* of only eleven years ago did not discuss these markets.

[20] J. R. S. Revell, *Changes in British Banking* (Hill Samuel Occasional Paper No. 3), p. 24, and *Midland Bank Review* May, Aug. 1966, Nov. 1969.

[21] In Apr. 1964 the proportion to total borrowing was restricted to 20 per cent for loans up to one year and 15 per cent for loans up to three months, these per-centages to be achieved within the next few years.

[22] *Select Committee on Nationalised Industries*, No. 258, Question 140. Governor of the Bank of England: 'I think it would be fair to say that now they [the other financial intermediaries] are fully susceptible to the requests which we make to them to conform to the same kind of restrictions on their activities as we ask the banks to endure.'

was similar and not unlike that of the clearing banks. In fact, the differences are wide for groups, for individual banks, and for liquidity arrangements. Thus the bank balances represent in the main activity in the inter-bank market and double counting has to be guarded against. Again, loans to local authorities include fixed-term lending, possibly for periods of years, and even short-term loans of this kind—as distinct from marketable bills—are not counted in the liquid assets of the clearing banks. The distinctive assets distribution for American banks results from the fact that Euro-dollar deposits are passed to head offices in New York and appear in British bank statistics as advances. But for the individual banks in all groups the components of assets under headings indicating liquidity differ, and in total they do not follow the 28 per cent ratio of the clearing banks.

As no liquidity ratio is observed special deposits could not be applied and another form of regulation, the 'cash deposits' scheme has been devised but not yet introduced. This would require cash deposits to be placed with the Bank of England and calculated as percentages of four groups of deposit liabilities; with no liquidity ratio to build on, the scheme might require rather high proportions. It would not, however, directly limit lending, but could reduce profits by diverting funds into comparatively low earning assets. The interest on cash deposits would be the same as on Treasury bills, and even this low return might be reduced by the authorities as a further penalty. For the time being, however, advances of such financial intermediaries continue to be subject to quantitative controls corresponding with those applied to the clearing banks.[23] Somewhat similar difficulties confront the regulation of finance houses by way of liquidity, where diversity in business and in institutions hinders ratio control. For many years past restrictions have included official regulations governing down payments and periods of hire purchase, and again quantitative controls on lending have been applied, but a scheme has still to be announced for running adjustments, by way of liquidity or earnings, to meet the requirements of monetary policy.

Regulation by ratios has advantages over direct controls, especially by allowing more competition, but in banking the method has still to be proved effective in action. This is partly because both the cash and liquidity ratios were formally applied in limiting conditions, when advances were directly restricted, and the

[23] Cf. n. 22 above.

authorities were more concerned with debt management than bank liquidity. Thus when the cash ratio was officially introduced, cash was not acting as the base for credit and, until recently, Treasury bills have been in ample supply, so that neither the cash nor liquidity ratios could act restrictively, though on occasions in earlier periods the pinch of liquidity had been felt, as when, in the thirties, the clearing banks complained of a bill famine, and again in recent years when investments have been sold. But although no fractional reserve system was demonstrably in operation in past years, the ratios have been a restraining influence on the activities of the clearing banks and also have enabled the authorities to conduct an active policy for short-term rates. Thus they have helped in the handling of the public debt, as well as by providing a base upon which special deposits can be imposed. Current pressures on bank liquidity represent a new situation when the liquidity ratio may be seen to operate as a regulator: over the past eighteen months, liquid assets have been scarce and deposits have been falling.

In these conditions, ratios are likely to extend their effectiveness on clearing bank activities and possibly they will be applied to other financial institutions as well, if only because of objections to direct controls on lending. The clearing banks prefer ratios to directives because these last have disadvantages besides the extent to which they lessen competition and hold back the efficient. In addition, they have discriminated in favour of unaffected lenders; they are arbitrary on base dates and incidence, and they stand in the way of a normative pattern of advances. Moreover, they strike with incalculable force because much of bank lending is still by way of overdrafts, and agreed aggregate limits substantially exceed the totals for outstanding borrowing, so that a bank is always vulnerable to an unexpected and inescapable growth in advances. This, too, is an objection to regulation through a ratio of advances to deposits, as suggested by the Radcliffe Committee[24] or to similar constraints on advances indirectly, as by a ratio to deposits of liquid assets plus investments.

Liquidity ratios, too, enforce restraints and, moreover, they provide a compulsory interest-free—or low-rate—loan to the government, acting thereby as a penalty solely on clearing bank activities, at least to the extent that ratio levels run above the needs of prudence. Then, too, they lack the inherent precision of selective controls on lending and the apparent immediacy of quantitative

[24] Para. 527.

restrictions. Even so, liquidity controls are less offensive than directives and allow greater flexibility than would result from using ratios of other assets. Hence the efforts to make clearing bank liquidity the main channel for regulation.

In the seventies, the ratios could be improved in technical application, and re-designed so as to sweeten restraint by being constructive in operation. A considerable technical refinement has already followed upon disclosure and other accounting adjustments. This year, banking figures have been clarified and made more nearly uniform as between the banks, and better figures have made possible better ratios. Thus ratios are now calculated for liquid assets as percentages of new-type gross deposits, of customers' moneys, and not, as for so long in the past, as proportions of old-type gross deposits, with all the uncertainties attaching to a figure that, until this year, included inner reserves, provisions and transit items. The effects of revising the method in this way are shown in Table 2 and the chart, and the improvement as a result of the new presentation of figures is evident. Besides closer relevance to customers' balances, an economy in liquid assets has resulted. This is welcomed because only the excess of liquid assets over the stated proportion is at the disposal of a bank; if 28 per cent is required, 28 per cent is alienated from other uses.

Then, too, the separate ratios for liquid assets and for special deposits give rise to questions, apart from the objection to the nature of special deposits themselves. In essence, special deposits, when called or repaid, take effect as variations in the liquidity ratio, and comparisons in operational detail with a variable liquidity ratio do not favour special deposits. The argument of the authorities[25] that special deposits, as a method for regulation, should not be seen 'principally as a device for government financing' is hardly sustainable since special deposits from the beginning have been passed to the Exchequer by taking up Treasury bills. Another official objection is that as the liquidity ratio is intended to maintain bank liquidity, it should not be regarded as part of the mechanics for regulating monetary conditions, but, in fact, this is just how it has come to be operated. Throughout, the authorities have spoken of both working ratios as in the first instance resting upon prudent banking practice, but if this was true of the past it is not so today. On several occasions the banks have said that both could be lowered without inconvenience or disturbance. And if banking

[25] *Bank of England Bulletin*, Dec. 1962.

practice is to be the guide, then the liquidity ratio should surely be adjusted over the year to allow for seasonal swings. The fact is that ratios remain fixed at existing levels and with particular components because the authorities determine and define them in this way, and take effect because the banks then closely observe the rules.[26] It is these conditions that make the ratios of operational significance, and not the levels at which they stand, nor the separation of special deposits, and there is point in the preference of the Radcliffe Committee for straightforward variable liquidity ratios.[27]

Technical aspects apart, the liquidity requirement might be made more constructive in various ways. For example, it might be helpful to vary percentages on a regional basis, so as to lessen the burden in areas where the full rate is not justified. Since the introduction of the scheme, the rate for special deposits for Scottish banks has been one-half that for the clearing banks, and in Northern Ireland banks are not subject to them at all. Differentials for special deposits or liquidity ratios could be considered in other regions if a practicable scheme could be devised. A major development could follow if the benefits of freedom to lend—when this arrives[28]—were to be made worthwhile by relaxations in the ties, long strengthened by official support, that link so closely to Bank rate the interest rates allowed on bank deposits and charged on advances, and if appropriate adjustments in liquidity requirements could be made. In the operations of the large banks, rather less rigidity in their rates policies is likely to prove rewarding. Depositors have shown themselves sensitive to rates, and a modest flexibility, for example between rates for deposits for varying periods of notice, might meet with a surprising response. Borrowing rates and charges, too, could move over a somewhat wider range to help to provide for the higher costs of resources and to bring a selectivity on type of risk more acceptable than that imposed by directives. In these ways the banking service could be more closely tailored to public needs, and the process could be aided by liquidity requirements varying with the periods of notice for deposits. A particular instance where bank liquidity easements could be of assistance is in

[26] See n. 12 above.
[27] *Radcliffe Report*, para. 508. For liquidity ratios generally, see *Midland Bank Review*, May 1970, pp. 3–8.
[28] The omens are not good. A sharp rise in bank advances last July was followed by a reminder from the Bank of England that the restrictions on lending still applied, with a request to bring about a slower rate of growth in lending.

small savings accounts at the banks. These could be encouraged by the offer of more attractive conditions if such accounts were excluded from the penalty of liquidity ratios, at any rate to the extent of compensating tax benefits enjoyed by depositors in official savings institutions.[29]

Should these hypothetical conditions be fulfilled, it is not to be supposed that the associated rise in clearing bank resources would be very great. First, the rates that would then emerge, if no longer uniform among clearing banks, would not be likely to show wide variations: competitive forces would operate to bring rates of individual banks fairly closely into line, probably at somewhat higher levels, even if understandings did not again do so, and such understandings were not again encouraged and endorsed by the authorities. Secondly, the going rates in the parallel markets are nowadays the London rates quoted for sizeable balances from home and abroad, and already the clearing banks compete actively and successfully in these fields through subsidiaries that are not subject to liquidity rules. In this sense the banks collect at their side doors funds that escape the ratio penalties applied to those passing through front ones and, within current credit restrictions, the subsidiaries use those resources for lending somewhat different in character from that of the parent bank, with the pattern of rates on a higher level.

In recent years, then, the clearing banks have been on the move in structure and practices, not only to gain advantages of scale and range of activities, but also to avoid, as far as possible, restrictions and liquidity penalties. For the next stage, even modest improvements in regulation by liquidity depend in large measure upon other reforms, and for more ambitious developments the necessary changes would be far-reaching. Then, too, in some directions other intermediaries have led the way with financial innovations, and they also are confronted with proposals for regulation by the authorities. If the clearing banks remain under the harrow of liquidity, and thereby eventually escape from directives, for other institutions proposed controls have still to be tried and to show that

[29] The National Savings Bank (formerly the Post Office Savings Bank) and the Trustee Savings Banks have recently announced that the rate offered on ordinary deposits is to be raised from $2\frac{1}{2}$ per cent to $3\frac{1}{2}$ per cent and the amount of interest free of tax from £15 to £20, thus maintaining at £600 the balance enjoying this privilege. The Post Office Savings Bank had formerly allowed interest at $2\frac{1}{2}$ per cent since it was established in 1861.

they could bring similar relief. The schemes announced do not rely upon liquidity ratios, and the most satisfactory development, an acceptable regulatory method applicable to all intermediaries, has yet to be found. Suggestions include establishing for all institutions proportions to deposits of advances, or of the other main assets taken together, but both would involve relinquishing the primacy of liquidity in the regulation of the clearing banks. Meanwhile, the change in monetary policy during the past eighteen months has given room for manoeuvre and for the authorities to provide the financial setting for the progress of further initiative in the seventies.

Discussion Papers

(*a*) R. F. G. ALFORD

(*London School of Economics*)

THE conventional treatment of liquidity begins by looking at the liquidity of an individual asset. Liquidity here is a two-dimensional concept involving (1) a time dimension for the expected ability to exchange out of the particular asset and into cash (shiftability or marketability) and (2) a value dimension showing the extent to which the asset is expected to maintain its value when it is exchanged for cash (capital safety). The liquidity of an asset is then shown by the range of paired values for these two dimensions, and the datum asset with which the liquidity of other assets is to be compared is cash, the asset which has only a single pair of extreme values in these two dimensions, giving the holder certain command *now* over its *full value*.

But it is not the liquidity of individual assets that we are normally really interested in, but rather the liquidity of a bank's whole balance sheet position. Then in addition to the objective asset structure and its expected ability to produce cash, we have to look at the objective liability structure and its expected pattern of cash requirements. In the case of the London clearing banks, a group of banks in substantially similar circumstances, these complications have been covered by certain rules of thumb (whose emergence is described in the paper) relating adequate balance sheet liquidity to the proportions to gross deposits of certain assets selected because of their high rating on the conventional view of liquidity—expected ability to produce *full value, now*. But if we look at a bank with a more varied term structure of liabilities than a clearing bank, relating the liquidity of its balance sheet in this way to its expected ability to secure *full value, now* from its assets could be misleading. Instead the criterion must be the more general one of the capacity of its assets to produce *full value, when needed,* the latter component reflecting amongst other things its term structure of liabilities. Simple rules of thumb may well emerge for some groups of such banks (indeed, the Bank of England appears to require the observance of rules of thumb of this kind by the Accepting Houses) but there is no reason why these should have any close resemblance to those of the clearing banks, for the banks in the two groups are different in many ways, apart from relative size. For example, while for a bank the exogenous change one first thinks of is an associated change in bank deposits and cash assets, the clearing banks are also faced with exogenous associated changes in bank advances and cash, arising from changes in the degree of usage of agreed overdraft facilities, something which does not face those banks who do their lending business by way of loans. And while through the deposit rate agreement the clearing banks restrict themselves to subsequent adjustment on the assets side of their balance sheets, banks which are free to quote competitive rates for customers' deposits and to borrow at competitive rates in the inter-bank market or through the issue of certificates of deposit can adjust their position through inducing changes on their liabilities side as well as on their assets side. In fact, as the paper implies, the liquidity of a bank's balance sheet is a matter of its adaptability in the face of likely exogenous changes, and its objective liability and asset structure may be only a rather imprecise guide to this.

The paper displays considerable enthusiasm for regulation of the clearing banks through liquidity controls (preferably in the form of a variable liquid assets ratio), as this would be less arbitrary in its incidence and would have less effect on bank competition and efficiency than the present system of direct controls on lending. But, as the paper admits elsewhere, there is no clear reason to suppose that without the support of direct controls of some sort the authorities could exercise any useful control in this manner. The trouble is that the distinction between liquid and non-liquid clearing bank assets does not coincide with any significant distinction at the macro-economic policy level. Liquid assets include both private and public sector debt and so do non-liquid assets; hence a change in the required liquid assets ratio need not cause any change in lending to the private sector (the main target of policy in the past), but only its reallocation between liquid and non-liquid forms of such lending. Nor is it true that the authorities have any market control over the volume of liquid assets, which together with the liquid assets ratio would enable them to control the volume of deposits; one liquid asset in particular—U.K. commercial bills— is determined by the banks and their customers and the volume has shown itself very elastic in the past. Altogether, it is far from clear how the authorities could exercise significant control through the liquidity ratio alone; supplementary direct controls, such as control over commercial bills, would be required and this would bring back a substantial element of arbitrariness, the avoidance of which is a major purpose of the exercise.

The paper also raises the question of how far a reserve ratio which has become an official requirement can then fulfil its original purpose of ensuring bank liquidity; the answer to this will depend upon the specification of the official reserve requirements, which in the U.K. have some degree of flexibility (relating as they do to roughly mid-monthly points, and allowing some temporary transgression although at rising marginal cost in terms of official disapproval). But perhaps the better question is, if we have two separate targets, individual bank liquidity and macro-economic control, why should we try to pursue both by means of one policy instrument—liquidity requirements? Surely it would be better to follow the more orthodox approach of looking for two separate instruments with which to pursue the two separate targets.

Looking at the first instrument, aimed at ensuring bank liquidity, we have already mentioned some of the different practices which would cause difficulties in the specification of rational liquidity requirements covering all banks. But even if we were to confine ourselves to requirements for one group of banks, say the clearing banks, it would seem that a rational system of liquidity requirements would have to be fairly complex to take account of the complexities of the banks' actual situation, and it would have to cover both equilibrium and disequilibrium situations. Even with this single limited target, therefore, there are difficult problems of evaluation and choice to be made between: a rational but fairly complex system of requirements (presumably subject to frequent revision as practices and markets change); allowing these banks complete freedom in managing their balance sheets (much fuller and more frequent information being necessary for the first, and desirable for the second so that public knowledge can reinforce bankers' natural sense of self-preservation); the present system, not very rational but at least known to be viable; or some variant of one of these.

Turning to the second instrument, one for macro-economic control, interpreted here as one for controlling the level of bank deposits, it has been suggested above that liquidity controls could not in any case perform this function. Here there are two broad alternatives; first, we can look on the supply side for something that is rigidly complementary to bank assets, and which is controllable by the authorities. One obvious possibility would be bank cash with a fixed ratio, except that this would intrude upon the separate arrangements relating to bank liquidity. Another possibility is a system in which a bank holding £100 million of assets would be required to hold licences covering this amount. The licences in various denominations would be marketable, with a fairly short life and hence a considerable turnover, and the authorities would control the issue (or sale) of new licences. Second, we can look at the demand side and use interest rates as a means of inducing changes in the demand for bank deposits, which in the British monetary system could be expected to change their volume. In a simple comparative equilibrium world, supply side and demand side methods of control over bank deposits could give the same results, being alternative means of reaching a single point on a demand for money function which, given money income, relates bank deposits and the rate of interest. It is difficult to guess how far such symmetry might hold in the real world in the short run or in the longer run.

If and when it does prove possible in the 1970s to remove the present structure of direct controls on bank lending, it is likely that there will be a substantial backlog of changes, or demands for change, which have been held back by the exigencies of policy. The paper sees the deposit rate agreement as one candidate for removal, and the restrictions on the asset holding practices of the clearing banks and the discount houses will be increasingly hard to justify, as will rather arbitrary liquidity requirements, particularly if the authorities should conclude that these are of little value for macro-economic policy. In these circumstances the clearing banks might well acquire much greater freedom to manage their liquidity as they thought fit.

Discussion Papers

(b) J. Michael Parkin
(Professor of Economics, University of Manchester)

I am going to divide my remarks on Mr. Wadsworth's paper into two sections. First, I am going to comment briefly on the concept of liquidity to see what we might learn from what Mr. Wadsworth has to say about the changes in the assets which have served as liquid. Second, and more extensively, I am going to look at Mr. Wadsworth's ideas about using liquidity ratios as devices for controlling the volume of deposit liabilities of banks and non-bank intermediaries.

What is Liquidity?

This is a question which has occupied all of us who were brought up on the Radcliffe Report and which is rarely answered satisfactorily. The trouble with the way the question is traditionally asked is that the questioner usually has in mind as the answer a single number to represent the liquidity, not only of the balance sheet of an institution, but that of the whole economy. Even the former is not a sensible thing to look for. Liquidity can only sensibly be thought of as one of the attributes attaching to a particular asset. Each asset has two economic attributes:

(1) a rate of return
(2) an acquisition/liquidation cost.

Both of these may be stochastic. The term liquidity may be attached to either the level of the liquidation cost or its variability. Once we see things in this light we begin to appreciate immediately why some assets are highly liquid at some times and less liquid at other times. Liquidation costs can vary both in terms of level and predictability. This is especially true in the case of large classes of Government debt under different monetary policy regimes.

In specifying econometric models of financial behaviour, especially when they are designed to explain long period behaviour, we should attempt to include liquidation cost distributions as variables. Almost all our past and present generation models of financial behaviour (e.g. all the work on the demand for money function) implicitly include liquidation costs in the parametric structure of the demand functions with which they deal. This factor could explain 'shifts' in such functions over long time periods. Including liquidation costs as variables would be one explicit way of incorporating in models what is often referred to (but never explicitly defined) as 'increasing financial sophistication'.

Monetary Control Through Ratios

The first point to be made here is obvious and well known: it is, however, one which is often overlooked and one whose relative neglect seems to me to lead to a little confusion in Mr. Wadsworth's paper. There is a clear distinction to be made between conventional ratios and required ratios. This is easily shown. Suppose a bank had no required reserve ratios at all but that it was observed to operate with an 8 per cent cash ratio and a 28 per cent liquid assets ratio. Suppose that the authorities then decided to name those observed ratios as required ratios. Would that have any effect on the behaviour of the bank? Clearly it would.

In the former situation the banks were presumably holding 8 per cent of their assets in cash and a further 20 per cent in other liquid assets so that they would not have to liquidate bonds and/or advances in a hurry in the event of cash losses.

In the second situation, a requirement always to have 8 per cent cash and 28 per cent liquid assets would mean that a cash drain would have to be met by a sale of bonds or a reduction of overdrafts.

Thus, in the first situation the 8 per cent cash and 28 per cent liquid assets are *liquid reserves*. Once those ratios become required ratios, the liquid reserves have vanished completely. There are no reserves at all. Reserves would have to be built up above those levels to provide low cost sources of cash. It is important, therefore, not to convert observed reserve ratios into required ratios without exploring in detail the predicted balance sheet adjustments to which this would give rise. Let us now ask whether required ratios are necessary at all to control deposits, and, if they are, let us also ask which asset might serve best as the mean through which deposits are controlled.

To make the discussion simpler, consider the following three equations:

$$X_B = f(R, r) D \qquad (1)$$

$$X_B = \bar{X} - X_P \qquad (2)$$

$$X_P = g(r, W) \qquad (3)$$

X is some asset held by the banks. Let us not say which asset it is at this stage. The demand for that asset by the banks is given by equation (1). D is deposits, R is the required ratio of X to deposits and r is the differential between the interest rate on asset X and that on other earning assets. Thus, $f(R, r)$ is the observed ratio of asset X to total deposits. The supply of the asset X to the banks is given by equation (2). $\bar{X}$ is the total supply of the asset, and X_P is the demand for X by the public. Equation (3) gives the demand function for X by the public. This demand is postulated to depend on the interest rate differential between X and other assets and the wealth of the public (W).

Now if we embed these equations into an aggregate general equilibrium system of the Hicks–Hansen variety we shall get a determinate solution for the interest rates, the volume of bank deposits, the allocation of X between the banks and the public, and, of course, for variables such as the levels of income, consumption and prices not mentioned in equations (1–3). Given $R, r, \bar{X}$ and W, the volume of bank deposits is given by equation (4). That is:

$$D = \frac{1}{f(R, r)} [\bar{X} - g(r, W)] \qquad (4)$$

What this says is very familiar. The volume of deposits is equal to the reciprocal of some asset ratio (actual—not required) times the amount of that asset available to the banks.

Now, can the authorities control deposits by controlling $\bar{X}$? Further, what is the role of R, the required reserve ratio, in this control process?

Clearly, the authorities can control D provided (a) that they can control $\bar{X}$, and (b) that equations (1) and (3) (the demand functions for X by the banks and the public) are well determined equations with stable and predictable interest, required reserve and wealth coefficients and small stochastic terms.

Now what asset, or group of assets might X be in order that these requirements be met? There are many logical possibilities but only three will be discussed here. They are (1) cash, (2) 'liquid assets' and (3) total government debt. First cash. How does this look as an effective means of controlling D? First we know that, for cash, equation (1) is rather well determined. We know quite a lot about the behaviour of the London clearing banks' and the Scottish banks' demand function for cash, but less about that of the foreign and overseas banks! The demand for cash by the public, equation (3), is quite well understood. It seems to be stable and is probably simpler than the form in (3). Furthermore, in principle the authorities have control over the supply of cash except for that which enters the system as discounts and advances. This factor, however, requires no serious modification to the equation system. A relationship determining the volume of discounts and advances could easily be specified and estimated. Hence, if X is cash it looks as if we have a reasonably reliable linkage mechanism for controlling D.

What if X was 'liquid assets'? In this case the demand function for X by the banks, equation (1), is not so well understood. First, X is now an aggregate of different assets. It is difficult to make predictions about demands for groups of assets in terms of a small number of explanatory variables. There are two published studies by Brechling and Clayton[1] and by Parkin, Gray and Barrett[2] of the demand for liquid assets by the banks. Though they achieve coefficients of the determination of the order of 0·9 they use a large number of explanatory variables in order to do so. Such relationships are probably too complex to be used for policy purposes. Second, the total stock of liquid assets is not controlled by the authorities. The private sector also issues debt in this category in the form of commercial bills and call loans. Third, the demand for liquid assets by the public, equation (3), is not at all well understood. To my knowledge there are no published empirical studies on the demand for that aggregate. All this suggests that liquid assets control (a) is not possible and (b) if it were possible would not give very predictable control over the total volume of bank deposits.

[1] F. P. R. Brechling and G. Clayton, 'Commercial Banks' Portfolio Behaviour', *Economic Journal*, June 1965, pp. 290–316.

[2] J. M. Parkin, M. R. Gray, and R. J. Barrett, 'The Portfolio Behaviour of Commercial Banks', Ch. 9 in K. Hilton and D. F. Heathfield (eds.), *The Econometric Study of the United Kingdom* (London: Macmillan, 1970).

Finally, suppose X was total government debt. This is a suggestion put forward by Bain.[3] The same objections arise here as in the case of liquid assets except that the authorities can, in this case, control the total quantity outstanding. However, we certainly do not at present know enough about the behaviour of the demand for government debt either by the banks or the public to enable us to use it as an instrument for controlling deposits. In principle, of course, the necessary knowledge could be obtained but work already done by Norton[4] and Parkin, Gray and Barrett,[5] as in the case of liquid assets, has not produced the kind of simple stable relationships needed for policy purposes.

All this leads me to conclude that in the present state of knowledge, the most precise control of deposits can be obtained by controlling the stock of cash (currency plus bankers' deposits) outstanding.

The second question posed above concerned the role of a required reserve ratio in the control process. Do required reserve ratios make any difference? Is not the observation that people follow certain behaviour rules enough for us to be able to predict the outcomes of controlling certain variables? Required ratios can be important in improving the predictability of the control of deposits.[6] If we consider there to be a stochastic error in equations (1) and (3) then we have

$$X_B = f(R,r) D + \epsilon_1 \tag{1'}$$

$$X_B = \bar{X} - X_P \tag{2'}$$

$$X_P = g(r, W) + \epsilon_2 \tag{3'}$$

where ϵ_1 and ϵ_2 are stochastic errors. The volume of deposits is given by

$$D = \frac{1}{f(R,r)} [\bar{X} - g(r, W)] + \frac{1}{f(R,r)} (\epsilon_1 - \epsilon_2) \tag{4'}$$

The stochastic component on this deposits determination equation is $[1/f(R,r)](\epsilon_1 - \epsilon_2)$. Clearly the larger is the required reserve ratio, the larger will be $f(R,r)$ and the smaller the stochastic term

[3] See Ch. V of this volume.

[4] W. E. Norton, 'Debt Management and Monetary Policy in the United Kingdom', *Economic Journal*, Sept. 1969.

[5] Loc. cit.

[6] This is not what I said in introducing the discussion on Mr. Wadsworth's paper. I am grateful to David Laidler and David Rowan for pointing out my mistake.

on D. The limit, of course, would be a required reserve ratio of unity with no stochastic error on D. This may not be optimal in a broader sense because of the effects of the required reserve ratio on the interest elasticity of the supply of money.[7]

A required ratio is important from quite another point of view, because it imposes a tax on the banks by forcing them to hold more of a lower yielding asset than they would otherwise hold. Whether such a tax is the best that could be devised is a question which goes beyond the scope of these comments.

What about dual asset ratios? Is there any purpose served by having, for example, both cash ratio and liquid assets ratio requirements such as we currently have in the case of London clearing banks? Given what I have said about the role of a single required reserve ratio in the monetary control process the answer to this question must be no. There is clearly no point in having a multiplicity of ratios for the purpose of improving monetary control. All that a multiplicity of ratios achieves is a distortion in the balance sheets of the institutions on whom these requirements are placed. The distortions must, in the nature of things, lead to Pareto inefficient resource allocations and have repercussions for intertemporal efficiency in general.

This brings me to the prescriptive aspects of Mr. Wadsworth's paper. He hints that he would like to see an extension of ratio controls to non-bank intermediaries as well as to the banks. If what I have said above is correct, then from the point of view of the efficiency of monetary control this is not necessary. Perhaps, though, what Mr. Wadsworth has in mind is that such control would be justifiable on the grounds that it is unfair to levy a tax on the banks without levying similar taxes on non-bank intermediaries. If required reserves were explicitly designed as a method of taxation there would be a case for extending them to other institutions. However, to look upon reserve requirements in this light forces us to consider the argument that there are better ways of taxing banks and financial institutions than by forcing them to hold quantities of public debt in excess of what they otherwise would have held. These arguments, though, lead us far beyond the scope of this comment.

---

[7] For a discussion of the optimal interest elasticity of the money supply function see W. Poole, 'Optimal Choice of Monetary Policy Instruments in a Simple Stochastic Macro Model', *Quarterly Journal of Economics* 84, May 1970, pp. 197–216.

SUMMARY OF THE GENERAL DISCUSSION

Professor Parkin's comments were the source of much discussion. There was a high degree of unanimity amongst the academic theorists that Parkin was right in asserting that only one ratio was required (the cash ratio) to give the authorities control over bank deposits and that there was no advantage to be gained, and several disadvantages, in increasing the number of control ratios. It was agreed that the higher the ratio the greater the predictability of control.

Dr C. Goodhart of the Bank of England, on the other hand, thought that this view neglected reality and the nature of the problems facing the authorities. He argued against Parkin's conclusions on the grounds that they depended on his assumption that the volume of high-powered money was given by the authorities. In reality the volume of high-powered money (X) the authorities were obliged to create (assuming a closed economy) depended upon the public sector borrowing requirements (F), the volume of debt maturities (M), and upon sales of public sector debt (S). Thus:

$$X_t - X_{t-1} = F + M - S$$

The authorities had to regard F and M as given in the short-run. Sales of public sector debt, however, were functionally related in a behavioural equation to a number of arguments. There was no certainty that these relationships were well specified or stable. So the control of high-powered money was subject to uncertainty. This was the problem faced by the authorities, and it could not be ignored by assuming the volume of high-powered money to be given.

If the relationships were well specified and stable, and if the system was free of restraints, the authorities could control the money supply by varying the rate of return on public sector debt, relative to the yield offered on alternative assets, particularly on bank liabilities, until the public wished to hold public sector debt rather than bank deposits. For this purpose the existence of specified minimum cash ratios, or any other ratios, was totally unnecessary. A rationale of the present control system was the belief that the relationships were unstable, and the consequent fear that an active open market operations policy would lead to marked interest rate instability in the system. It was largely to reduce such instability that the authorities sought to restrain and to direct the banking system in certain ways, with the co-operation of the banks. The return for this co-operation, from the banks' point of view, was that the sharp adjustments that would be forced upon them, if they were operating in a completely free system, were not enforced by the authorities. Pressure had not been applied to make the cash ratio effective, and pressure on the banks via the liquidity ratio had up till now been very mild.

The discussant believed that the financial system could be controlled either by relying more on restrictions and rationing or by accepting free markets and a greater degree of instability. The substantive issues were two. First, how much more instability in financial markets did one have to accept as restrictions on the system were lifted (what was the shape of the trade-off function between the two)? Second, what was the optimal point or combination of freedom and control at which to aim (what was the optimal point on the function)? Arguments on the role and functions of cash or liquidity ratios were only about subsidiary technical matters.

Some discussants thought that the rate of interest was too important a variable to be subject to excessive instability, but also thought that the authorities should reduce their present excessive reliance on directives and other discretionary controls and make more use of control techniques which utilized market forces. They regarded ratio control as the best of these techniques. To be effective, however, they thought the ability of the financial system to create liquid assets would have to be nullified by the authorities restricting the class of assets eligible for inclusion in the liquid asset ratio.

Parkin's reply to the above was that the instability/rationing trade-off argument ignored the problem of whether the control mechanism placed the burden of adjustment in the economy on quantity or price variations. The Bank of England's interest rate policy was only compatible with a control system of price adjustments if it always knew the level of the rate of interest required to give the desired level of output and employment in the economy. In terms of an aggregate general equilibrium system of the Hicks–Hansen variety this meant that the authorities not only determined the position of the *LM* curve, but did so in full knowledge of the position of the *IS* curve. The problem was that in reality the Bank of England determined the position of the *LM* curve in ignorance of the true position of the *IS* curve, and in consequence their interest rate policy placed the burden of adjustment in the economy on to changes in the levels of output and employment. The monetarists' preference for a price adjustment policy rather than a quantity adjustment policy was one of the reasons why they argued for a control policy based on regulation of the growth of the money supply. He was in favour of a price adjustment control mechanism, but recognized that in a world of positive financial transactions costs the monetarists position was less strong. For this reason he allowed that it might be desirable to have some trade-off between price/quantity adjustments.

Concerning the interest rate instability issue, it was argued that increased instability was unlikely to result if the authorities relaxed their interest rate support policy. One discussant argued that the authorities' belief in the inherent instability of interest rate variations in a competitive market assumed that the United Kingdom financial sector equalled the world financial sector. This was not the case and he thought that international competition and capital flows could be relied upon to prevent interest rate instability. He did not think that the authorities would experience difficulties with the increased volume of capital outflows and inflows which would result from a freeing of the market. The authorities' apprehension over the consequences of more short-run capital inflows and outflows was an undesirable by-product of their concern with economic restraint rather than economic growth. Other discussants agreed that greater interest rate instability was unlikely to follow a relaxation of the authorities' interest rate policy. They disagreed as to whether rates would fall or rise in the long-run with increased competition in the financial system, but they were agreed that, irrespective of what happened to the level of interest rates, the move towards greater reliance on the market allocative mechanism was in itself desirable.

There was a discussion of the efficiency of the banking system. In particular, several discussants thought that inefficiency was promoted by the fact that only the commercial banks were subject to minimum required reserve ratio control. The taxation of the banks inherent in the requirement to hold certain quantities of low interest bearing public sector assets, quantities greater than they would hold if free to determine their own liquidity structure, placed them at a competitive disadvantage with the financial intermediaries which were exempt from reserve ratio control requirements. This source of inefficiency could be removed either by paying the going market rate of interest on all minimum holdings of required reserve assets, or by an extension of ratio control methods and requirements to other financial institutions. The latter course of action suffered from the disadvantage of applying a form of taxation that was a by-product of the monetary control system rather than a well-designed tax decided upon in terms of general fiscal policy. However, it was pointed out that while the removal of this implicit tax would improve the efficiency of the banking system, it was not necessarily a Pareto Optimal strategy. The removal of the tax on bank asset holdings would increase the interest cost of managing the public sector debt and thus alter the distribution of income. The general tax paying public would be worse off and the commercial banks better off.

There was a debate between the participants from the commercial banks on the desirability and feasibility of reducing the cash and liquidity ratios. They agreed that the current ratio levels no longer reflected the liquidity requirements of the banks and served only to facilitate monetary control. They disagreed, however, on the question of the magnitude of the desired reductions. One discussant thought that the cash ratio was already at its minimum level, but that the liquidity ratio could be substantially reduced. Another discussant thought that both the cash ratio and the liquidity ratio could be reduced, but that the scope for reducing the liquidity ratio was limited by precautionary considerations. The lower cash and liquid asset ratios of the Scottish commercial banks were mentioned as evidence of the possibility of working with much smaller ratios. This was thought to be irrelevant because of the special links that existed between the Scottish commercial banks and the London clearing banks.

At the end of the discussion Mr. Wadsworth restated the main points of his paper. He argued that the message of his paper was that in the next few years adjustments would have to be made in the system of monetary control, and that on the basis of past experience it would be wise to introduce these changes slowly. His own preference was for an extension of ratio control to non-bank financial intermediaries.

VII

ON THE NORMATIVE THEORY OF
BALANCE-OF-PAYMENTS ADJUSTMENT

J. H. WILLIAMSON

Discussion Papers
(*a*) M. H. MILLER
(*b*) P. M. OPPENHEIMER

VII

ON THE NORMATIVE THEORY OF BALANCE-OF-PAYMENTS ADJUSTMENT*

J. H. Williamson
(*H.M. Treasury*)

Introduction

In a well-known paper,[1] Mundell claimed that it was both possible and desirable to reconcile 'internal and external balance' under fixed exchange rates by an appropriate choice of the mix of fiscal and monetary policy. He postulated that demand depends inversely on the restrictiveness of both fiscal policy (which one may conceive as being measured by the high-employment budget surplus, g) and monetary policy (measured by 'the' interest rate, i), so that the locus of points of 'internal balance' in the i/g plane is downward-sloping as shown by IB in Figure 1. The trade balance is constant along IB and greater below it than above it. Since a rise in interest rates would improve the capital account of the balance of payments the overall balance would increase as one moved rightwards along IB, so that the locus of points of 'external balance' (EB) must be steeper than IB. Hence the two curves must intersect at some point (i^*, g^*) where one can simultaneously attain 'internal and external balance'.

This model has sometimes been challenged on the grounds of the supposed non-feasibility of the recommended strategy, most often

* This paper arises from work undertaken while the author was Reader in Economics at the University of York. He was an Economic Consultant to H.M. Treasury at the time when the paper was presented, but views expressed do not necessarily reflect those held in the Treasury. He is indebted to A. B. Atkinson, P. Geary, P. H. Lindert and G. J. Wyatt for helpful comments on a previous draft.
[1] R. A. Mundell, 'The Appropriate Use of Monetary and Fiscal Policy for Internal and External Stability', *IMF Staff Papers*, Mar. 1962.

because of a belief that international capital movements are better described by a stock-adjustment theory than by a flow theory. But, even if long-term capital movements are sufficiently well described by a flow theory to save the model as a positive model of how one could reconcile zero reserve changes with constant unemployment, it deserves no status as normative economics; for there are no circumstances in which it would be desirable to pursue Mundell's strategy.

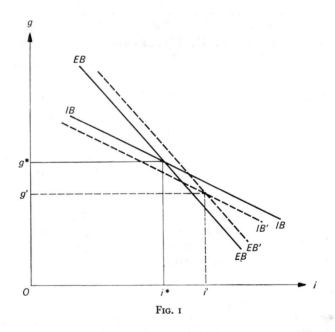

Fig. 1

It is possible to demonstrate this assertion as follows. Consider an alternative initial situation from that shown by the solid lines in Figure 1, which differs only in the country having a slightly higher price level. Because of its lesser competitiveness it will have a less favourable current account at the designated unemployment level; achievement of internal balance will therefore require a more relaxed fiscal-monetary policy mix, as shown by *IB'*. But the worsened current account will require the attraction of a greater capital inflow to maintain external balance, so that *EB* will move rightwards to *EB'*. Fiscal policy will be looser, monetary policy tighter, and international indebtedness greater than in the first situation. It follows that in the next period the interest burden of debt finance will be greater and the investment ratio will be lower, thereby reducing productivity gains and increasing the inflation resulting from the given rate of wage increase. These effects would again push *IB* inwards and *EB* outwards as compared to the trajectory implied by the solid lines. It follows that the trajectories traced out by Mundell's prescription from differing initial conditions necessarily diverge. In contrast, the optimal trajectories that result from maximizing inter-temporal welfare starting from different initial conditions have been found to converge asymptotically in a wide range of problems. Hence, unless this rather striking uniformity has arisen as a coincidence, Mundell's strategy cannot maximize any interesting welfare function; and it therefore cannot be admitted as normative economics.

Professor Johnson[2] has previously recognized that a policy of manipulating the capital account to offset whatever current account surplus or deficit emerges from pursuing full employment with historically-given cost and exchange-rate levels is scarcely likely to lead to an efficient pattern of international investment. What is remarkable is that such a trivial proposition can ever have been doubted; yet a recent book by no less an authority than Scitovsky[3] is based upon the view that the adjustment problem is pre-eminently a matter of inadequate facilities to finance current-account flows rather than of inadequate means to alter them. The first moral that one can draw from the failure of Mundell's model to stand up to rigorous scrutiny is that an efficient adjustment mechanism must include a means of adjusting the current account.

There is a second, and perhaps more fundamental, moral. This concerns the limitations of the Tinbergen–Meade 'theory of economic policy', or targets–instruments analysis, as a basis for normative economic theory.[4] At worst this analysis can be seriously misleading, as shown above. But even at the best it suffers from two important inherent limitations. First, it is unable to indicate appropriate policy in those cases where the targets are mutually

[2] H. G. Johnson, 'Theoretical Problems of the International Monetary System', *Pakistan Development Review*, spring 1967.

[3] T. Scitovsky, *Money and the Balance of Payments* (London: Allen and Unwin, 1969).

[4] For a previous critique of this analysis see J. M. Fleming, 'Targets and Instruments', *IMF Staff Papers*, Nov. 1968.

inconsistent. It is true that it advises one to seek another policy variable that will eliminate the inconsistency, and there have no doubt been occasions (as in indicating the need for incomes policy?) when this advice has been valuable. But policy still requires formulation if this search is unsuccessful, or if (as is perhaps usual) the introduction of a new policy variable also serves to introduce new distortions and thereby to increase the number of targets that must be listed. The second limitation is its adoption of *a priori* targets for variables that are only proximate goals. A payments surplus, or a high growth rate, is a means to an end and in no sense an end in itself; and it is the task of economists to derive means and not, as the targets-instruments approach does, to accept them as data.

Both of these limitations may in principle be overcome by constructing a social welfare function that is a reasonable reflection of the ultimate ends of economic activity and maximizing this subject to the constraints imposed by the positive economy. Value judgements about trade-offs between ultimate objectives are expressed explicitly in the social welfare function, while appropriate values of the proximate objectives are derived as an automatic by-product of inter-temporal optimization analysis. The remainder of this paper is devoted to examining the extent to which such a welfare-maximizing approach is able to yield qualitative theorems regarding the desirable macro-economic management of an open economy.

A Simple Model

It is useful to start by analysing a very simple model, even though this omits several essential aspects of reality. Assume an open economy in which the exchange rate, price level, capital stock and technology are fixed. The trade balance depends negatively on income as in the theory of the foreign trade multiplier; the payments surplus, which is also the rate of accumulation of foreign assets, is the sum of the trade balance and the investment income yielded by the existing stock of foreign assets. The authorities can manipulate fiscal policy to induce any level of income they desire. The problem is to characterize optimal demand-management policy in such an economy.

Since the policy deemed optimal depends on the welfare criterion employed, it is important to select a social welfare function that will prove widely acceptable. In the present context it is difficult to envisage objections to

$$\int_0^\infty W(C)\,e^{-\delta t}\,dt \tag{1}$$

where $\delta > 0$ is the pure rate of social time preference and $W(C)$ has the customary properties of a utility function. Maximizing (1) subject to the constraints listed above is essentially similar to the problem originally studied by Ramsey,[5] since in both cases future consumption is increased by present accumulation but accumulation requires a restriction of current consumption; the only difference is that the trade-off between consumption and accumulation is due to technological constraints on output in the Ramsey model and to the additional imports generated by a rise in consumption in the present context. The solution is therefore similar to that derived by Cass in his analysis of the Ramsey problem with positive discounting,[6] provided that the marginal rate of return on foreign assets straddles the rate of time preference and is non-increasing. That is, there exists a steady-state stock of foreign assets where the marginal rate of return on foreign assets is equal to the rate of time preference (the 'Modified Golden Rule'), and this position is approached asymptotically. The asymptotic stock of foreign assets, and level of consumption, depend positively on the yield of foreign assets and negatively on the rate of time preference.

It is also possible to develop comparative-dynamics theorems concerning the determinants of the speed of adjustment towards steady state. Simple as the present model is, a full treatment of this subject would be quite a major undertaking. Nevertheless, it may be of interest to indicate the results that have been established, and the proof of one of the more surprising results is presented in the Appendix.[7] Assume that the initial stock of foreign assets is below the steady-state level.

1. A reduction in the initial stock of foreign assets would not change the steady-state solution, while it would reduce consumption and increase the payments surplus at time zero.

[5] F. P. Ramsey, 'A Mathematical Theory of Saving', *Economic Journal*, Dec. 1928.

[6] D. Cass, 'Optimal Growth in an Aggregate Model of Capital Accumulation', *Review of Economic Studies*, July 1965.

[7] pp. 250–6 ff. below.

2. An increase in the rate of time preference would decrease the steady-state levels of foreign assets and consumption, while at time zero (or indeed for any time at which the stock of foreign assets is the same) it would increase consumption and reduce the payments surplus.

3. A uniform increase in the return on foreign assets would increase the steady-state levels of foreign assets and consumption, while at time zero (or for similar stocks of foreign assets) the payments surplus would be larger. Consumption would be smaller if the stock of foreign assets were zero or negative, but the effect is ambiguous for a positive stock.

4. An increase in the marginal propensity to import would not change the steady-state stock of foreign assets but it would reduce steady-state consumption; at time zero it would reduce the payments surplus but have an ambiguous effect on consumption.

5. A change in the import propensity which increased the marginal propensity but left the average propensity unchanged at the previous steady-state would reduce the payments surplus and increase consumption at time zero. (See Appendix for proof.)

6. An increase in exports would reduce the payments surplus and increase consumption at time zero.

It is to some extent possible to give an intuitive interpretation to these results, by observing that the optimal speed of adjustment depends positively on the benefits of being close to steady-state and negatively on the costliness of adjusting towards it. But where (as with an increase in the marginal but not the average import propensity) a change increases these benefits and costs simultaneously, it is necessary to resort to a more formal analysis in order to establish a definite result. Some of the results are in fact quite striking, since they recommend that a change which tends to improve the payments position should be overcompensated so as to worsen the actual outcome. One would, of course, expect this result to be fundamentally modified if uncertainty were introduced into the analysis.

Optimal Adjustment with Fixed Exchange Rates

But the problem of adjustment is not in reality a simple parallel to the theory of optimal capital accumulation in a closed economy, for the preceding model omits no less than five elements of essential importance. First, there is the fact that the current account depends on competitiveness as well as income and the state of international

indebtedness. This means that, in a world where inflation is determined by a Phillips-curve mechanism, income deflation can produce
long-run benefits to the current account through lowering relative
international prices, as well as through accumulating additional
interest-yielding foreign assets. Second, a plausible specification
of social objectives would seem to require the inclusion of inflation
as an argument in the social welfare function, since the public
pronouncements of those responsible for guiding economic policy
indicate that they dislike changes in the price level for their own
sake quite independently of any implications they may have for
the balance of payments. The instantaneous utility function is
therefore postulated as:

$$W(C, \dot{P}/P) \qquad \text{where } W_1 > 0, \ W_{11} < 0,$$
$$W_2 \gtreqless 0 \text{ as } \dot{P}/P \lesseqgtr 0, \ W_{22} \leqq 0.$$

Third, capital accumulation can take a variety of forms. In particular, one might wish to distinguish domestic capital, long-term
foreign assets, short-term private foreign assets, and reserves.
Fourth, the rest of the world can more realistically be considered
as enjoying steady-state growth and inflation than as being in the
stationary state. Fifth, relative international prices influence real
income through the terms of trade.

It is no doubt self-evident that a model incorporating all of these
factors would be formidably complex. The primary difficulty is
that the model must include at least two state variables (the price
level and the stock of reserves or short-term foreign assets), and
preferably one or two others as well (other forms of capital). This
means that the customary solution by phase diagram, which would
require a minimum of four dimensions, is excluded and so a complete analytical solution is not possible. One must therefore be
content with more limited results, most of which concern asymptotic
solutions.

The asymptotic rate of inflation must be such as to maintain an
unchanging payments position over time. If steady-state is possible,
and with an exogenous natural rate of growth, this internationally-
consistent rate of inflation will be that which satisfies equation (5a)
on page 106 of H. G. Johnson's *International Trade and Economic
Growth*.[8] If this asymptotic rate of inflation differs from the internally-optimal rate of inflation—i.e. the rate that results when demand

[8] London: Allen and Unwin, 1958.

is held at a point where the marginal utility of the additional output is equal to the marginal disutility of the additional inflation—the maintenance of fixed exchange rates imposes welfare costs even in the long run. These costs are of two types. The first and obvious cost is that the country is constrained from achieving the combination of absorption and inflation that it would prefer with its existing capital stock. The second, and surprising, cost is that it transpires that the country indulges in sub-optimal accumulation of domestic capital (relative to the level that the Modified Golden Rule indicates as desirable in a closed economy) in the case where its tastes for inflation are internationally excessive. The moral to be drawn is that, at least in the absence of adaptive expectations of the kind postulated by Phelps,[9] it is important to economic efficiency in a world of fixed exchange rates to ensure that the international authorities agree on a representative, positive price trend as a collective policy target.[10]

Consideration of the terms of trade reinforces this argument. Consider a country whose internally-optimal and internationally-consistent rates of inflation are the same. If the authorities ignored the feedback from domestic income to the terms of trade, they would accumulate capital until the net marginal product was equal to the rate of social time preference. But if they recognized this feedback, they would again curb domestic capital formation since lower domestic output would yield a terms-of-trade gain. But this gain is only a national gain and implies an equal loss in welfare for other countries, so that the net effect on world welfare is negative. Alignment of national and world welfare therefore requires an internationally-consistent rate of inflation in excess of the internally-optimal rate. A search for absolute price stability could therefore be doubly damaging to world welfare.

These conclusions require important modifications if inflation is in fact subject to an adaptive-expectations mechanism. In that event, the country is precluded from exercising any choice over its steady-state rate of unemployment, which must settle down at the 'natural' level. On the other hand, the theorem regarding sub-optimal capital accumulation merely requires reinterpretation; it

---

[9] E. S. Phelps, 'Phillips Curves, Expectations of Inflation, and Optimal Unemployment over Time', *Economica*, Aug. 1967.

[10] This has been previously argued by Tobin in W. Fellner, F. Machlup, and R. Triffin (eds.), *Maintaining and Restoring Balance in International Payments* (Princeton, N.J.: Princeton University Press, 1966), Ch. 16.

remains true that constraining the domestic rate of inflation to that of the world at large will curtail the domestic capital stock if the world rate of inflation is less than the country would choose to settle down at in a closed economy.

A Digression on Definitions

The preceding discussion has been couched in terms which interpret 'the adjustment process' as one whereby the authorities return the economy to its asymptotically-optimal trajectory from initial conditions off that trajectory. But this is clearly too general, for one would scarcely wish to assert that a country was suffering from a payments problem if non-steady-state was solely attributable to an inadequate capital stock. That would be to make the problem of payments adjustment definitionally synonymous with that of economic development! It may be that the two are not separable; that is an empirical question that rests upon whether all the trajectories from different initial conditions with the same wealth endowment converge on a common path much more quickly tha the paths from different wealth endowments converge. If they do then one can treat adjustment as an independent problem and define it as the problem of returning the economy to the common path that is asymptotically optimal for the particular wealth endowment.[11]

But there are two reasons that could prevent one drawing this convenient distinction. The first would arise if the time taken for convergence were much the same whatever the cause for a divergence in initial conditions. Commonsense suggests that this is not an important possibility; payments problems are not of the same order of intractability as underdevelopment or slow growth. The second reason stems from the possibility that there may not be a common path that is independent of the adjustment mechanisms available to the authorities. For example, the asymptotically-optimal demand pressure may depend on the availability of exchange-rate policy. There is nothing one can do about this ambiguity other than to recognize its existence.

[11] The assumption that this would necessarily be the case lay behind the author's distinction between 'basic adjustments', conceived as those which accomplished this return, and 'quasi-adjustments', which merely eliminate a payments imbalance at the cost of an indefinite departure from the optimal trajectory. See J. H. Williamson, 'The Crawling Peg', *Princeton Essays in International Finance*, 1965, p. 10.

Further Remarks on Fixed Exchange Rates

The asymptotic path towards which adjustment takes place depends upon the traditional factors of productivity and thrift in the traditional directions; for example, a rise in the marginal social return on foreign investment, or a fall in the domestic rate of time preference, will increase the optimal current-account surplus. But it will depend on *nothing but* thrift and productivity *only* under rather special conditions, e.g. when the feedback via the terms of trade is unrecognized and the internally-optimal rate of inflation is equal to the internationally-consistent rate. In other circumstances 'monetary' factors will influence optimal real accumulation, even in the long run.

Consider the case of a country whose values and tastes satisfy the special conditions stated above. Suppose that it has an initial position with excessive prices and deficient reserves, so that it has an adjustment problem that requires an improvement in competitiveness and reserve rebuilding. These aims require a deflation of income below the internally-optimal level; this produces both an income effect that conserves reserves and a gradual improvement in competitiveness that will aid subsequent reserve replenishment. Indeed, in order to aid this reserve accumulation it is optimal for the price level to overshoot its asymptotic level, and to go through a subsequent phase of inflation. Likewise, reserves will oscillate around their optimal level, lagging behind the price level. This is qualitatively the same behaviour as that implied by the gold-standard adjustment mechanism, where reserve changes induce proportionate changes in the money supply which in turn induce income changes and thence price changes. Hence one might speculate on the possible existence of an inverse-optimum theorem which would assert that, for a suitable choice of the monetary multiplier, the gold-standard adjustment mechanism would maximize a welfare function of the form postulated previously. Even if such a theorem can be established, however, it will be of rather limited significance, since reserves serve the function of enabling a country to avoid adjusting to transitory disturbances as well as to optimize the rate of adjustment to underlying changes. Rigid adherence to the gold-standard 'rules of the game' prevents reserves fulfilling the former function.

No rigorous results have been established concerning the optimal speed of adjustment. However, it seems intuitively clear that (for a deficit country) the optimal payments surplus will be larger:

(a) the lower the rate of time preference;
(b) the greater the marginal rate of return on the foreign assets that can be acquired with the present current surplus;
(c) the greater are the costs of reserve depletion or of such substitutes as reserve borrowing;
(d) the less the country resents large departures from the internally-optimal level of demand.

The Exchange Rate Question

One of the principal theorems yielded by the targets–instruments approach is Meade's proof that a country's internal and external objectives can be reconciled by supplementing demand-management policy with an active exchange-rate policy.[12] It is natural to ask what becomes of this result using the welfare-maximizing approach. The type of exchange-rate flexibility being analysed is managed floating, in which the exchange rate is a policy variable.

It is obvious that the result cannot be accepted as it stands, since the concept of aiming to achieve a limited number of arbitrary targets is alien to the approach. Instead, one needs to compare the level of welfare that is achievable under flexible exchange rates with the level under the optimal policy subject to the constraint of a fixed exchange rate. Since the authorities can always choose not to exercise their freedom to vary the exchange rate, it follows immediately that welfare cannot be reduced, and will in general be increased, by giving the authorities the power to vary the exchange rate; subject to the proviso that conditions in the rest of the world are unchanged. And the equations describing the optimal flexible-rate trajectory do not in general coincide with those describing the optimal fixed-rate trajectory, so that this is a freedom that the authorities of an individual country could advantageously exercise except under special circumstances. Meade's theorem is, therefore, valid; but it is still interesting to establish the special circumstances under which an active use of the exchange rate would not be advantageous.

In discussing this question it is again helpful to consider separately the asymptotic solution and the process of adjusting towards it.

[12] J. E. Meade, *The Balance of Payments* (London: Oxford University Press, 1951).

In the absence of adaptive expectations, a set of jointly-sufficient conditions for an unchanging exchange rate are:

(a) that the country does not exercise a perceptible influence on its terms of trade (or fails to recognize the effect of the terms of trade on welfare);
(b) that the internally-optimal rate of inflation be equal to the internationally-consistent rate of inflation;
(c) that the rate of time preference be zero.

If the first of these conditions fails to hold, the country can benefit by restricting output somewhat and exploiting the (greater) gain in real income resulting from the improved terms of trade consistent with the same trade balance. The lower output will result in less inflation and will require a continuous appreciation of the exchange rate. This result provides an example of the proviso noted above. The gain in national welfare is achieved at the expense of a greater loss in foreign welfare, since the improved terms of trade impose an equal loss on foreign countries while there is no gain in the rest of the world to offset the loss in domestic output. Hence if all countries pursue nationally-optimal policies it is possible that they will all lose, just as the general imposition of nationally-optimal tariffs can result in a general reduction in welfare. Fixed exchange rates have the virtue of preventing such a self-defeating scramble for terms-of trade gains. If condition (b) fails to hold, then the country will seek to avoid importing inflation (if its internally-optimal rate of inflation is the lower) by appreciation, or (in the converse case) to avoid undesired deflation by depreciation. Where the third condition fails to hold, the country will never be prepared to make the current sacrifices needed to establish the 'ideal' position, and will again end up with appreciation and lower output. It would be possible for the exchange rate to be unchanging in steady state even if these conditions did not all hold together; but only if the incentive to depreciate provided by an 'inadequate' foreign rate of inflation were exactly offset by the terms-of-trade effect and/or positive time preference.

The conditions for an asymptotically-constant exchange rate are significantly different in the presence of adaptive expectations. The terms-of-trade effect becomes irrelevant, because the asymptotic pressure of demand is not a subject of choice. Jointly-sufficient conditions are that there be zero inflation in the rest of the world and that the rate of time preference be zero. Positive inflation in the rest of the world will lead the country to undertake an offsetting appreciation. Positive time preference (with zero inflation abroad) will result in depreciation, since the country will not be willing to make the sacrifice necessary to wipe out expectations of inflation. (This is in striking contrast to the result with non-adaptive expectations.) There will be combinations of positive foreign inflation and positive time preference where these factors will offset one another and lead to an asymptotically-constant exchange rate. But the most significant point is, perhaps, that the presence of adaptive expectations does not in itself mean that a country is unable to gain long-run benefits by exercising the degree of insulation from the rest of the world that can be provided by the exchange rate. The lack of choice over the pressure of demand means that the value of this freedom is reduced; but it is not necessarily eliminated.

In general, therefore, asymptotic welfare can be raised by the utilization of exchange-rate flexibility. The important exception concerns a country with zero time preference and tastes for inflation that are typical of the international community. Even a country which satisfies these conditions can in general reduce the costs of adjusting toward steady-state by an appropriate employment of exchange-rate variations. There is one particular case where this is particularly clear: a country whose optimum position is disturbed by some change that alters its competitiveness but nothing else. Unless the country dislikes sudden price changes more than the same amount of inflation or disinflation spread over a longer period (which is formalized in the model by setting $W_{22} < 0$), the optimal strategy involves a step change in the exchange rate sufficiently large to restore competitiveness immediately.

It was stated previously that the presence of adaptive expectations tended to reduce the value of exchange-rate flexibility in raising asymptotic welfare. Although it has not been established by the mathematics in the Appendix, one may conjecture that the same is not true of the adjustment process. Particularly for a country with a small foreign-trade sector, the welfare cost of altering competitiveness by manipulating the internal price level would be magnified by the need to alter price expectations and subsequently to reverse the initial change. For a more integrated economy, on the other hand, the process of altering the exchange rate could itself create expectations of further price changes that might be more costly to eradicate than reliance on manipulating the pressure of demand.

Even though exchange-rate flexibility is helpful in the management of an individual economy, Meade's theorem does not in itself imply anything about the desirable exchange-rate regime. Other issues are involved here, including the possibility that active exchange-rate policies will impose external costs on other countries; the effects of different regimes on uncertainty, transactions costs and speculation; the degree of built-in stabilization provided; and the discipline question that arises if governments are better characterized as myopic profiteers than as the omniscient guardians of the social interest whose actions are prescribed in the present paper.

The Capital Account

Since this paper opened by a criticism of one of the prescriptions regarding the role of the capital account in the adjustment process, it is appropriate to close by sketching the conclusions that emerge when this subject is analysed in the welfare-maximizing framework.

Although manipulation of the capital account cannot provide a permanent solution to a balance of payments problem, the analysis should not be construed as implying that there is no useful role for policies to manipulate capital flows. The analysis shows that the availability of these policies does not alter the desirable steady-state solution, but it can also show that they have a valuable potential role as quasi-adjustments during the transition to steady-state. A country that has a liquidity problem, or that wishes to finance a current-account deficit because of the costs of eliminating that deficit rapidly, may well wish to induce a temporary capital inflow. The desire for such an inflow is likely to be mitigated, but not disposed of, by exchange-rate flexibility: even with a flexible exchange rate, there could be a need for capital inflows immediately after a depreciation in order to finance the temporary current-account deficit produced by the 'J-curve'. (If the country has a dislike for sharp price changes it might also prefer to spread out the depreciation over a longer period.)

Interest rate policy is one method that could be employed to induce a desired inflow, but the extent to which its use is desirable depends on how much distortion it causes to the consumption-investment mix compared to the distortions to capital flows involved in imposing direct controls. Reserve borrowing may facilitate a worthwhile relaxation of the policies that would be needed to obtain the desired improvement in the capital account through the private sector.

It transpires that the nature of the optimal policy is importantly influenced by the factual question as to whether a stock theory or a flow theory provides the better description of international capital movements. If a stock theory is best, it follows that there is no gain in accepting current distortions in the aid of building up reserves to a level above that which is currently necessary, even if the present situation seems to carry the threat of a future crisis, since the necessary inflow can be engineered if and when the future crisis materializes. But, in contrast, if a flow theory of capital movements is the correct one, this conclusion needs to be reversed; any threat of a future liquidity crisis should lead one to tighten up on capital outflows with a view to conserving reserves to meet the threat. This is still a far cry from a policy of always seeking to prevent reserve changes through manipulating interest rates.

Conclusion

The aim of this paper has been to provide the framework for the systematic analysis of what is desirable in the way of macro-economic policy. Not surprisingly, the use of such a framework does not yield any revolutionary conclusions that had eluded previous thinkers. Its results are more modest, but one may hope nonetheless valuable:

(a) One may hope that an increase in the rigour with which normative problems are approached will avoid future confusion of the possible and the desirable. Surprising as it may seem, some of the leading writers in international monetary economics are still on occasion guilty of such errors.

(b) The approach permits a critical assessment of the existing literature on nationally-desirable adjustment policies.[13] In essence the accepted analysis comprises three theorems. The first states that demand should be reduced (increased) if it is currently greater (lower) than required in the interests of both domestic and external objectives. This result is so trivial that it has not been discussed in this paper. The second is Meade's theorem on the value of exchange-rate policy in reconciling domestic and external objectives. This theorem is valid. The third is Mundell's proposal to vary the fiscal-monetary mix to prevent reserve changes without depressing or inflating demand. This theorem is false.

[13] As expressed in Fellner, Machlup, and Triffin, op. cit., or OECD, *The Balance of Payments Adjustment Process* (Paris, 1966).

17

(c) The analysis has yielded certain new qualitative theorems. For example, it was proved that in a very simple model the optimal level of consumption was greater with a larger marginal propensity to import (assuming that the average propensity in steady state remains unchanged); it was shown that there were possible monetary conditions which would lead to the optimal policy producing sub-optimal capital accumulation in comparison with the level that would be desirable in the absence of monetary complications; and the conditions under which a non-use of exchange-rate flexibility would be optimal were shown to be more restrictive than intuition might have suggested.

(d) The analysis has illuminated the critical role that certain factual questions play in determining the character of desirable policies. The two outstanding examples concern the presence or absence of adaptive expectations under a system of flexible exchange rates, and whether the capital account is best explained by a stock theory or a flow theory.

(e) The technical approach developed in the paper has emphasized the analytical value of breaking the problem down into asymptotic and transitory components. The 'adjustment problem' has been interpreted as essentially concerning the latter, although a sharp distinction is not necessarily possible.

MATHEMATICAL APPENDIX

The purpose of this Appendix is to provide a sketch of the proofs of the propositions discussed in the text. The analysis is somewhat condensed, and familiarity with the Maximum Principle of Pontryagin is assumed.

Notation

C = Consumption
F = Foreign assets (net)
$f(U)$ = Phillips curve
H = Hamiltonian
I = Investment
K = Capital stock
M = Imports
P = Price level
R = Foreign interest income
T = Trade balance (in foreign exchange terms)
U = Unemployment
W = Welfare

X = Exports
x = Exchange rate
Y = Output
z = Expected rate of inflation
α = Import content of output
$\beta = \gamma/(1 + \gamma)$
γ = Marginal propensity to import
δ = Rate of time preference
ψ_i = Shadow price of ith constraint
π = Competitiveness
μ = Rate of depreciation
ρ = Foreign rate of inflation
λ = Rate of adjustment of expectations

I. *The Simple Model*

Welfare function:

$$\int_0^\infty W(C)\,e^{-\delta t}\,dt, \qquad W_1 > 0,\ W_{11} < 0.$$

Control variable: C.
Income determination:

$$Y = C + T$$
$$M = \gamma Y$$
$$T = X - M = X/(1 + \gamma) - \beta C.$$

Balance of payments:

$$\dot{F} = R(F) + T, \qquad R_1 > 0,\ R_{11} < 0. \tag{1}$$

Hamiltonian:

$$H e^{\delta t} = W(C) + \psi[R(F) + X/(1 + \gamma) - \beta C]$$

Optimum conditions: (1), appropriate transversality conditions, and:

$$\frac{\partial H}{\partial C} = W_1 - \psi\beta = 0, \tag{2}$$

$$\dot{\psi} = (\delta - R_1)\,\psi. \tag{3}$$

The asymptotic solution: requires $\dot{\psi} = \dot{F} = 0$. (3) and $\dot{\psi} = 0$ imply that F is accumulated to the point where the marginal rate of return is equal to the rate of time preference. Define this as F^*. Then (1) implies that in steady state $T = -R(F^*)$.

Adjustment: The phase diagram implied by (1) to (3) is Figure 2. The asymptotic solution is, as usual, a saddlepoint that is approached monotonically. The size of payments surplus varies inversely with F on the optimal trajectory.

Comparative dynamics: Redefining (1) around steady state gives:

$$\dot{F} = R(F) + T^* - \beta(C - C^*). \tag{4}$$

A change in the import propensity that increases the marginal propensity but leaves the average unchanged in steady state is represented by an increase in β.

From (2): $\quad W_{11}\dfrac{\partial C}{\partial \beta} = \psi + \beta\dfrac{\partial \psi}{\partial \beta}.$

From (4): $\quad \dfrac{\partial}{\partial \beta}\left(\dfrac{\partial F}{\partial t}\right) = R_1\dfrac{\partial F}{\partial \beta} - \beta\dfrac{\partial C}{\partial \beta} - (C - C^*)$ (5)

so $\quad \dfrac{\partial}{\partial t}\left(\dfrac{\partial F}{\partial \beta}\right) = R_1\dfrac{\partial F}{\partial \beta} - \dfrac{\beta}{W_{11}}\left[\psi + \beta\dfrac{\partial \psi}{\partial \beta}\right] - (C - C^*).$

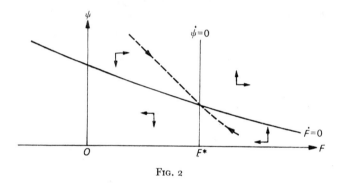

FIG. 2

Construct a phase diagram of the deviations of ψ and F caused by the change in β (see Figure 3). From (5), the equation of $(\partial \dot{F}/\partial \beta) = 0$ has a negative slope. It cuts the S.W. quadrant for $F < F^*$ and therefore $C < C^*$.

From (3): $\quad \dfrac{\partial}{\partial \beta}\left(\dfrac{\partial \psi}{\partial t}\right) = (\delta - R_1)\dfrac{\partial \psi}{\partial \beta} - \psi R_{11}\dfrac{\partial F}{\partial \beta} = \dfrac{\partial}{\partial t}\left(\dfrac{\partial \psi}{\partial \beta}\right).$

Clearly $(\partial \dot{\psi}/\partial \beta) = 0$ intercepts the origin and has a positive slope. Since $(\delta - R_1) \to 0$ as $F \to F^*$, the curve $(\partial \dot{\psi}/\partial \beta) = 0$ rotates anticlockwise through the origin through time, and coincides with the vertical axis in steady state. Clearly $\partial F/\partial \beta = 0$ both at time zero and in steady state. During the transitional period, however, one must have $\partial F/\partial \beta < 0$, since any attainable point to the right of the vertical axis gives $(\partial F/\partial \beta) > 0$ for all subsequent t. Hence the payments surplus is smaller at time zero; it is also smaller at any point during the adjustment process than it would have been for the same size of capital stock.

To see that consumption is increased at time zero, note that from (5):

$$\beta \frac{\partial C}{\partial \beta} = R_1 \frac{\partial F}{\partial \beta} - (C - C^*) - \frac{\partial}{\partial t}\left(\frac{\partial F}{\partial \beta}\right).$$

The first term is necessarily zero at time zero, the second is positive for $F < F^*$ and the third is positive in view of the fact that the optimum trajectory in $(\partial\psi/\partial\beta, \partial F/\partial\beta)$-space leaves the vertical axis to the left.

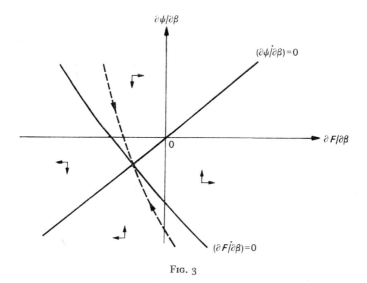

FIG. 3

II. *The General Model*

Welfare function:

$$\int_0^\infty W(C, \dot{P}/P)\,e^{-\delta t}\,dt, \qquad W_1 > 0,\ W_{11} < 0,$$

$$W_2 \gtreqqless 0 \text{ as } \dot{P}/P \gtreqqless 0.$$

Control variables: $C, I, \dot{x}/x$. (Note that it is only legitimate to treat both C and I as controls so long as the authorities in fact have adequate degrees of freedom to vary them independently. It is implicitly assumed here that the fiscal-monetary mix provides the necessary flexibility. The last stage of any problem of the sort being considered here is to select the values for fiscal and monetary policy needed to attain the desired levels of consumption and investment. This step, which may be considered as the 'Tinbergen-Meade stage of the problem', is not discussed further.)

Income determination: $Y = C + I + g(T,\pi)$ where $g(T,\pi)$ represents the output needed to earn a trade balance T defined in foreign-exchange terms at terms-of-trade π, so $g_1 > 0$ and $g_2 \geqq 0$.

$$T = T(Y,\pi), \qquad T_1 < 0,\ T_2 > 0.$$
$$U = U(Y,K), \qquad U_1 < 0,\ U_2 > 0.$$

The differential equations:

$$\dot{\pi}/\pi = \rho - \dot{x}/x - \dot{P}/P. \tag{6}$$

$$\dot{P}/P = \alpha(\rho - \dot{x}/x) + (1 - \alpha)\,(f(U) + Z). \tag{7}$$

$$\dot{Z} = \lambda(\dot{P}/P - Z). \tag{8}$$

$$\dot{K} = I - \mu K. \tag{9}$$

$$\dot{F} = R(F) + T. \tag{10}$$

The Hamiltonian:

$$H\mathrm{e}^{\delta t} = W(C,\dot{P}/P) + \psi_1(1 - \alpha)\,(\rho - \dot{x}/x - f(U) - Z) + \psi_2(I - \mu K)$$
$$+ \psi_3(R(F) + T) + \psi_4\lambda(\dot{P}/P - Z).$$

The optimum conditions:

$$\left.\begin{array}{l} \dfrac{\partial H}{\partial C} \\[2mm] \dfrac{\partial H}{\partial I} \end{array}\right\} \text{imply} \left\{\begin{array}{l} W_1 = \psi_2. \\[2mm] W_1(1 - g_1\,T_1) + \psi_3\,T_1 \\ \qquad + (W_2 - \psi_1\pi + \psi_4\lambda)\,(1 - \alpha)\,f'\,U_1 = 0. \end{array}\right. \tag{11}$$

$$\frac{\partial H}{\partial(\dot{x}/x)} \text{ implies } W_2\,\alpha + \psi_1\,\pi(1 - \alpha) + \psi_4\lambda\alpha = 0. \tag{12}$$

$$\dot{\psi}_1 = \delta\psi_1 + W_1(g_1\,T_2 + g_2) - \psi_3\,T_2 - \psi_1(1 - \alpha)\,(\rho - \dot{x}/x - f(U) - Z) \tag{13}$$

$$\dot{\psi}_2 = (\delta + \mu)\,\psi_2 - (W_2 - \psi_1\pi + \psi_4\lambda)\,(1 - \alpha)\,f'\,U_2 \tag{14}$$

$$\dot{\psi}_3 = (\delta - R_1)\,\psi_3$$

$$\dot{\psi}_4 = (\delta + \lambda)\,\psi_4 - (1 - \alpha)\,(W_2 - \psi_1\pi + \psi_4\lambda). \tag{15}$$

In addition there are (6) to (10) and appropriate transversality conditions.

III. *Solution: Fixed Exchange Rates, Non-Adaptive Expectations*

In this case one has $\dot{x}/x = 0$, $Z = 0$; and (8), (12) and (15) do not hold.

Case A: $\rho = g_2 = 0$. (The latter assumption means that the country does not recognize the implications for real income of changes in its terms of trade.)

$\rho = 0$ and $\dot{\pi} = 0$ imply $\dot{P}/P = 0$ and therefore $W_2 = 0$.

From $\dot{\psi}_1 = 0$ and (13), and noting that the final term drops out in steady state, $\psi_3 - g_1 W_1 \gtreqless 0$ as $\psi_1 \gtreqless 0$.

But in that case (11) is satisfied only for $\psi_1 > 0$, $\psi_3 - g_1 W_1 > 0$.

$\psi_1 > 0$ implies that competitiveness is undesirably low even in steady state.

Substituting $W_2 = 0$ and (11) into (14), and recognizing that $-U_2/U_1$ is the marginal product of capital:

$$(\delta + \mu) \psi_2 = [\psi_2 + (\psi_3 - g_1 W_1) T_1] MPK$$

or

$$\delta + \mu = (1 - \epsilon) MPK < MPK$$

which shows that the steady-state capital stock is less than the 'Modified Golden Rule' level.

Case B. Assume $g_2 = 0$ and $\rho = \tilde{\rho} =$ the 'internally-optimal rate of inflation', which is characterized by the condition that

$$W_1 + W_2(1 - \alpha) f' U_1 = 0.$$

Then (11) and (13) are consistent if and only if $\psi_1 = 0$ and $\psi_3 = g_1 W_1$. Hence competitiveness and capital accumulation are both optimal.

Case C. Assume $\rho = \tilde{\rho}$ and $g_2 > 0$. The additional positive term in (13) now implies that (11) and (13) are consistent if and only if $\psi_1 < 0$ and $\psi_3 > g_1 W_1$. The latter implies that capital is below the MGR, as in Case A.

IV. *Asymptotic Solution: Fixed Exchange Rates, Adaptive Expectations*

One still has $\dot{x}/x = 0$ and (15) does not hold.

$\dot{Z} = 0$ implies $f(U) = 0$ and $Z = \rho$, so there is no scope for choosing the pressure of demand or rate of inflation.

In a closed economy, the asymptotically-optimal rate of inflation and asymptotic demand pressure are characterized by:

$$W_1 + (W_2 + \psi_4 \lambda)(1 - \alpha) f' U_1 = 0. \tag{16}$$

If ρ is such that (16) holds and $g_2 = 0$, then (11) and (13) together with $\psi_1 = \dot{\pi} = 0$ are satisfied only for $\psi_1 = 0$ and $\psi_3 = g_1 W_1$, which imply absence of undercompetitiveness or sub-optimal capital accumulation.

But if g_2 is positive or if the left hand side of (16) is positive when inflation is equal to ρ (i.e. the country has more inflationary tastes than its partners), one will again have $\psi_1 > 0$ and $\psi_3 > g_1 W_1$. The latter again implies sub-optimal capital accumulation.

V. *Asymptotic Solution: Flexible Exchange Rates, Non-Adaptive Expectations*

Z and ψ_4 are necessarily zero and (8) and (15) do not hold.

But (12) does hold. This is the additional optimality condition permitted by flexible exchange rates. Welfare will always be increased by varying the exchange rate except when this condition happens to be satisfied with the exchange rate constant.

After substituting (12), (11) simplifies to:

$$W_1(1 - g_1 T_1) + \psi_3 T_1 + W_2 f' U_1 = 0. \tag{17}$$

Consider the case where $g_2 = \delta = 0$.[1] When $\dot{\psi}_1 = \dot{\pi} = 0$, (13) implies that $\psi_3 = g_1 W_1$. Substituting in (17) gives $W_1 + W_2 f' U_1 = 0$, which is the condition for $f(U) = \bar{\rho}$, the internally-optimal rate of inflation.[2] So if $\rho = \bar{\rho}$, $\dot{\pi}/\pi = (1 - \alpha)(\rho - \dot{x}/x - f(U)) = 0$ implies $\dot{x}/x = 0$.

Conversely, the asymptotic optimum will involve appreciation:

(a) When ρ exceeds $\bar{\rho}$. Note that if $W_{22} = 0$, unemployment will remain at the internally-optimal level $\hat{U}$ and $\dot{x}/x = \rho - f(\hat{U})$. (In the converse case of $\rho < f(\hat{U})$, the optimal policy involves depreciation.)

(b) When $g_2 > 0$. Then (13) implies $\psi_3 > g_1 W_1$, so (17) implies $U > \hat{U}$; and hence if $\rho = \bar{\rho}$, $\dot{\pi}/\pi = 0$ implies $\dot{x}/x > 0$.

(c) When $\delta > 0$. Simultaneous satisfaction of (11), (12) and (17) is possible only for $\psi_1 > 0$, $W_2 < 0$, and $\psi_3 > g_1 W_1$. With $\rho = \bar{\rho}$ the latter implies $U > \hat{U}$ by (17), and hence $\dot{x}/x > 0$ again.

VI. *Flexible Exchange Rates, Adaptive Expectations*

Since $f(U) = 0$ to satisfy (8), $\dot{x}/x = \rho - \mathcal{Z}$.

Jointly sufficient conditions for asymptotic non-use of exchange-rate policy are $\rho = \delta = 0$. This is shown by substituting (12) into (15) and noting that $\dot{\psi}_4 = 0$ implies $W_2 = 0$ which implies $\dot{P}/P = 0$ and so $\dot{x}/x = 0$. Although $g_2 = 0$ is not necessary for non-variation of the exchange rate, it is necessary to avoid sub-optimal capital accumulation; since otherwise (13) does not imply $\psi_3 = g_1 W_1$, which is necessary for (14) to yield the Golden Rule.

Case A. $\rho > 0$, $\delta = 0$. Since $(1 - \alpha)(W_2 - \psi_1 \pi + \psi_4 \lambda) = W_2 + \psi_4 \lambda$ from (12), (15) implies $W_2 = 0$ and so $\dot{P}/P = 0$. Since $f(U) = 0$ one must have $\mathcal{Z} = 0$ and so $\dot{x}/x = \rho - \mathcal{Z} = \rho > 0$.

Case B. $\rho = 0$, $\delta > 0$, $g_2 = 0$. Then (11) to (13) yield a contradiction unless $\psi_1 > 0$; hence $(W_2 + \psi_4 \lambda) < 0$ by (12), and so $W_2 < 0$ by (15). This implies $\dot{P}/P > 0$ and so $\dot{x}/x = \rho - \dot{P}/P < 0$.

---

[1] Strictly speaking the condition $\delta = 0$ implies that $\int W$ does not converge, so that a rigorous treatment would require reformulation in terms of a limit.

[2] Under fixed rates the condition for the internally-optimal rate of inflation is $W_1 + W_2(1 - \alpha) f' U_1 = 0$. The difference arises because with flexible rates an increase in domestic wage inflation produces an additional feedback to the price level through the induced depreciation.

Discussion Papers

(a) MARCUS H. MILLER
(London School of Economics)

THE first element in Professor Williamson's criticism of accepted balance of payments theory, is the latter's focus on the *overall* balance (i.e. on current and capital accounts) as the target of government policy. Implicitly in the work of Mundell's which is cited,[1] and explicitly in his book on *International Economics*, the balance of payments is defined as 'the difference between the values of the goods plus securities sold and bought abroad'.[2] Just as the overall balance of payments measures the change in the (net) international *liquid* asset position of the domestic economy, the current account alone (in the absence of revaluations) measures the change in the (net) international asset position taking all assets into account. And it is Williamson's contention that it cannot be good welfare economics to ignore the current account position *per se*, that is to ignore the development of the foreign net worth of the economy. Mundell is not unaware of this point for he does concede that 'discomfort is provided by a bad *composition of the balance*'. Citing the Canadian experience from 1950 to 1962 as an example, he concludes that 'what is involved here is an additional goal implicit in the system: the level of net external indebtedness. Increasing indebtedness causes discomfort because it introduces present feelings of future insecurity.'[3]

Though Mundell is aware of the point, it is Williamson's contribution to provide the framework for taking this extra goal into account. As is suggested in the last quotation from Mundell, current account deficits and surpluses signify intertemporal shifts in domestic 'absorption'; but this implies that normative results can only be arrived at where intertemporal welfare comparisons are possible. Williamson's second criticism of accepted balance of

[1] See p. 235 n. 1 above.
[2] Robert A. Mundell, *International Economics* (New York: The Macmillan Company, 1968), p. 205.
[3] Ibid., p. 207.

18

payments theory is the postulation of arbitrary 'targets' or goals in circumstances like these; instead he uses the criterion of maximizing the discounted sum of utilities of consumption over time. The formal result is to treat balance of payments problems as applications of capital theory; and this is surely the right approach. It is certainly preferable to derive an optimal strategy from such explicit utility maximization, rather than to extract 'assignment' rules from the stability conditions of arbitrary patterns of adjustment towards chosen targets, as is the case with Mundell. Indeed it is only in so far as Mundell's policy guides can be rationalized by such utility maximization that they can be considered optimal behaviour.

To make the maximization of utility rather than the attainment of targets the kingpin of the normative analysis does not avoid the charge of arbitrariness laid against the choice of targets. For, as Koopmans noted in his survey of Optimal Growth Models,[4] 'the entire shape of the optimal path where it exists depends on the entire shape of the utility function'. Indeed, he goes on to observe that 'pertinent ethical judgments are perhaps more easily called forth by a comparison of optimal growth paths implicit in alternative utility functions than by a direct and aprioristic comparison of these utility functions'. This is especially true when it comes to choosing a discount rate, for low rates of utility discount can lead to the non-existence of an optimal path. The fact remains that even though different utility functions change the desired policy just as different targets do, it is only in the framework suggested by Williamson that the different implications can be adequately drawn out.

While this is not the occasion for any detailed consideration of the theorems derived for the complex general model specified, one question does arise. It is asserted that policies to manipulate capital flows have a 'valuable potential role as quasi-adjustments during the transition to the steady state'; but where in the model are the lags which give rise to the J-shape response of current account to devaluation which needs 'financing', or the speculation that needs countering? How can policies have a role in a model which does not explicitly include the occasion for their use?

Having expressed my agreement with the framework proposed by Williamson, I turn now to points which must arise when applying

[4] Tjalling C. Koopmans, 'Objectives, Constraints and Outcomes in Optimal Growth Models', *Econometrica*, 35(1), Jan. 1967.

this approach to countries like the U.K. which play the role of an international financial intermediary.

The first point is to do with the problem of measuring changes in a country's international net worth. Balance of payments statistics do not include revaluation effects in principle, but nor are data normally collected which would allow one to compute such revaluation effects. The Bank of England has, however, published in its *Quarterly Bulletin* inventories of U.K. external assets and liabilities. The estimates of the end year stock position are available for 1962, 1964 and annually from 1966, a total of six observations to date. These figures do highlight the inappropriateness of taking the balance of payments on current account as a measure of the change in net worth, because the U.K. current account from 1962 to 1969 showed a cumulative *deficit* of £0·5 billion, signifying a run down in foreign net worth, while the inventory position shows an *improvement* of £1·2 billion. The difference of £1·7 billion is largely accounted for by the boom in world stock markets in the early part of the period, and the devaluation of sterling in 1967 which secured a capital gain of at least £0·5 billion. Care must clearly be taken to use the correct measures for the concepts of the theory. A second point is that countries do not just invest their foreign net worth in external assets, but the sum of net worth and of borrowing. For the U.K. at the end of 1969 the magnitudes were £2·7 billion of net worth and £28·4 billion of liabilities. For a country like the U.K. it is not merely the foreign net worth position but the *level* of financial intermediation which must be determined optimally.

A closely related point is that the *structure* of both borrowing and lending have likewise to be chosen to maximize welfare. This requires the application of the theory of portfolio selection, complicated by the fact that world capital markets are far from perfect. Since international asset portfolios are highly diversified, and since risk is clearly a factor here (e.g. the dangers of expropriation by foreign governments), it may be necessary to make returns stochastic and maximize the sum of discounted expected utility.

While it may be stretching a point to see Williamson's framework as leading inevitably to a portfolio selection approach for the external asset position, it is unquestionable that by stressing the intertemporal aspects of balance of payments disequilibria he has convincingly demonstrated the applicability of capital theory to the problem of balance of payments adjustment.

Discussion Papers

(b) P. M. OPPENHEIMER
(University of Oxford)

JOHN WILLIAMSON's paper represents, so far as I know, the first attempt to apply Ramsey-type theory to balance-of-payments questions. This is a notoriously difficult branch of theory, and Williamson deserves congratulations on his pioneering effort. The following comments will look first at the general nature of his analysis and then at a few particular points which arise in the course of it.

Williamson contrasts his treatment with the targets-and-instruments approach of Tinbergen–Meade and Mundell. In doing so he seems to me a little hard on Mundell in particular. It is perhaps true that Mundell underemphasized the limitations of his analysis and thus caused it to be misunderstood by policymakers.[1] However, it is surely going too far to say that Mundell's theorem 'deserves no status as normative economics' (p. 236 above). Like the Tinbergen–Meade approach in general, it is concerned with necessary rather than sufficient conditions and with a Keynesian short-run policy horizon. Within this framework it says something valid about how monetary and fiscal policy should *not* be used, given that the exchange rate is fixed for the time being (however untenable such fixity may prove in the longer run) and that liquid funds are internationally mobile. Williamson's own remarks in the penultimate section of his paper on the short-run manipulation of capital flows seem to me very much in the spirit of Mundell's analysis.

Of course, there is no denying the incompleteness of the targets-and-instruments approach from the welfare point of view. Static welfare theory teaches that optimum adjustment of the balance of payments will take place on current rather than capital account; and that the correct policy weapon for achieving it is the exchange

---

[1] See p. 235 n. 1 above. I doubt, however, whether anyone misled by Mundell would be able to understand Williamson's refutation of him.

rate (or, if available, the money-wage rate). Restrictions on trade and on capital movements should be imposed if and only if they serve to cure a 'market failure' situation and so improve the allocation of real resources. None of these propositions can be established by the targets-and-instruments approach either in its Tinbergen–Meade version or in the modified 'optimizing' version proposed by Niehans.[2] On the other hand, neither do they require intertemporal analysis of the Ramsey type. So Williamson's criticism of Tinbergen–Meade is rather distinct from his own positive contribution.

This contribution consists primarily in defining the optimum behaviour over time of a country's external surplus on current account. A steady-state optimum is a situation in which the marginal social return on foreign assets is kept equal to the marginal social rate of time preference. Starting from an arbitrary initial position the problem is to steer the economy along an adjustment path which converges (asymptotically) on the steady-state optimum. Balance-of-payments equilibrium in the IMF sense may or may not exist initially. It must, of course, be achieved in steady state if not before; but this is incidental to the main object of accumulating the optimum stock of foreign capital assets. As a secondary point, Williamson aims to integrate real and monetary aspects of the problem by incorporating the impact of inflation both on the asymptotic optimum and on the adjustment path. In other words, along with the trade-off between present and future consumption, he is also concerned with a possible Phillips-curve trade-off between marginal output and price stability.

Impressive as Williamson's analysis is, it has one or two questionable features. First, it treats the domestic capital stock as being determined independently of the external capital stock. This means that the social rate of time preference, being equated in steady state with the marginal social return on foreign assets, may be quite different from the marginal return on domestic assets—an odd result in a normative model, to say the least. Incidentally, I do not see why Williamson thinks it surprising that a country with a fixed exchange rate should indulge in sub-optimal accumulation of domestic capital when 'its tastes for inflation are internationally excessive' (p. 242 above). Since such a country is forced to accept a lower level of real income than it would like, it would be surprising

[2] J. Niehans, 'Monetary and Fiscal Policies in Open Economics under Fixed Exchange Rates: an Optimizing Approach', *Journal of Political Economy*, July/Aug. 1968, Part II.

(Keynesian consumption function!) if capital accumulation remained *un*affected.

Secondly, there are some problems about Williamson's treatment of inflation. Suppose first that there is no adaptive expectations mechanism. The case for including inflation as an argument in the social welfare function must then rest on its income-distribution effects. But in that case income distribution is presumably not being taken care of by lump-sum transfers, so there ought to be an income-distribution term in the social welfare function anyway.

Now suppose that there is an adaptive expectations mechanism. Inflation to which everyone adapts does not affect income distribution, so the previous case for including it in the welfare function disappears. Presumably the reason for including it now is the cost and inconvenience of actually adapting.[3] But, first, it is doubtful whether this cost exists in steady state. And secondly, it presupposes that adaptive expectations do not cause the inflation to explode completely—in other words, that the modified Phillips curve remains some way short of a vertical position. For if inflation is completely explosive it cannot be permitted to take hold; in which case there are no costs of adapting to it and no reason to include it in the social welfare function. Price stability is then a *constraint* rather than a desideratum.[4] If, on the other hand, adaptive expectations are indeed such that inflation is incompletely explosive, then it is not true, as Williamson more than once asserts, that the country is prevented from exercising *any* choice over its steady-state rate of unemployment.

Finally, a word about governmental omniscience and the choice of exchange-rate regime. Williamson has two basic arguments for allowing some flexibility in exchange rates. First, he points out that in a world of fixed exchange rates economic efficiency requires governments to 'agree on a representative positive price trend as a collective policy target' (p. 242 above). As this is difficult to achieve it constitutes a good prima facie case for exchange-rate flexibility. Later on, Williamson puts forward a different argument: 'Since the authorities can always choose not to exercise their freedom to

---

[3] As discussed, for instance, by Sir John Hicks, 'Expected Inflation', *Three Banks Review*, Sept. 1970.

[4] This raises the further point that, in the case of fixed exchange rate, dynamic equilibrium is impossible for the home country if the rest of the world has non-zero inflation. I thus find it difficult to follow the argument in the last paragraph of the section on 'Optimal Adjustment with Fixed Exchange Rates'.

ERRATUM

p. 262, the second full paragraph and the footnotes should read as follows:

Now suppose that there is an adaptive expectations mechanism. Inflation to which everyone adapts has no effect on income distribution, so the previous case for putting it in the objective function does not arise. One possible reason for including it now is the cost and inconvenience of actually adapting.[3] It is doubtful, however, whether there is any such cost in steady state, provided that a competitive rate of interest is paid on all money balances. The problem arises rather when the rate of inflation is changing and/or is imperfectly anticipated. A more convincing reason for disliking inflation in the long run is the difficulty and uncertainty of keeping it down to any particular (equilibrium) rate. There is always the danger that institutional or political factors may cause it to explode and threaten a general breakdown of the country's monetary system. In so far as this is the basic objection, price stability is more in the nature of a *constraint* than of a desideratum. Another minor point in the same context is that adaptive expectations do not necessarily, as Williamson states, prevent the country from exercising *any* choice over its steady-state level of unemployment. They do so only in the special case where the steady-state Phillips curve is vertical.[4]

[3] As discussed by Edmund S. Phelps, 'Phillips Curves, Expectations of Inflation and Optimal Unemployment Over Time', *Economica*, Aug. 1967, especially pp. 271–2; and by Sir John Hicks, 'Expected Inflation', *Three Banks Review*, Sept. 1970.

[4] The original version of this paragraph erroneously asserted that a vertical Phillips curve necessarily implies explosive inflation, whereas in fact it is compatible with any equilibrium rate of inflation that society happens to light on. I am most grateful to John Williamson for the correction.

vary the exchange rate, it follows immediately that welfare cannot be reduced, and will in general be increased, by giving the authorities the power to vary the exchange rate; subject to the proviso that conditions in the rest of the world are unchanged.' (p. 245.) On a purely logical level this argument is less convincing than the first. As advocates of freely floating rates would hasten to point out, the case for flexible exchange rates is not the same thing as the case for governmental discretion in exchange-rate policy. The latter, unlike the former, assumes that governments know how to stabilize the economy by discretionary means. Admittedly, Williamson assumes throughout his paper that the government knows the socially optimal rate of accumulation of foreign assets in the long run; but this is a different kind of knowledge.

SUMMARY OF THE GENERAL DISCUSSION

THE opening topic of the discussion was Professor Williamson's assertion that Mundell's model was misleading, as it led to the recommendation of a strategy which deserved no status as normative economics, and that it should be replaced by a welfare maximizing approach similar to the one presented in his paper. While only one discussant went so far as to suggest that Williamson's model and Mundell's model could not be compared, and that Williamson's model was more of a contribution to growth theory than a contribution to balance of payments' adjustment theory, several discussants argued that the approach was complementary with Mundell's analysis rather than competitive.

Williamson argued that the differences between his own analysis of the short-run manipulation of capital flows and Mundell's model were fundamental. Mundell had implied that current-account adjustment could be dispensed with by manipulating the capital account. This doctrine had had a pernicious influence on policy and almost certainly contributed to the persistence of recent payments imbalances. In addition, Mundell attached a significance to the maintenance of a constant reserve level which was simply inappropriate: the purpose of reserves was to act as an inventory to even out short-run fluctuations and to provide time for the employment of the best available adjustment mechanism. In contrast, his own analysis treated reserves as a constraint and emphasized that it was only worth accepting distortions if that constraint were otherwise liable to be violated.

On the content and form of the model, the first difficulty which was discussed was that of the indeterminancy of the time period involved in the approach to the asymptotic solution of the model. Was the asymptotic solution approached in the long run, and, if so, how long was the long run? It was thought that these questions would require clear answers if the model was to be of use in formulating policy. Williamson did not think that this was a serious drawback. He pointed out that with a relatively high rate of discount the asymptotic solution was approached in a short period of time, 5–10 years, so that the time horizon considered in the model was in the near future and not the distant future.

Another difficulty had to do with the problem of specifying the exact form of social welfare function employed in the model. It was argued that the usefulness of the model depends on the existence of a consensus about the exact form of the function, since in the absence of such a consensus the terminal conditions would be arbitrary and there would be a large number of optimal growth paths.

Amongst the discussants those most closely connected with the formulation and implementation of policy argued that Williamson's model was severely limited by its failure to allow for the class of problems which necessitated 'quasi' balance of payments' adjustment policies. They argued that the authorities were not always in the position of being able to neglect short-term 'bread and butter' problems and pursue policies which were 'desirable' in terms of the long-run solution. However, another group of discussants argued that one of the worthwhile features of the kind of approach under discussion was that it forced attention on to the need to look at the long-run consequences of particular policy strategies and led to the formulation of policies which were designed to achieve the end goals of policy and not subsidiary proximate goals. They argued that in the past the authorities had frequently paid too much attention to short-run 'bread and butter' problems and as a result of this they had made the attainment of the end goals of policy more difficult. They further thought that the approach served a useful purpose in emphasizing the need to analyse and formulate balance of payments' adjustment policy in a framework for the analysis and formulation of macro-policy in general.

Williamson's treatment of inflation was the subject of another part of the discussion. Doubt was cast on the validity of his reason for introducing inflation as an argument in the social welfare function. He referred to the public pronouncements of those responsible for guiding economic policy indicating that they disliked changes in the price level for their own sake. It was argued, however, that the welfare loss association with inflation depends on whether inflation is anticipated or unanticipated. In the former case inflation is not necessarily disruptive. Some discussants also thought that his analysis of inflation was confusing in that it involved use of a Phillips Curve mechanism and an adaptive price expectations mechanism. Several discussants thought that the speed of the adaptive price expectation process was inadequately treated in the analysis.

The final part of the discussion had to do with the role of exchange rate flexibility in the model. The absence in the paper of any analysis of the part played by expectations in the foreign exchange market was thought to detract from the usefulness of Williamson's conclusions. Williamson agreed that the role of exchange rate flexibility in the model needed to be analysed in more detail. However, he did not regard the difficulties of agreeing on a representative price trend as a major argument for flexibility. He believed the important consideration to be Meade's argument concerning the greater efficiency of economic management that is possible with the use of the exchange rate as an additional policy variable. This is an argument for government-controlled flexibility rather than for freely floating exchange rates; the latter was a separate topic that his analysis was unable to illuminate.

The discussion ended on a note of accord. It was generally agreed that the approach presented in the paper was important and provided a basis for future development.

PARTICIPANTS IN THE SHEFFIELD SEMINAR ON 'MONETARY THEORY AND MONETARY POLICY IN THE 1970s'

Organizing Committee
Professor J. C. Gilbert (University of Sheffield): Chairman
Professor G. Clayton (University of Sheffield)
Mr. R. Sedgwick (University of Sheffield): Secretary

Professor M. Gaskin (Aberdeen)
Professor J. R. S. Revell (Bangor)
Mr. C. R. Barrett (Birmingham)
Mr. D. K. Sheppard (Birmingham)
Professor J. M. Fleming (Bristol)
Professor R. Barro (Brown, U.S.A.)
Professor H. Grossman (Brown, U.S.A.)
Professor W. B. Reddaway (Cambridge)
Professor B. Thomas (Cardiff)
Professor M. Friedman (Chicago)
Mrs. M. Friedman
Professor A. G. Hines (Durham)
Mrs. A. V. Crowther (Edinburgh)
Dr. D. Fisher (Essex)
Mr. M. T. Sumner (Essex)
Professor T. Wilson (Glasgow)
Sir Roy Harrod
Professor J. S. G. Wilson (Hull)
Professor L. Fishman (Keele)
Dr. M. J. M. Neumann (Konstanz)
Mr. R. F. G. Alford (L.S.E.)
Mr. B. Griffiths (L.S.E.)
Professor H. G. Johnson (L.S.E./Chicago)
Mr. M. H. Miller (L.S.E.)
Professor L. S. Pressnell (L.S.E./City)
Mr. R. L. Harrington (Manchester)
Professor D. E. W. Laidler (Manchester)
Professor J. M. Parkin (Manchester)

Professor F. P. R. Brechling (Northwestern)
Professor R. W. Clower (Northwestern)
Professor J. C. Parkinson (Nottingham)
Dr. R. G. Opie (Oxford)
Mr. P. M. Oppenheimer (Oxford)
Professor G. W. Maynard (Reading)
Professor C. Nishiyama (Rikkyo, Japan)
Professor P. E. Davidson (Rutgers, New Jersey, U.S.A.)
Emeritus Professor G. L. S. Shackle
Mr. A. Gabor (Sheffield)
Professor K. Hilton (Southampton)
Mr. A. R. Nobay (Southampton)
Professor D. C. Rowan (Southampton)
Mr. M. I. Townsend (Southampton/Ulster)
Professor A. D. Bain (Stirling)
Professor N. J. Gibson (Ulster)
Miss V. Chick (University College London)

Mr. M. J. Artis (National Institute of Economic and Social Research)

Mr. R. L. Sammons (O.E.C.D./FEDERAL RESERVE BOARD)

Mr. A. J. C. Britton (H.M. Treasury)
Mr. A. H. Lovell (H.M. Treasury)
Mr. M. V. Posner (H.M. Treasury)
Professor J. H. Williamson (H.M. Treasury)

Mr. L. A. Dicks-Mireaux (Bank of England)
Dr. C. A. E. Goodhart (Bank of England)
Dr. M. J. Hamburger (Bank of England/Federal Reserve Bank of New York)
Mr. C. W. McMahon (Bank of England)
Mr. A. J. G. Wood (Bank of England)

Mr. G. I. Lipscombe (Lloyds Bank Ltd.)
Mr. P. K. Marks (Midland Bank Ltd.)
Mr. J. E. Wadsworth (Midland Bank Ltd.)
Mr. D. E. Fair (National and Commercial Banking Group Ltd.)
Mr. D. F. Lomax (National Westminster Bank Ltd.)

Dr. W. E. Norton (Reserve Bank of Australia)

Mr. D. M. Andrew (Shell International Petroleum Company Ltd.)
Mr. A. F. Peters (Shell International Petroleum Company Ltd.)
Mr. H. van der Schaaf (Shell International Petroleum Company Ltd.)

Mrs. C. M. Cunningham (Social Science Research Council)

INDEX

(Entries printed in italics are references to particular authors or their works)